States . . . shall regard astronauts as
Envoys of Mankind in outer space.

Treaty on Principles
Governing the Activities of States
in the Exploration and Use of Outer Space,
Including the Moon and Other Celestial Bodies
Article 5, 1967

Envoys of Mankind

A DECLARATION OF FIRST PRINCIPLES FOR
THE GOVERNANCE OF SPACE SOCIETIES

George S. Robinson
Harold M. White, Jr.

Prologue by Gene Roddenberry

Smithsonian Institution Press
Washington, D.C.   London

Library of Congress Cataloging-in-Publication Data
Robinson, George S., 1937–
Envoys of mankind.

Bibliography: p.
Includes index.
Supt. of Docs. no.: SI 1.2:En8/4
1. Space law.   I. White, Harold M., 1949–
II. Title.
JX5810.R63 1986   341.4'7   86–6707
ISBN 0-87474-820-8

The authors wish to express their appreciation to
the following for permission to quote from certain
works: To Jeremy P. Tarcher, Inc., for several passages quoted from *The Aquarian Conspiracy*,
© 1981, by Marilyn Ferguson. To Random House,
Inc., for passages quoted from *Cultures beyond
the Earth*, © 1975, by Philip Singer and Carl R.
Vann, edited by Magoroh Maruyama and Arthur
Harkins. To Yale University Press for three brief
excerpts from *The Nature of the Judicial Process*,
© 1921, by Benjamin N. Cardozo. To R. Walter
Cunningham for two passages quoted from his
The All-American Boys, © 1977, published by the
Macmillan Company. To Farrar, Straus & Giroux
for an excerpt from *Carrying the Fire,* © 1974, by
Michael Collins.

For my wife and sons

George S. Robinson

For my wife, Rita,
daughter Camie,
and family

Harold M. White, Jr.

Contents

Preamble: The Spacekind Declaration of Independence

In Representative Assembly of Space Migrants
The Unanimous Declaration
of the Communities of Space Migrants

Recognizing the distinction between thought processes that occur in space and those that respond to the influences of inhabiting Earth's surface;

Believing that the habitation of space should be characterized by the full expression of the limitless varieties of human-related cultures;

Believing that an accurate understanding of the biological foundations of value-forming processes in a space environment will contribute substantially to lessening the fruitless competition and violent conflicts among Earth civilizations;

Desiring to elevate the evolution of *Homo sapiens* to its next logical stage,

Be it therefore DECLARED:

WHEN IN THE COURSE OF HUMAN EVOLUTION it becomes necessary for progeny to dissolve the political and biological bonds which have connected them with their progenitors, and to assume among the powers of the solar system and galaxy the separate and equal station to which the Laws of Nature and their Creator entitle them, a decent respect for the opinions of earthkind requires that they should declare the causes which impel them to their separation into spacekind . . .

Acknowledgments

The authors are grateful to many people for the time and help given them during the research, writing, and production of *Envoys of Mankind*. Although our special thanks go to each person who has helped us in any way during this project, there are a few people whose contributions are so significant that they require specific acknowledgment.

Our first thanks, of course, go to our families, whose patience, assistance, and advice were indispensable in bringing this project to fruition. This is particularly true of Rita Lauria White, our research, editorial, and administrative assistant, whose logistical support and literary and managerial skills greatly facilitated the completion of the manuscript.

Particular mention must also be made of Felix Lowe, director of the Smithsonian Institution Press, whose commitment and quiet, consistent enthusiasm for the manuscript nudged us over the occasional hurdles of self-doubt. Our thanks also go to Walter Boyne, director of the National Air and Space Museum, whose support for the project and hard criticism were critical elements in whatever success we have been able to achieve in our effort. We are also grateful to Catherine D. Scott, who gave invaluable assistance in verifying a great many bibliographical details.

Special thanks are due our friends and critics, Max Lerner, David C. Webb, Wilton S. Dillon, and Gene Roddenberry. While many others read, criticized, and commented on parts of the manuscript, these gentlemen read and commented on the entire work. Although the authors bear ultimate responsibility for the nature or quality of the work, all who have helped us contributed greatly to improving the first and second drafts, and we shall be forever indebted to them.

We are also appreciative of the work done by our legal intern, Ed Schorr, of the Stanford University School of Law, whose capacity for detailed research and ferreting out of fascinating anecdotes gave us much-needed encouragement. Finally, our thanks to the patient and always helpful staff of the Smithsonian Institution Press and to our final-draft editor, David Howell-Jones, whose professional touch has considerably softened the rough edges and has saved us and this book too many times to count.

George S. Robinson Harold M. White, Jr.
Washington, D.C.   Chapel Hill, N.C.
            30 January 1986

Prologue

Gene Roddenberry

> The Smithsonian Institution . . . [is con-
> cerned with] all cognate ways of learning
> and knowing — experimental, exploratory,
> historical and aesthetic. . . . What counts is
> that we recognize the boundaries we draw
> as a matter of convenience only: between
> science and technology, between science
> and history . . . and even between science
> and art. We are all collaborators on a funda-
> mentally unitary enterprise of learning and
> knowing, and within as well as around that
> enterprise there should be no real bounda-
> ries at all.
>
> *Robert McCormick Adams*
> *Proceedings of the*
> *National Academy of Sciences*
> *Annual Meeting, 1984*

If you have ever pondered the puzzle of what you are, who you are now, and where you seem to be going, read on and enjoy! The authors begin by compressing billions of years into a couple of minutes, taking you on a journey from the beginnings of the everything up to the now. It is a strangely exhilarating description of the way our universe first burst into existence as space-time-light-energy-gravity and matter, a gigantic cloud of hydrogen whose atoms and molecules grew ever more complex as they expanded to become all the galaxies of stars, solar systems, comets, meteors, space dust — everything that makes up our universe. The authors then examine the evolution of the universe, how it has continued growing in complexity until, upon this particular dust speck planet named Earth, there has evolved an even more complex you, whose conscious thoughts are at this very moment considering the way everything began and grew into the now.

Quite a leap! The authors continue by considering the many possible and even probable tomorrows of our special life form. They explore the startling implications of our present move into and occupation of space. Perhaps this unfolding odyssey will even leave some feeling uneasy, but it should leave many feeling that everything is no doubt happening to us exactly as it was meant to happen and that the way our evolution is happening strongly suggests that something about us is an important part of the entire scheme of things. What is described has infinitely more grandeur and hope than the common belief that a god—or whatever—simply patty-caked moist clay into an *us* in its own form. Equally hopeful is the implication that our universe was somehow *meant* to go from hydrogen atom simplicity to now's complexity, which has shown itself capable of evolving at least one conscious entity with the potential to engage in similar powers of creation itself. This certainly suggests that our kind of conscious intelligence and the force that created everything may have some primal relationship with each other.

I met the authors several years ago when we were addressing the same professional meeting. I was speaking on a subject somewhat related to the theme of this book. They were puzzled that they, as practitioners and teachers in the conservative and tradition-bound profession of law, could find themselves intrigued by a Hollywood producer-writer's comments about society, space, and the human future. This led to a friendship during which we learned more about the way both science and art are in essence seeking answers to the same questions and how the two different work methods and perspectives are infinitely less conflicting than they are complementary.

I did feel some trepidation, however, about accepting their invitation to write this prologue to their book. Just as there is an antiscience bias among some artists, there are people concerned with science who are biased against so-called popular art, particularly when it attempts to reflect or interpret the world of scientific methodology and its empirically generated data. Thus, I believe the authors showed some courage in inviting me to open their book with my observations and thoughts—and perhaps I showed a fair measure of courage in accepting. Some people may well believe that, as the creator and executive producer of the television series *Star Trek,* I considered that series to have been "an inspired vision of the human future." In *1984,* George Orwell stated that every human being has one great nightmarish fear, and mine is a terror that friends and associates might think that I bed down at night in space admiral's pajamas!

These questions did not trouble me when I stood before my first audience, more than twenty years ago, to comment on space and the human future. At that time I had been considering a television idea, which only later became *Star Trek*. So I had been researching current thinking about the future at places such as the RAND Corporation and the California Institute of Technology. I had also been interviewing prominent writers on the subject. When a former law professor of mine heard of what I was doing he asked me to come to the local Harvard Luncheon Club and talk about what I had learned.

On the appointed day in 1964 I found myself addressing a group of successful Harvard graduates, telling them that it seemed certain we human beings would soon break away from this ancestral egg we call Earth. I summarized for them what the aerospace scientists and engineers had said about orbital space stations and eventual human colonies within our solar system, explaining the economic attractiveness of manufacturing in zero gravity and zero temperatures, of mining iron ore and other minerals from asteroids and moons, and of watching weather happen from way out there. And when I was done, the luncheon club had just one question: "Who invited the cuckoo?"

It is worth remembering that barely twenty years ago this fairly typical group of educated, prominent, and successful men considered space to be wild fantasy. I think they were quite pleased with the world as it was, and they seemed to believe that God would respect their wishes. Yet only five years after that luncheon a man walked on the moon, and since then the world around us has continued to change and complexify even more rapidly with each passing year.

The rapidity of change in our world today is simply mind-bending. There are many people in science and art who now agree that 1961 is a fair approximation of the year in which we human beings began doubling our knowledge every seven years. Although some estimate that knowledge is growing a bit faster or a bit slower, 1961 has the advantage of being about the time the number of science papers published throughout the world began to double every seven years.

A good way to appreciate the meaning of this phenomenon is to imagine that back in 1961 humanity constructed a library large enough to hold all the knowledge ever gathered. Since human knowledge in 1961 had already progressed to the beginnings of the space program, television, jet airlines, computers, and much more, a library capable of holding all that knowledge would have required an enormous structure.

Let's say that we were continuing to store knowledge in that same fashion in 1968, which means that to store it would then require two of those enormous structures—and here is where the mind-bending begins.

Seven years later, in 1975, the doubling of human knowledge had revealed itself in the genetics revolution, in microminiature electronics, and in equally astonishing progress elsewhere—and, of course, similar storage for that knowledge would have required four such enormous libraries.

Seven years later, back in 1982, a doubling of knowledge saw humanity changing much of its view of the history of Earth and of its parade of life forms and of human evolution, and some lovely new realizations came about, including a genuine understanding of the need for equality between men and women. In addition, there were other manifestations of our steadily evolving social consciences, such as the nationwide provision of ramps and reserved parking spaces for the handicapped, and one can find considerable optimism in the fact that these kinds of understanding also seem to be doubling and redoubling, while the growth rate of new knowledge of weaponry, by some measurements, may even have begun to decline!

And in 1982, the same way of storing our accumulated knowledge would have required eight of those huge libraries. In other words, we human beings increased our scientific knowledge an incredible eight times in just twenty-one years.

Staggering? Absolutely! Our knowledge had hardly increased that much in the preceding two centuries!

Seven years from then, in 1989, it appears that our knowledge will have zoomed to sixteen times what it was in 1961.

In seven more years, in 1996, human knowledge will have skyrocketed to an amount thirty-two times as great—and many who read these words will have half or more of their lives still ahead of them.

Can human beings physically, psychologically, and culturally endure such a flood of change? Yes, of course! What alternative is there? We've been successfully handling an exponential rate of change for more than a million years, and we seem to have been evolving a progressive capacity to handle even the incredible amount of change that we are now facing— and will face. It has been estimated that the billions of neurons now present in a typical human brain have a potential thought pattern greater than the number of stars in our galaxy.

This torrent of change in our world appears to have made artistic speculation about the meaning of change, and its impact on human purpose and direction, as necessary and valuable as scientifically empirical speculation. Although interpretive artists may work or speculate with well-informed and disciplined imaginations, they are perhaps not quite so much constrained by the precision and rigors of universal applicability and peer justification. The artist has a license to work with greater freedom than the scientist or engineer, and this encourages a considerable amount of unrestrained inventing of possible human futures, especially by dramatists, whose emphasis is on people and feelings and ethics and values. After all, the artist must help ascribe human values and purpose to the unfolding, hard data of the scientists and engineers. This, in turn, helps prepare all the rest of us to adjust to, accommodate, and use for the benefit of all humankind the flood of change that might otherwise prove overwhelming and destructive to whole civilizations, if not to the human species itself.

How do science fiction writers manage so often to guess correctly about tomorrow? Beyond the disciplined imagination of the interpretive artists, a principal reason is undoubtedly that no one penalizes or even criticizes them—especially the storytellers—for inventing futures that seem impossible or implausible. Indeed, the artist will even be rewarded for an impossible dream if it is sufficiently entertaining. A scientist, presenting precisely the same ideas, even as a speculation based on empirical data, may well risk a loss of status and professional reputation, even though the extrapolation or prediction may someday be proven completely accurate. Scientific and academic communities are very much aware of the danger of predicting the future accurately too soon.

Fortunately, this attitude has also started to change. The example closest to me came when the Smithsonian Institution decided to hang the original eleven-foot model of *Star Trek's* fictional starship in its National Air and Space Museum in Washington, D.C. The Smithsonian continues to recognize the importance of societal aspirations and the interpretive importance of the arts and artists to space exploration and habitation. In September 1984 the National Air and Space Museum opened a show of paintings by space artist Robert McCall which, in large part, are symbolic of human space habitation and life styles and several of which depict scenes from *Star Trek* productions. Of course, these are not really statements about the *Star Trek* television or motion picture series, but rather the Smithsonian's recognition and acknowledgment of the fact that, even before the tale of Icarus was first related, the artists were usually the first to penetrate the veil of the future and encourage scientists and others to follow.

While many people will readily accept that the business of the artist is not only the depiction of perceived reality but also the creation of alternative realities, only rarely do the same people understand that alternative realities are also the business of the scientist. Most people, indeed many scientists, believe that the scientist's concepts *are* reality. The authors delve into some of the logical and scientific reasons this is not altogether true. Science can give us a conception of reality that may, at a given level of human evolution, knowledge, and technology, seem to explain our world and our universe best. Fortunately for us, however, the conceptions of science never explain everything completely. Loose ends keep appearing, and it is in the careful reexamination of these loose ends that the old scientific ideas are expanded and reshaped into new ones.

The physical world that college science courses now portray to students is considerably different from that studied by their parents. Going back further, it was only a dozen centuries or so ago that the best of our scientists were pronouncing the universe to be composed of earth, air, fire, and water. It is the incredible distance that science has come that makes it all the more annoying to me that a strong antiscience faction still thrives in society today—and that much of that faction's most powerful propaganda is put forth by some of my fellow artists.

This seems to me particularly unfortunate because I have always suspected that the scientist and the artist perform a closely related kind of work—that they perhaps represent the two faces of a special kind of human being whose profession is rooted in intelligent thought. It is difficult to study Einstein, for example, without seeing the artist at work with his creative inspirations. Or can anyone deny the physical scientist that exists in many great composers, or the social scientist in George Orwell, or the balanced mixture that existed in Leonardo, and so on throughout history?

The dramatist or storyteller can easily recognize the importance of both scientist and artist to early human space societies. The authors take a good look at early Earth societies in order to bolster the suggestion of this dual importance. The scientist-engineer was probably the discoverer and worker of flint, while society's early verbal memory reposed in the artist-storyteller. There could hardly be a more potent combination for expanding human knowledge and developing human intelligence.

There are some good reasons to believe that science and art, perhaps first separated by the enviable theatrics of the shaman or priest and later by the various secular priesthoods of the scientific schools and artistic guilds, can now begin to work more closely together again. Perhaps that goal might be brought nearer if both disciplines would adopt the Roman god Janus as their joint symbol, its twin faces representing science and art in combination, scanning the entire far horizon. Alone, science or art can see only part of that horizon, but in combination they can hope to scan it all.

How can an artist's view of that far horizon have anything near the value of a scientist's vision growing out of known information? What can be more reliable than carefully collected, well-verified data? Part of the answer is that while the scientist usually proceeds from the superior data base, this tends to limit that scientist's speculation to areas of known information. The artist, with no obligation to proceed according to any particular kind of logic, can speculate in any direction, with imagination fueled by personal prejudice, emotional needs, anger, love, or anything that feels right at the time. While this produces considerable waste and nonsense, of course, it can also add considerable perspective to humanity's view of itself and its world.

It is a massively complex undertaking to make compassionate sense of the never-ending loose ends and ambiguities of human life, especially in a new and unique environment like outer space. Yet this is precisely the task undertaken by George Robinson and Hal White in *Envoys of Mankind*. They have therefore necessarily drawn on both science and art to illustrate their disciplined social and jurisprudential speculations and suggestions concerning the human settlement of the final frontier. As jurists and educators, professions of synthesis, they have used the Janus of art and science, melding empirical data with disciplined imagination and rational speculation to create a plausible projection of the genesis of spacekind, our own extraterrestrial progeny.

The potential is great, so the stakes are high. A good part of our ability to reach the potential of humanity, to surmount the rising odds against us, lies in international cooperation and the capacity of human beings to articulate effective laws that maintain both social order *and* individual freedom. We must not forget that even with all our doubling and redoubling of human knowledge, it is still possible for more people to starve to death now in, say, Africa or South Asia than a century ago.

A few years ago I found myself growing angry upon reading an article describing millions of deaths from famine in Africa. Considering our growth in knowledge and the improvements constantly being made in agriculture, remote sensing from space, and ocean-shipping technology, the world should be threatened by obesity, not hunger! And why all today's petty nationalisms, its foolish religious hatreds, and the fearsome arms race? What happened to the promise of humanity moving toward racial adulthood? We're acting more like infants who have got hold of a butcher knife without even being potty-trained yet! Are these the cultural values we wish to send into space with our envoys?

Considerable anger! With imagination being fueled by emotion, I began to block out a science fiction story in which I could retain my optimism about humanity by blaming our present problems on some sort of villain. Ah! Why not say that human organizations are to blame. Why not call them socio-organisms and claim them to be as much a life form as any other. In fact, why not call them a higher life form, a new kind of life form in which the individual cells no longer have to be in physical proximity to each other— in which individual cells can also be part of more than one of these socio-

creatures. Perhaps this is why this new creature is more powerful than human beings, who were the last dominant species.

All this can be made to sound plausible (I told myself) by claiming that the same natural laws that governed the evolution of life forms have also produced socio-organisms. And I'll claim that these constitute Earth's new dominant species and that human beings are the cells of these new creatures. Some human individuals have already surrendered to this new life form and some others are still battling to stay free.

It is an artist's conception—my own—depicting an alternative reality. Yet it is also one the authors seem to be addressing in their calls for diversity and individual sovereignty in the face of the unavoidable social engineering for the establishment of biotechnologically integrated space habitats. It is a conception that the authors, in their capacities as students of legal philosophy, are trying to illuminate with rational synthesis and a postterrestrial set of human perceptions. Indeed, the authors have found that human beings in space will be biotechnologically integrated and completely dependent upon social structure and complex organization for survival. These space communities possess the knowledge that no one individual can. They are truly socio-organisms in which the human component cannot survive by itself in the alien and synthetic life-support environment of a space habitat.

My original conceptualization of this idea came about some years ago, and the science fiction story behind it has never been completed. I don't know that I actually began to believe that this new dominant species was really replacing humanity, but neither have I discarded a suspicion that it could be true, as our sons and daughters, relying upon ever newer technology for survival, replace their mothers and fathers and their diminishing capacities to cope.

I've also had much pleasure from embroidering tales around the concepts of metalaw that the authors have included in this book. Since metalaw embraces general principles of relations between any and all sentient entities, Earth-indigenous or otherwise, it has seemed to me that the most exciting dimensions of metalaw will not be found in space admiralty regulations or even in solar system exploration law, but rather in a revolutionary concept embracing both space law and Earth law. My storyteller's instinct tells me that there are dramatic possibilities in a human demand for a kind of freedom advocated as long ago as the time of Jefferson, Locke, and Rousseau—a theory embracing individual and societal freedom.

In his description of the social contract Rousseau held that in the presocial state, human beings were timid and far from warlike. He believed that laws were the natural result of the acquiesence of participants to the surrender of some individual freedom of action for the sake of mutual protection and access to community knowledge–but the community's prime requisite, its raison d'être, was to facilitate the full actualization of every individual's potential. Each individual was basically free to travel the Earth as he pleased. In essence, each individual was a citizen of the world first and of a particular community second, so long as his movements did not do damage to other individuals or communities. It was a theory that presupposed that any form of government—or socio-organism—any formal embodiment of willing compromises on the freedom of individual action, must truly rest on the freely given consent of the governed.

I feel certain that the next few decades will see a growing worldwide belief, then a growing insistence, that the nations of Earth are nothing more than different forms of tyranny being imposed upon individuals and that the only legitimate and legal citizenship that can exist is Earth citizenship—human citizenship. The authors of this book have helped blaze a trail in understanding of the uniquely unifying knowledge required for a spacekind declaration of independence and a constitution underlying a free spacekind citizenship.

The premise of my view is that no political subdivision on Earth has a right derived from natural law to deny the inhabitants of this planet their right to free access to all parts of their home. Nor do these sociopolitical entities have any right to separate human beings one from the other, or in any way to compel them to contend against other members of the human family of Earth. Again, the authors have attempted to resurrect and breath life into the basic rights of natural law found in such diverse documents as the Magna Charta, the Virginia Declaration of Rights, the Declaration of Independence of the United States, the Bill of Rights of the Constitution of the United States, the French Declaration of the Rights of Man and Citizen, and the Universal Declaration of Human Rights of the United Nations. These documents represent a kind of evolutionary continuity in the types of values that the authors advocate for sending envoys of mankind into space and for creating a globally recognized spacekind citizenship—a social order in space that responds in the first instance to the needs of spacekind and in the second instance to the needs of their earthkind cousins.

It seems to me inescapable that the continuing growth and application of human knowledge will convince each human being that the geopolitical divisions of the nations of the world have no legitimate right, beyond the self-arrogation of raw force, to claim ownership of us and our spacekind progeny on the basis of geographical accidents of birth and heritage. I like to believe that the same remarkable people who formulated the greatest documents of freedom in history would have no hesitation in also subscribing to the principle that all human beings possess additional inalienable rights that

transcend nationality and that no law can restrict those rights without negotiated reasons that are consistent with and protective of them.

Concepts such as these are also necessary to space law, of course, as
it encompasses a new frontier, a totally new arena of human community
with new matrices of social arrangements. The concept of planetary or
human citizenship must of necessity be embodied in what some space lawyers are beginning to refer to as astrolaw, the body of law that governs
human relations in space, principles of social order flowing from the unique
natural requirements of human space existence.

George Robinson and Hal White are telling us that our children, whom
we are sending into space as our cultural couriers, our intelligence agents,
are constantly growing different from us and that this must be recognized
and accommodated if we are to help ensure the ongoing survival of *Homo
sapiens* and its envoys—its progeny—*Homo spatialis*. Grow, change, or
perish.

As parents we must be willing to sever the umbilicus while providing
friendship and support, always hoping that the children never really do leave
home, no matter how different they become as individuals. Indeed, as long
as the focus of law is the human creature, then the jurisprudential concepts
for Earth and space cannot be separated. However far our children may
travel toward the stars, their biological and cultural roots are in this Earth
below and flow from the loins of earthkind. We have arisen from the mud of
the primeval shores of planet Earth to begin our return to the stars. As we
become the increasingly sophisticated creatures of the future, we need to
remember and savor both our origins and our odyssey. It has been said that
Earth's mud between our toes is what has enabled us to dance—and the
loss of the human ability either to laugh or dance is too sad to contemplate,
even in story form.

Introduction: Cosmic Origins

In the beginning was the Word; and the
Word was with God; and the Word was
God.

John 1:1

And the Earth was without form and void;
and darkness was upon the face of the
deep. And the Spirit of God moved . . . and
God said, Let there be light: and there was
light.

Genesis 1:2-3

It all began with a big bang, most astronomers agree. Some 15 to 20 billion years ago an infinitesimally small and infinitely dense primordial energy mass emerged in an extremely hot explosive fashion. The ensuing expansion cooled the energy mass so that subatomic particles combined and atoms formed. The resultant gases dispersed and cooled to the point of invisibility, revealing a constantly expanding blackness of increasingly open space.

These invisible gases were about 93 percent hydrogen and 7 percent helium, the simplest and lightest of atoms, having only one and two protons, respectively. Nevertheless, under the force of gravity, a sufficiently dense concentration of atoms can lead to thermonuclear fusion—ignition— the formation of a star. Thus were the early stars formed, which themselves seemed to be drawn together by gravity into great spiraling masses of stars, called galaxies.

As we examine the human future in space we begin, in part 1, with the large perspective offered by space and time. In later chapters we shall focus our view like a movie camera approaching its subject for a close-up. But we begin our look at the next human migration, at our emerging space pioneers, our envoys of mankind, with a look at the basic nature of our makeup. We shall quickly trace the evolution of our star-stuff envoys from the primordial big bang, to the primitive communities of early *Homo sapiens* and, in part 2, to the organizational and episodic histories of our space explorers.

As we look back over our shoulders to the future we are struck by increasing hierarchies of community, from the original community of sub-atomic particles to the ever-evolving and complexifying communities of atoms, molecules, celestial bodies, organisms, human beings, and finally socio-organisms, great and small, including families, tribes, cities, states, and nations such as the Soviet Union and the United States.

As we continue our inward focus in part 3 we look at the kinds of people that have been and will be going into space as progenitors of long-duration and permanent inhabitants. We also see why our socio-organisms are sending them. We are especially concerned with the kinds of values they will be taking with them, so in parts 4 and 5 we shall examine the envoys' special physiological, psychological, and communal needs.

After we examine this ecological basis for the formation of values by individuals and communities in space we shall finally look, in parts 6 and 7, at the way the irreducible foundations of space community can and should be embodied in space jurisprudence. Throughout we shall attempt to catch at least a glimmer of what the natural values and institutions of future communities in space may be like.

Perhaps such a broad examination by a couple of early space lawyers may seem a classic example of reach exceeding grasp, especially in the non-legal areas of science and technology. Yet the nature of space law itself requires just such an interdisciplinary examination. Perhaps the best way to illustrate this assertion is to look at just what the nature of space law really is.

For ease of conceptualizing we can break the subject of space law into two broad subtopics. First, there is the evolving body of national and inter-national law relating to the essential and mundane aspects of a space law practice, such as spacecraft insurance, satellite broadcast licenses, NASA contracts, and international treaty law.

Second, there is the more exotic aspect of the evolving discipline—its underlying philosophy, grand internal model, paradigm, or metaphysical con-ception. This jurisprudential and jurimetric perspective is concerned with the relations between earthkind and spacekind and among spacekind them-selves.

While we will glance at the most important aspects of both types of space law, our primary focus will be on the more exotic jurisprudential aspects. Why? Because even the nuts and bolts embodied in the first, more workaday topic of space law are really best understood, used, and even cre-ated on the basis of reason, values, needs, perspectives, prejudices, and knowledge—the province of the second, more philosophical subtopic. In addition, whenever we encounter a new realm of human activity or knowledge we are forced to confront our most basic concept through paradigmatic shifts in both individual and social consciousness.

This second, jurisprudential subtopic reveals a critical challenge, a challenge that is the close-up focus of this book—that is, as humanity moves to populate the stars, it is our generation that will establish the jurisprudential matrix from which the ultimate principles of social order in space communities will be born. How shall we rate as founding fathers and mothers?

Embryonic Astronauts

1   Extraterrestrial Children

> To begin with . . . there is . . . unresolved
> simplicity, luminous in nature and not to be
> defined in terms of figures. Then, suddenly,
> came a swarming of elementary corpus-
> cles, both positive and negative. . . . Then
> the harmonic series of simple [arrange-
> ments] strung out from hydrogen to ura-
> nium on the notes of the atomic scale. Next
> follows the immense variety of compound
> bodies in which the molecular weights go
> on increasing up to a certain critical value
> above which . . . we pass on to life. This
> fundamental discovery that all bodies owe
> their origin to different arrangements of a
> single initial corpuscular type is the beacon
> that lights the history of the universe to our
> eyes.
>
> *Pierre Teilhard de Chardin*
> The Phenomenon of Man

Stars have life expectancies just as people do. The violent, explosive deaths
of certain of the larger stars have actually been witnessed and chronicled by
many peoples and cultures since the beginning of recorded human history, a
very brief period on the cosmic time scale. Some of these violent novas,
such as the famous one that occurred in 1054, were so bright for short
periods that they could actually be seen in broad daylight, despite being
hundreds of light-years away.

Early novas spewed out clouds of heavy atoms—those with more protons, neutrons, and electrons—such as carbon, nitrogen and oxygen, which
had been formed by the intense thermonuclear fusion or combining of the
light hydrogen atoms in the early stars. It is in such an interstellar cloud of
dust and gas that we find the atoms of our embryonic envoys approximately
4 billion years ago. Our bodies are composed of the same elements that
drifted in this presolar nebula. So it is that our envoys are star children. Our

very atoms and early molecules were captured at the outset by the gravity of the newly formed, primeval Earth, which accreted from this presolar nebula, as did the sun and the other planets.

Human beings have always demonstrated an interest in genesis, the process of creation that led to our consciousness. This is no less so in the Space Age than it was at earlier times in history. The majority of our most sacred and passionate beliefs center in one way or another on some version of the story of creation. Apparently there is a deep need within humanity to understand the nature and meaning of existence. Intelligence seeks purpose, and jurisprudence consists of the interpretations and conventions of common purpose and perception.

Philip Morrison suggested that the compulsion to investigate and understand our natures is the most telling feature of our overall conscious nature. He observed that

We are creatures who construct for ourselves, not only separately and singly, but also together in our collectivities, internal models of all that happens, of all we see, find, feel, guess, and conjecture about reality. It is fair to say . . . that our language, our myth and ritual, our tools, our science, and indeed our art, are all expressions translated in one way or another . . . [from] this grand internal model. The presence of that internal model and its steady need for completion, the obviously adaptive need of its leading edges to have continuity, not to fade off into the nothing or the nowhere; this is the essential feature of human exploration.

Morrison was saying that our institutions, conventions, and inventions are products of our continually refined perceptions of reality. Therefore, we see that no part of the natural order, or of our grand internal models of that order, are irrelevant to our modern social constructions, whether technological or institutional. Jurisprudence, philosophy, science, and religion are thus all concerned with accurate translation of our perceptions. They are concerned with the way these perceptions are related to reality and truth. They are concerned with the extent to which our social and scientific technologies are in balance with nature.

The long view of the processes involved in creation and the origins of humanity reveals a tendency to become more complex in the course of time. This tendency seems to be a basic property of energy and matter in arrangement and interaction. Pierre Teilhard de Chardin, in *The Phenomenon of Man,* noted that the suppleness and mobility of even the mineral world can scarcely be imagined. A perpetual transformation of mineral species, vaguely analogous to the metamorphosis of living creatures, takes place even in solid rock. Occasionally we feel the movements or see the molten interior spew forth from a crack.

This sense of perpetual motion prepares us for one of the most important processes of geochemistry in the benign interface of our lithosphere and hydrosphere. That process is polymerization, a chemical reaction in which two or more small molecules combine to form larger molecules. Polymerization is also defined as the reduplication of parts in an organism, more broadly as the process of association. It is the process of synthesis leading to life and to higher levels of interaction and consciousness.

It was a mathematical description of this kind of synthesis that earned Ilya Prigogine the 1977 Nobel Prize in chemistry for his theory of dissipative structures. The theory describes the workings of open systems, in which there is a constant exchange of energy and matter with the outside environment. A human being is such a system, using or dissipating energy in order to retain its organization and activity. The human being, for example, takes in food and oxygen and excretes waste. In fact, a truly closed system is only a theoretical conception, like a perpetual motion machine, unattainable.

So Prigogine's theory assumes great importance, since theoretically it applies to all known systems, including human social systems, chemical reactions, ecosystems, and all other systems that depend upon a continuous flow of energy from outside. Prigogine showed that as the energy flow increases or becomes more complex, it can cause fluctuations greater than a system can absorb, thus forcing it to reorganize. Each reorganization produces greater complexity and therefore greater likelihood of random fluctuations. The natural result of those fluctuations is even greater instability, further reorganization, and a quickened transformation of living matter into new structures—evolution—precisely the type of elemental polymerization we were discussing.

The impetus for this flash of intuition came from Prigogine's observation of the so-called Benard instability. It occurs when a liquid is heated from below. As heating intensifies, the mixture begins to "self-organize, taking on a striking spacial structure sometimes resembling miniature stained-glass cathedral windows, with ovals of brilliant colors arranging themselves in kaleidoscopic patterns." The patterns resemble living cells, ordered molecular motion occurring within each cell. Prigogine realized that this self-organization represented a critical link between animate and inanimate matter and that it could even "provide a clue to the spontaneous eruption of life's beginnings."

Thus came the birth of the biosphere of the Earth, an envelope of life within the hydrosphere of the planet. Here we can see even more clearly how our intelligence and consciousness developed from increasingly complex interactions and organizations of organic compounds, among which we live and of which we are made. During an immensely long period the chains of carbon molecules, amino acids, and proteins arranged themselves into a molecular spiral, a double helix, deoxyribonucleic acid (DNA).

This tendency of matter to complexify, to polymerize, to dissipate energy, or to evolve into or invent new arrangements led inexorably to biology and the concomitant potential for conscious awareness within matter. Perhaps it was just such a realization that led the Nobel committee, in announcing its award to Ilya Prigogine, to state that he had "created theories which bridge the gap which exists between the biological and social scientific fields of inquiry."

2 From *Cosmos* to *The Ascent of Man*

> Mankind in its totality is a phenomenon to
> be described and analyzed like any other
> phenomenon: it and all its manifestations,
> including Human history and values, are
> proper objects for scientific study.
>
> *Sir Julian Huxley*

Modern humanity is gradually coming to recognize that evolution involves something far more magnificent than simply the survival of the fittest or the accidental mutation of a monkey into a man. From the Darwinian continuum through Einstein's space-time continuum to Jacob Bronowski's synthesis of current findings on *The Ascent of Man,* we see recognition of the inherent nature of our existence as unfolding and ever changing since the very beginning of time.

In some ways, of course, this is not merely a modern view. Perhaps we are witnessing intuition at work within recorded history when we observe that many of the world's religions have interpreted history as some form of divine process, with an identifiable beginning and an ultimate destiny. The Greeks grounded philosophy — "love of wisdom" — on just such a concept. The "Indians" of the New World had myths and creation legends that envisaged an unfolding process. But in the late twentieth century the perception is heightened. We can see the change. We can "feel" it.

Alvin Toffler called this feeling *Future Shock.* New life forms are created in laboratories — cultural biotechnology — as life consciously operates upon itself. We see panoramas of far worlds in living color. We uncover long-lost secrets of science and medicine. We hear communication theorists discuss cultural and biotechnological break boundaries — points at which systems transform themselves into recognizably different systems. Elderly human beings on planet Earth today, one generation of people, have experienced a revolution in knowledge. They personally have lived through the transformation of a handcraft and animal-labor society into fossil-fuel, jet-age, atomic-age, electronic-age, computer-age, and space-age societies.

Indeed, as we have seen by piecing together information from several disciplines, we can provide a broad outline of the way in which the universe has progressed, slowly, through billions of years, from the featureless light of the primeval big bang to the complexity of the present world order. We can picture a universe gradually establishing organization through the several billions of years that followed the plasma era. We can still see the processes of complexification and polymerization taking place as we begin to focus on the ascent of man from his early forms to his currently unfolding form.

One of the most beautiful metaphors of this continuously unfolding process of creation is Carl Sagan's Cosmic Calendar, which compresses the 20-billion-year history of the cosmos into a single calendar year. On this scale, each month represents 1.25 billion years, each day 40 million years. The plasma era thus occupies most of January.

The first stars and galaxies form in February and March, and we see our solar nebula beginning to form in late August. By early October life has appeared in the tidepools of the newly accreted earth, and by late October it is a profusion of single-celled organisms and algae mats. During November photosynthetic cells colonize the land and produce an oxygen-rich atmosphere, while the underwater species specialize and proliferate. By early December the lungfish amphibians crawl out onto the land, and by December 30th, 65 million years ago, they develop and proliferate into the reptiles, birds, and mammals.

As we examine the Cosmic Calendar we are struck by the fact that even the most primitive human beings do not appear until about 9:00 or 10:00 P.M. on December 31st, the last day of the cosmic year. The discovery of fire and the invention of agriculture take place only in the last few minutes of the last hour of the last day. All of recorded history fits into the last ten seconds of the Cosmic Calendar!

Poised upon either the last millisecond of this cosmic year or perhaps the first millisecond of the next, let us use our vantage point to examine the last two or three calendar hours of creation since the appearance of manlike animals some 5 or 6 million years ago. During that period we see evolutionary transformations, increasing biological complexity, and increasing intelligence and awareness, all witnessed in ever more rapid succession.

Information storage, exchange, and increase—at first exclusively a function of molecular DNA—came to be accomplished by the external technologies, tools, or media developed by the "consciousness" or intelligent self-awareness permitted by the evolution of DNA. The first "technology" of this consciousness may have been a rudimentary form known as cooperation. We see cooperation in the wolf pack, in the group hunt, in the very processes of association, polymerization, and complexification that we have already discovered.

Nevertheless, with *self*-consciousness we are definitely seeing something new in the unfolding and development of matter. By 750,000 B.C. we are finding the remains of campfires and an increasing array of stone tools. The creature now stands erect and has an even larger cranial capacity than his big-game-hunting predecessors. We call him *Homo erectus.* He is the source of several innovations such as bigger brains, prolonged infant dependency, loss of estrus, the coming of the family, and taboos and traditions. His discoveries drove his evolution at an even faster rate than that of earlier prehuman species. This time, in only 500,000 years the transformation was made from *Homo erectus* to *Homo sapiens.*

Since *Homo sapiens* began to dominate the scene some 200,000 years ago, the evolution of intelligence and society have been moving at an ever more rapid pace. *Homo sapiens* has evolved in stages through several subspecies or types, such as Neanderthal man, the caveman who appeared approximately 75,000 years ago. Even Neanderthal man, before his disappearance 35,000 years ago, represented a significant step in the evolution of our envoys. He was almost certainly religious, engaging in the ritual of burial, which implies concern for the individual and a new attitude toward death.

By 40,000 B.C. we see Cro-Magnon man, an early type of modern human being, virtually indistinguishable from people of today. Cro-Magnon man advanced even more rapidly than the subspecies that had come before, blending into thoroughly modern man by 10,000 B.C. In *The Emergence of Man,* John Pfeiffer called this period between 40,000 and 10,000 B.C. "the Golden Age of Pre-History." We find Cro-Magnon man living within social structures that represent a significant step toward the full-fledged tribe.

The early tribe was essentially an association of family and hunting bands, which were held together not only by marriage, but also by shared traditions and problems. Gene Roddenberry would probably classify these early tribes as the first socio-organisms, thus equating our social development with our biological development.

Socio-organisms act in many ways like bio-organisms. Individual human "cells" (persons) make up the organs (tribes, cities, and so on) that evolve into organisms (states, cultures, enterprises, civilizations). These entities have identity, pride, and an instinct for self-preservation. It might be possible to make too much of the analogy, but at least the vestiges of embryonic jurisprudence are to be found here. *Biojuridics,* or the jurisprudence that relates to the biological foundations of human values, and *biojurimetrics,* or the quantifiable aspects of biojuridics, are born. Institutions have always been survival technologies. These early cultural technologies included rituals for coming together and staying together, such as incest taboos and kinship rules, which say who can mate with, marry, and live with whom. These practices created even more intricate and cohesive relationships among ever larger numbers of individuals.

As the exchange of information and communication skills grew, the accompanying growth of the power of conceptualization led to more social and technical invention. Between 20,000 and 13,000 B.C. we find the bow and arrow in use and the making of physical objects as symbols. Between 13,000 and 10,000 B.C. we find cave art and the use of personal adornments, some of which suggest secret ritual and ceremony.

These prehistoric human beings were doing many interesting things with their art and their caves. Even more than the campfire, the caves represent protoinstitutional sites, before the coming of specialized, engineered institutions. The caves may have served as prehistoric archives, shrines, offices, schools, vigils, and theaters. Without alphabetic technology, the only information technologies available were art, symbols, and rituals. Cro-Magnon man bequeathed us these early sociotechnologies.

With the advent of modern man around 10,000 B.C. comes the final phase of human prehistory. Population pressures and fertile lands led to agricultural settlements in the fertile crescent of the Middle East sometime between 9,000 and 10,000 B.C. According to the wave-of-advance paleontological model, agriculture led to larger populations and slowly spread over much of the world in all directions at the rate of about two thirds of a mile a year—thus reaching Britain, for example, by 5,000 B.C.

Thus begins the decline of the hunt as an activity essential to the community. At this point in our outward journey from creation we are already almost at home in modern times. The native populations of most of North America were still in transition from hunting and gathering to agriculture as recently as 200 years ago. In his sequel to *The Emergence of Man,* appropriately titled *The Emergence of Society,* John Pfeiffer showed how the rise of agriculture brought more rapid social change wherever people settled into communities.

The tradition of hunting and gathering was one of basic equality—no hierarchies other than deference to the superior capabilities of group leaders, or chiefs. Even this position was largely ceremonial and carried few powers or prerogatives. But with organized communities this natural equality declined. A rise of hierarchies and elites coincided with the increasing social complexity, interaction, and geographical immobility brought on by agriculture and its attendant cities. The hunt was no longer available as an outlet for the curiosity and competitiveness of *Homo sapiens.* After a long egalitarian past, when human beings were equals among equals, social forces were released that brought into being the big man, or the strong man.

Perhaps this rise of hierarchies was unavoidable. Cities with large agricultural surpluses had to be defended from the slowly decreasing bands of marauding hunters who still roamed during this late period of prehistory. The growing personal wealth of those with the knowledge and instrumentalities of agriculture, as well as of those with control of the land, had to be justified and defended. For the first time in history people were found working, expending personal energy to acquire or produce goods for more than immediate needs. They were working longer hours and maintaining new urban, year-round agricultural environments.

Palaces and ceremonial structures began to appear. Walls were built around many of the early cities, so that they also became military hierarchies or organizations. It is not difficult to see that many of the tensions of our own times had their origins in this period. Hierarchies, which seem always to have been essential for organizing people on a large scale, appear to have encouraged exclusions and discriminations from the very beginning. Pfeiffer suggests that studies of these first social relations can help us in our search for "nothing less than the underlying laws of hierarchy and state formation."

As we continue our search for the jurisprudential nature of our envoys, we find the invention of writing around 3000–4000 B.C. Before writing, oracular ceremony and repetitive memorization had been the only means of ordering matter, or storing information. It had been the only means of learning "the tribal encyclopedia," a body of knowledge that Pfeiffer says was "imprinted on the brain of the community." Writing, therefore, brought important changes to a world in which tradition had always been imparted by repetition and rhyme.

Modern society is still very much under the influence of the old social technology of pomp, circumstance, and ritual. Nevertheless, writing began to moderate, refine, and define the purposes and limits of social organization and power. It began to change the nature of personal practice and public ceremony and therefore the nature of thinking itself.

The invention of writing marks the official end of prehistory and the beginning of the symbolic, physical, or technological accumulation of knowledge. Both Bronowski and Pfeiffer observe that a unity had been shattered. Religion, the arts, entertainment, military planning, community organization, and schooling had all been pursued together within the limits and the immediacy of ceremony. With the advent of writing these subjects became specialties. A new analytical device had been created. It now became possible to conduct continuing investigations into fleeting or remote phenomena, whose manifestations and characteristics could be recorded and preserved.

The capacity of the collective brain had been enlarged. Only since the invention of writing have we been able to document the conscious, conceptual, and continuing efforts of humanity to improve, even to bring into harmony with nature, its social organizations and institutions, such as law, government, and organized religion. Since the invention of writing and with the development of each successive element of information technology, the growth of knowledge has accelerated.

3 Discovery and Invention

The time has come to realize that an interpretation of the universe—even a positivist
one—remains unsatisfying unless it covers
the interior as well as the exterior of things;
mind as well as matter.

Pierre Teilhard de Chardin
The Phenomenon of Man

Something unprecedented had already happened by the beginnings of
recorded history. Pfeiffer, Bronowski, and Sagan all discuss it with great
beauty. Humanity is seen not merely as a new species. Rather, the intelligence and self-consciousness of humanity are seen as representing another
order of being. Human beings are thus pioneers of a newly recognized kind
of evolution, that of intelligence itself.

Of course, human beings still depend on their genetic makeup. They
inherit the brains that make them human. But they also learn and pass accumulated knowledge from generation to generation through the use of cultural and technological devices. They make their own coverings, shelters,
weapons, and, to a growing extent, their own environments.

The imagination and reason of a human being help make it possible
for him or her to modify the environment rather than simply accept it.
Bronowski notes that the series of inventions by which man through the
ages has remade his environment is a different kind of evolution. Though it
is a product of conscious biological action, it is not strictly biological evolution, but biocultural evolution.

Learning and tradition have acquired a new order of importance. As
Pfeiffer puts it, "Cultural evolution has come to dominate genetic evolution." Modern human beings don't always wait for change to act upon them
from the outside. They are, in some sense, self-propelled. They generate
their own pressures. They deliberately create change, thereby creating new
conditions, to which they must adapt in new ways.

We shall not adapt to the space environment, for example, merely
through traditional biological mutation and natural selection, but rather by

cultural selection—cultural transformation—the use of perceptive intellect to industrialize and fashion technology, which in turn is used to fashion new variations of traditional biology. Culture, like biology, can be seen as directed toward specific aims and characterized by complexity, functionality, and interdependence of parts.

According to L. L. Cavalli-Sforza, of the Stanford University Medical Center, these cultural qualities are realized, "are transmitted . . . with rules entirely different from those of living organisms, being transmitted, in fact, *by* living organisms." Natural selection is here replaced by cultural selection. We reform the environment, joining it as an agent that affects choice and change.

It is interesting to note that more and more the resolution of biocultural threats to humankind on Earth depends upon the cultural equivalent of biological mutation—that is, invention, which occurs with ever greater frequency within cultural forms than within biological forms. In fact, as implied earlier, cultural invention has even increased the frequency of biological mutation through toxicity, radiation, and direct pharmaceutical and surgical interventions into genetic coding.

Space activity is only a recent example of a long series of such newly invented conditions. Looking back upon a list of such human inventions, Bronowski says they compose a "brilliant sequence of cultural peaks" that make up *The Ascent of Man*. "I use the word ascent with a precise meaning," he says. "Man is distinguished by his imaginative gifts . . . plans, inventions, new discoveries . . . [which] become more subtle and penetrating. . . . So the great discoveries of different ages and different cultures . . . express in their progression a richer and more intricate conjunction of human faculties, an ascending trellis of [human] gifts."

In this growth of human conciousness we see the process that has been going on from the very beginning of our cosmic, physical, and biological evolution. Every new arrangement of matter that occurred, from the subatomic on, created greater potential and increased the physical experience of matter, thereby creating more information. What we see is something even more than a genetic drive toward greater complexity and information. We also see molecular and atomic tendencies toward arrangements necessary for awareness and intelligence.

If we are to cultivate Space Age internal models as the basis for our international and interplanetary jurisprudence, then we must take advantage of Space Age information. We must look for the unifying factors, the least common denominators in the unfolding process of creation. Julian Huxley suggested that Teilhard de Chardin did just that in his view of the process of complexification. Teilhard identified complexification as a primary unifying factor in nature and as a form of consciousness itself. To him complexification represented an all-pervading tendency. He defined "full consciousness," or "self-consciousness," as the "specific effect of organized complexity."

Teilhard indicated clearly the general evidence of constantly ascending mind consequent with, and throughout, the ascending phyla of life. Teilhard could not believe that any natural phenomenon, such as intelligent self-awareness, could be an isolated phenomenon. Even an irregularity in nature can only be regarded by science, he said, "as the sharp exacerbation, to the point of perceptible disclosure, of a property diffused throughout the universe, in a state which eludes our recognition of its presence."

He felt that we must therefore infer the presence of at least potential mind in all material systems, by extrapolating backwards from the human to the biological and from the biological to the inorganic. He saw a possibility that mindlike properties might exist in elemental matter throughout the universe. An all-pervading consciousness, of course, has been a constant preoccupation of philosophy and the metaphor of almost all the religions since the beginnings of recorded history. Many religions maintain that the kingdom of God is within.

Throughout the rest of our search for our emerging envoys of mankind, we shall look at many of the ways in which the consciousness that has emanated from the heart of matter, this tendency or inner drive toward increasing mind, has affected the sociobiological or cultural-institutional evolution of the human species. We shall continue our search at this point by looking at the way this selfsame inner drive has taken us from argonauts to astronauts and is carrying us farther into the Space Age and beyond.

"Oh you swimmers in the far sea of space," mused Ray Bradbury. From the earliest origins of human beings on the planet Earth, we have been space voyagers, astronauts aboard spaceship Earth. And now that we have achieved the ability to construct our own spaceships, it becomes even more important to understand the drives that have led us to do so.

Science is finally beginning to take a more serious look at the question of consciousness, at the inner nature of matter. In *God and the New Physics*, Paul Davies stated that "it is ironical that physics, which has led the way for all other sciences, is now moving toward a more accommodating view of mind, while the life sciences, following the path of last century's physics, are trying to abolish mind altogether." He quotes psychologist Harold Morowitz in the same vein:

What has happened is that biologists . . . have been moving relentlessly toward the hard-core materialism that characterized 19th Century physics.

At the same time, physicists, faced with compelling experimental evidence, have been moving away from strictly mechanical models of the universe to a view that sees the mind as playing an integral role in all physical events.

Davies described some of the new experimental evidence in his discussion of the quantum theory and its famous principle of uncertainty, which indicates that it is impossible to predict both the location and direction of any particle of energy from moment to moment. Only probabilities exist. The cosmos is portrayed as inherently spontaneous and unpredictable. At the same time, quantum physics is seen to have provided a loophole to the age-old assumption of entropy, that you can't get out as much as you put in. Instead, physicists now talk about a self-creating universe. Davies observed that

Physicists began to realize that their discoveries demanded a radical reformulation of the most fundamental aspects of reality. They learned to approach their subject in totally unexpected and novel ways that seemed to turn commonsense on its head and find closer accord with mysticism than materialism.

Teilhard argued that even entropy has a dual nature, that it is at least two-dimensional or bipolar, just as the cosmos is multidimensional. He imagined entropy as a whole effect, with positive and negative poles, or with an inner and an outer nature. It degrades physical systems irreversibly and is an unavoidable cost of transforming energy, but it thereby facilitates the basic changes in the arrangement of matter that are essential if complexity, communication, and thus consciousness are to increase.

Almost the same description was used by science writer Robert B. Tucker concerning the influence of Ilya Prigogine's work in physical chemistry on dissipative structures. Tucker indicated that classical science had contented itself with examining the effects of entropy on theoretically closed systems, where the irreversible effect of entropy should be an equilibrium of total randomness, lack of order, or chaos. Such a view ignores, however, the more disquieting open or nonequilibrium systems. According to Tucker,

Rather than viewing non-equilibrium as a negative factor, Prigogine believed that it was actually a source of organization and order. In effect, he turned the second law of thermodynamics on its head and made it relevant to the natural world and its open, complex, non-equilibrium systems.

Even the prestigious Nobel committee noted that "Prigogine has fundamentally transformed and revised the science of irreversible thermodynamics. He has given it new relevance and created theories to bridge the gap that exists between the biological and social scientific fields of inquiry." Prigogine's self-organizing systems bring order out of chaos and thus seem to fit conveniently with Davies's self-creating universe and Teilhard's bipolar entropy.

As we move up the chain of life into the fields of bacteriology, botany, and zoology, the observation of conscious behavior, of the "within" of things, assumes greater importance. Any attempt to ignore the within aspect of nature breaks down completely with humanity, in which, says Teilhard, "the existence of a within can no longer be denied, because it is the object of direct intuition and the substance of all knowledge." Descartes expressed a similar insight when he said "I think; therefore I am."

Jurisprudence, philosophy, theology, sociology, psychology, and the other social arts and sciences can be seen, therefore, as almost entirely concerned with this inner nature of matter in arrangement, although the concern has perhaps not always been pursued with the degree of interdisciplinary vigor that those in the hard sciences would like to see. This should no longer continue to be so, however, for it is the purpose of all the disciplines to discover the universal hidden beneath the exceptional or transient manifestation. Ultimately, it is the purpose of all the disciplines to know the truth, and they are going to have to borrow from one another if they are to do it.

This human search for the truth has profound implications for the human experience and for future space civilizations. "In their ceaseless experimenting, they had learned to store knowledge in the structure of space itself," said Arthur C. Clarke in *2010: Odyssey Two.* "They could become creatures of radiation, free at last from the tyranny of matter. . . . They could rove at will among the stars and sink like a subtle mist through the very interstices of space."

Such metaphors are merely isolated examples of the almost giddy significance of consciousness when it considers itself. In the process of evolution, the mental properties of matter have become ever more important, until in humanity they have become the dominant characteristics of life. Perhaps this had already come to pass by the time of the cave painters. It almost certainly had become so by the time writing came into being.

There is no better place than with this early invention and discovery to begin to look for the answer to the question why we are moving into space, or to the questions, Why do we climb Mount Everest? Why do we attempt to conquer death, disease, and injustice? Why do we attempt to increase consciousness, experience, and awareness?

Curiosity, discovery, and invention, the inner characteristics of matter, are the reasons. They are synergy at work. They are axiomatic in humanity. And they will ultimately lead us to the evolving natures of our astronauts, cosmonauts, envoys, us.

We find these same inner characteristics as long ago as the early Greek argonauts. Homer described the world as a turquoise island within which a ring of earth protects the known sea — the eastern Mediterranean — from the roar of the "Infinite Ocean." The technology of exploration was advanced by early mariners such as Jason and his argonauts, who set out to explore beyond the known sea. Each exploration, from that of Jason, through Marco Polo, through Columbus, to our recent space explorers, pushed back the circumference of darkness a bit farther.

As the facts of nature and the laws of the universe began to be uncovered, one by one, it became obvious that nature itself facilitates free interaction and random, or free, experimentation. It became clear that our institutions are unnatural whenever they violate this nature. The beginnings of this realization in the seventeenth century gave rise to the Enlightenment, or the Age of Reason, in the eighteenth century. We are there able to witness the effects of natural insights and natural laws on institutions and jurisprudence in totally new environments.

At the time of the exploration and settlement of the New World, philosophers and jurists had been influenced greatly by the discoveries of science and the explorers in the New World, which served as a mirror for the hopes and aspirations of the dreamers, inventors, and naturalists of the Old World. That New World mirror helped to reawaken and illuminate an ancient sense of equality and freedom.

In a similar way, the very existence of space is a challenge to the mind. Space offers us a view of our lonely planet as a whole, and our perspective of Earth is now different. In what ways it is different we are, perhaps, not quite sure. But we have heard our astronauts talk about it. We may even have "felt" it as we watched fellow human beings walk on the moon or as we watched our exploring satellites send live pictures from other planets and then head silently out to the stars, carrying encoded plaques for possible extraterrestrial intelligence.

Space provides a more comprehensive view of the natural conditions that must be weighed in devising any system of social interaction which is in accord with natural law. A late twentieth-century group of musical lyricists, the Moody Blues, mused, "Vast vision must improve our sight. Perhaps at last we'll see an end to our home's endless plight and the beginning of the free."

Yet, before such a dream can be fulfilled, many obstacles must be overcome. Just as in the past, the transformations of energy in the Space Age have such awesome power potentials that many seek them in order to achieve hegemony rather than freedom and cooperation. As Einstein said, "Against every great and noble endeavor stand a thousand mediocre minds."

In Einstein's universe of constantly unfolding events no place was at rest. There was no perspective from which to study the universe that was in any way superior to any other. The ideas of natural freedom and intelligent arrangement were basic to Einstein. He once said, "In order to punish me for my contempt for authority, fate made me an authority myself." Yet, he also understood the modeling power of his consciousness, saying "Imagination is more important than knowledge."

Relativity meant that the laws of nature must be identical no matter from what point of view they are being described and no matter how differently they may be perceived as a result of differences in perspective, all of which are relative. If this were also to be true of social laws, such laws would have to be fundamentally based upon a substantial allowance for spontaneity and protection of diversity. Any other assumption, given the deep-seated cultural diversity of humanity, would presuppose a great tyranny.

Einstein often spoke of his concern about whether our social and conscious evolution were keeping pace with our technological revolution. He called for "a supra-national government based on law, to eliminate for all time the methods of brute force."

And so it is that now, at the advent of the Space Age, we find ourselves preoccupied with global survival. As our literary camera zooms in for a close-up of our Space Age voyagers, it reveals them afloat in a time of internationalism, and of many other *isms*. Unfortunately, it is still a time of brute force that harbors the potential for the destruction of the planet's biosphere, its envelope of consciousness.

But it is also a time in which another new frontier may serve as a mirror for our hopes and aspirations, just as it did for the enlightened hopes and dreams of the exploring and growing civilizations in the sixteenth and seventeenth centuries. President Kennedy envisaged this parallel:

The world was not meant to be a prison in which man awaits his execution. Nor has man survived the tests and trials of thousands of years to surrender everything, including its existence. . . . We will persist until we prevail, until the rule of law has replaced the ever dangerous use of force.

This is the dilemma we face as we move in for a closer look at the human and jurisprudential circumstances of our first space explorers. Indeed, it is particularly important to note that, so far, the newest earthbound astronauts of our unfolding epic are not simply individual scientists, theologians, or storytellers. Instead they are socio-organisms, great and anonymous entities, with names such as National Aeronautics and Space Administration, United States of America, and Union of Soviet Socialist Republics. NASA's organic identity has become as closely identified with the lunar landings as has that of Columbus with the discovery of America.

The existence of such vast socio-organisms and their pivotal roles in the human occupation of near and deep space raises some of the more vexing problems of our new space age developments. These developments require an ever greater recognition of natural law, of the sovereignty and sanctity of the individual human consciousness. This was the recognition enshrined in the Constitution of the United States by our forefathers, themselves children of the Enlightenment. This is why the theories of the early legal naturalists are still pertinent to us now. In discussing the early legal naturalists, Andrew Haley, one of the world's first space lawyers, said:

They gave the natural theory of international law its most searching examination at precisely the time when man was last faced with a major expansion in the effective size of his universe and with the resulting need to devise new systems of law. . . . We are on a similar threshold today.

We are entering an age in which access to information and to new frontiers is controlled by giant organizations. We have already lived through the first quarter century of an age when space explorations are conducted and space explorers are chosen on the basis of substantial military criteria. What does this imply for the policies that we should adopt concerning space? If space activity is to represent the promise of universal citizenship and personal liberty that has been widely perceived and sought through the ages, how is it to do so when it is a captive of the powerful and intoxicating social technologies of humanity? As Louis Halle put it in *Harvard* magazine:

Our perspective, which embraced almost four billion years at the beginning . . . has now been reduced to the point where we confront, close up, the practical problems of the day. These have to be resolved within the limits of economic feasibility and the present stage of technological development. The prospect set forth in what follows remains within these limits.

II   From Argonauts to Astronauts

4   Toward a Philosophy of Space

The Earth is the Cradle of Mankind; but one
cannot expect to remain forever in the cradle.

> *Konstantin Tsiolkavsky*

The spear, the bow, the gun, and finally the
guided missile, had given him weapons of
infinite range and all but infinite power.
Without those weapons, often though he
had used them against himself, man would
never have conquered his world. Into them
he had put his heart and soul. . . . But now,
as long as they existed, he was living on
borrowed time.

> *Arthur C. Clarke*
> 2001: A Space Odyssey

Until now, most of our important explorers have been the *conquistadores*,
the single-combat warriors of *The Right Stuff.* Single, or symbolic, combat
was common throughout the world in ancient times. In single combat, the
leader of one organization would fight his counterpart from another, as a
substitute for a pitched battle between their entire forces. The biblical story
of David and Goliath is a good example. The tradition lived on in the retreat
of an army when its leader fell, or in the greatest warrior becoming the
leader, a practice still often followed.

Our earliest astronauts played similarly symbolic roles, as the single-
combat warriors of the Cold War. They were thrust forward into this rarefied
ideological battle, which was a substitute for the unthinkable suicide of
total atomic war. Astronautics was seen by millions as the epitome of the
entire technological and intellectual capacity of the first two space powers
and as an indication of the character of their national identities. The astronauts and cosmonauts were thus given all the homage, fame, honor, and

heroic status of the ancient single-combat warriors. And, not surprisingly, they were military men, both by training and by allegiance. "Thus beat the mighty drum of martial superstition in the mid-twentieth century," said Thomas Wolfe.

From Jason and his argonauts to the Mercury Seven, our envoys have been on missions as representatives of organizational sovereignties—whether kingdoms, principalities, private enterprises, cities, or nations. They have been the very personification of the values and goals of the groups they have represented on every new frontier. Securing territory and resources, essential to the continued well-being and survival of any society, has been the primary thrust of these missions of exploration. The human territorial imperative is ancient and obvious. It is therefore natural to find that most explorations were conducted primarily for military or economic objectives.

Large-scale exploration merely for the sake of discovery has been particularly elusive. How many times in history has it really happened? Perhaps Marco Polo, Daniel Boone, and Charles Lindbergh were motivated primarily by wanderlust, but even their expeditions were sponsored. Essentially they were economic ventures, paid for by elites acting under the laws of existing public sovereignties.

The epic voyages of humanity were hard-won achievements. Christopher Columbus spent a year lobbying in Portugal and seven years at the court of Spain before he gained the reluctant blessing of the queen, and then only with the pledge of royal jewels by the Prince of Aragon. The queen's coffers were diminished by her military expenditures. She agreed to the venture only for its potential profit and strategic importance—the East Indies in sixty days! But the queen still required a loan guarantee!

Despite the magnificent upward-spiraling nature of evolution and intelligent consciousness, imaged in us is the tedious, timeless struggle of energy and matter in the procession of organization and reorganization. The march of discovery and civilization has been progress, but a slow, entropic process.

Yet we know that intelligence will continue assembling energy into different combinations, seeking balanced and evolutionarily productive or useful arrangements. Intelligence reorders random energy into resonance. It creates order from disorder. This is the "magnificent trend" we have been discussing.

A good example of the spontaneous, constructive irreversibility of entropy in the social or cultural setting is the idea that all innovations are introduced parochially. This means that whatever the ultimate influence or ripple effect of an event, the take-off point, the immediate effect, is localized in time and space. Like a pebble dropped into a pond, it takes time for an event to affect, or resonate with, increasing spheres of both the physical and social environments. Different resonances develop in separate and widely dispersed locations.

This is because human beings are both physical and conscious entities. Physically, human relations are inherently resource-using, because the human body occupies space and requires systematic interaction with its surroundings in order to survive. Consciously, those in the vicinity of an invention, innovation, or change may even attempt to block its diffusion if they perceive it as some sort of threat. This is the basis of *social* parochialism and prejudice and is the essence of Einstein's comment about mediocre minds arrayed against every great and noble endeavor.

When the species *sapiens* first appeared, it lived in tiny social units, families, whose relations with other similar units were dominated by fear and hostility. This appears to be a fundamental factor in the evolution of the political process on the planet Earth, because control of contiguous space is essential to all living forms. The individual organism is nothing if not a system organized in space, which can be annihilated if its vital components are penetrated or destroyed.

Early *Homo sapiens* was in constant danger from other species and from protohuman rivals. Survival required the resonance of cooperation, the merger of the ego with the collective identity of the kinship group, tribe, or other small social unit. The success of that strategy was reflected in these social units, these cultural technologies. As a result of cooperation they grew and became cities, states, nations, religions, enterprises, and organizations of all sorts. As noted earlier, the species became more recognizably human as it became more highly organized and developed higher orders of cooperation.

Thus we revisit the birth of the human socio-organism. We see it become a larger and more complex entity, surpassing the individual as the sole unit of sovereignty or society, as the sole possessor of sovereign regalia. And its point of view was initially parochial, directed toward group territoriality, subordination of the individual ego to the collective ego, and the expectation of violence. Its goal was survival, a goal that has persisted to this day, bringing ever greater reliance on the development of military technologies to achieve collective demands and value goals.

So perhaps Arthur Clarke was right when he speculated that the world would never have been conquered without weapons. Many of the first tools were weapons, weapons for the hunt. Even the development of agriculture only heightened the need for organized space. Perhaps without this territoriality and the organization and control that it requires and facilitates humanity would never have developed social technologies of sufficient complexity to permit activity and migration off the planet. Yet parochialism and territoriality have also caused much of the conflict and fragmentation in the human social order, an order that has finally developed military strategies with suicidal potential, a fact recognized in Clarke's further observation that we are living on borrowed time.

In *Law and Public Order in Space,* Myres McDougal, Harold Lasswell, and Ivan Vlasic said that the essential nature or goal of this military strategy is to segregate within a domain the values that are required "to encircle and penetrate, and to detach the significant assets of other participants for inclusion within a controlled and delimited space." Even the simple amoeba can be observed operating in this fashion, and since human beings are members of a physical-biological species, their primary need or expectation, like that of the amoeba, is for survival.

Survival was first on Thomas Jefferson's list. His specified inalienable rights were those of life, liberty, and the pursuit of happiness. These three simple expectations were meant to serve as a measure of the various needs, demands, and values that have been and will be important in the evolution of human society. Nor does the order of their listing appear to be mere coincidence. Jefferson was both equating them and putting them in some sort of order of priority. And, although he might not have thought of it in quite this way, it can be suggested that they represent distinct levels of social evolution, social ecology, and conscious expectation—that is, survival, social-transitional, and metaphysical-transcendental.

Survival, of course, has to do with Jefferson's first self-evident truth, life. *Social-transitional* relates to his second, liberty. And the third, pursuit of happiness, is the *metaphysical-transcendental* level. It is natural that those values which primarily support physical survival would have developed first. Survival is the supreme instinct of biology. And, as we have already seen, the survival level has dominated the social-transitional level in its cultural expression.

Although McDougal, Lasswell, and Vlasic suggested the existence of at least eight categories of basic values, needs, or demands in human cultural expression, we find that at least half of them are directly related to the first level of expectation, that of survival. They are power and security; health and well-being; physical control and learning; and wealth and resources. These values, needs, or demands are physical and territorial. They have necessitated control over space and have motivated the military strategies we have just discussed.

Jefferson's second important expectation was liberty, a social-transitional concept. It implies the absence of social coercion and the opportunity to exercise power and acquire skills in order to consume energy for health, well-being, and security, which is the exercise of sovereignty. Its McDougal values are respect and loyalty.

To the extent that these needs are of importance for effective social organization, they may not always have promoted civil liberty or individual civil rights as much as they promoted the survival of the group or the right to survive and function as a member of the group. This is because the development of hierarchies encouraged exclusions and discriminations from the very beginning. But if the hierarchies were also promoting survival by enlarging opportunity, increasing choice, and advancing social evolution through cooperation, then they were promoting liberty in the long run.

Robert McC. Adams reminds us that social organizations were not only parochial in perspective but were also internally creative and ecumenical. He said that cities were "seats of learning, sources of artistic and philosophical ferment, initiators and exponents of ecumenical ideas, and forges . . . of our persuasive symbols."

Ecumenical is a word with almost the opposite meaning from that of parochial. It means universal, worldwide, or totally interactive and cooperative. Ecumenism is implicit in the higher orders of cooperation that are necessary for the existence of the social system. It is the social expression of the processes of complexification, polymerization, and the dissipation of structural energy that were discussed earlier.

A similar perspective on the competition between social parochialism and ecumenism has been found in the works of philosophers from John Locke to Karl Marx, although Marx unfortunately used the perception to justify delay in the evolution of civil liberties by glorifying the parental role of the social system and nation-state. And his views have been even further distorted by Stalinism, Maoism, classism, and all the other totalitarian forms. Still, Marx saw that the existence of the hierarchy, the physical social structure, inherently limits some choices while it increases others.

So the very existence of the system limits civil rights to some irreducible extent. And yet, if there were no commonly agreed-upon systems of interaction, there would be few, if any, social or civil relationships within which rights could be exercised. This paradox is at the center of the argument in all countries as to what constitutes patriotic or unpatriotic, social or antisocial behavior. It is the reason freedom of speech does not include shouting "Fire!" in a crowded theater. It is the conflict between personal and group sovereignty.

The fact that social systems both create and restrict civil rights at the same time is part of something variously described as Catch-22, positivism, the Zen Paradox, and the Sufi Compromise. It is a result of the polarity or paradox in existence that we noted in the interplay of the "magnificent trend" and the "tedious, timeless process of organization and re-organization." It is because of irreversibility, because consciousness feeds on entropy to create ever higher states of ordered complexity or "interiority."

So the purpose of the system is to increase individual choice and increase intelligence through peaceful, civil, co-operative arrangements. This purpose is becoming clearer as we are forced to cope with the new perspectives and dangers of the Space Age. Ultimately, the only stable system of social interaction will be one that does justice to these more human social expectations of equal respect, social equality, loyalty, and cooperation.

Finally comes the most recently evolved level of expectation, that of the pursuit of happiness. It is the most intelligent, conscious, or interiorized expectation. Its McDougal values are the metaphysical-transcendental, intellectual, conscious, or psychic values of rectitude and enlightenment. And in due course we shall return to them and their important functions in reordering random energy into resonance.

But for now we simply note that all eight of McDougal's basic values, needs, or demands are at least to some extent characteristic of the human concept of sovereignty, which is control of space, freedom of action, and self-control. And yet, as we shall discuss in greater detail in later chapters, sovereignty has been primarily a synonym for collective forms of power: those that reside primarily in the survival and social-transitional realms. This, again, is because social organisms and cultural technologies are physical systems, whose primary function is survival. And, at least in the species *Homo sapiens,* it is also because the physical and biological needs evolved before the intellectual or conscious needs. The nature and tactics of the nation-state have thus been less enlightened than basic and rudimentary.

Aviation and aerospace provide good examples of the abiding dominance of biosurvival values such as territoriality and contiguity in the early Space Age. McDougal reminded us that "even the grasshopper-like technology of the airplane did not abolish the fundamental role of contiguity [territoriality]," suggesting that this is because of the dependence of planes upon surface bases and the military use and potential of aircraft. Yet territorial sovereignty over airspace is a principle much older than the airplane; its origin is ancient and obscure.

We know the Romans had such a principle. Named *ad coelum,* "to the heavens," it was a principle of property law to the effect that an owner's sovereignty over a piece of land went infinitely downward below the Earth, and infinitely upward above it. Perhaps this is a relic of the flat-Earth perception, but it illustrates well the continuing dominance of parochial security consciousness, which has in modern times assumed three and now four dimensions. When ships began to traverse around Earth and planes the ocean of air, territorial awareness became plainly three-dimensional. And when Einstein discovered the fourth dimension of "space-time," awareness assumed an even greater dimensional aspect.

But even Einsteinian events emanate from points localized in time and space. They may have vectors, velocities, and ripple effects, and they may only be arrangements of some underlying uniform field or metaphysical fabric, but they still display parochialism. So *ad coelum* has persisted in the law. It had to be addressed when the first airplanes trespassed the ascending columns of quasi-legal domain. It came to be understood that each person's legal column extended up only so far as beneficial use could be made of it. A modern example of beneficial use would be the skyscraper.

But what happened above there? Might it not even be a planetary domain equally accessible to all? Such an idea may seem fanciful now, but it was suggested and debated in the proceedings of the Institute of International Law in 1902, 1906, and 1911 and also in the Paris Conventions of 1906 and 1919. A scholar-statesman named Paul Fauchille advocated the proposition that "the air is free, subject to the right of security and defense of the subjacent state."

There is the catch! "Subject to the right of security and defense of the subjacent state" just about says it all. Group sovereignties have the columnar control above their underlying territories. The sovereign has always asserted exclusive, absolute dominion over the land and everything incident to it, regardless of whether the sovereign was thinking in two, three, or four dimensions. Even democratic and constitutional states, which legally recognize individual sovereignty, still retain such principles as the right of eminent domain, public imprisonment, police power, the military draft, the right of self-defense, and public control over national airspace and contiguous waters.

Yet Fauchille was not totally naive and unjustified in his hope for freedom of the air. He succeeded primarily in making the air free for some forms of commerce, just as the sea is, although the subjacent state always had the right to restrict its use. Many countries, for example, temporarily restricted access to aircraft of the Soviet Union as a protest against the shooting down of a civilian airliner over Soviet airspace in 1983, the KAL 007 incident. That incident essentially pointed up the true extent of worldwide freedom of the air. Everyone knows that there are military and other restrictions on aviation.

Yet there have been significant positive developments. Cooperation has proved essential to international aviation, just as it has to other elements of society. Significant conventions and international coordinating organizations were set up. There were the Chicago and Geneva Conventions on International Civil Aviation in the 1940s. The International Civil Aviation Organization was established to coordinate international air traffic and is now affiliated with the United Nations. Domestic organizations such as the American Federal Aviation Administration facilitated coordination with other nation-states and international organizations.

Throughout the world there exists a complex matrix of cooperation in many areas of endeavor, such as communications, weather, public health, and agriculture. Such arrangements are extraterritorial, requiring the merger, even if only within a specific and limited realm, of one territorial entity with another or of one sovereign's interests with those of another. Global arrangements emerged. The parochial unit began to be the planet.

Of course aviation was not solely responsible. Religion, ideology, science, history, education, seafaring, the printing press, radio, television, internal combustion, world war, and now satellites and space travel were also contributing factors. Whatever the interplay of factors, however, *home* was being redefined, perhaps not all at once, and perhaps not toward metamorphic transcendence quite yet, but it was being redefined measurably just the same. Global interaction was strengthening the demands for social-transitional values, for cooperation and social equality.

These social values are transitional because they mediate between individual and organizational demands and between the strictly physical or survival needs and the metaphysical-transcendental ones. These higher values are the values that must predominate in any successful international public order and within and among any truly evolved states. Given the hair-trigger status of our nuclear world, we have already come to the point in evolution when the social values of loyalty and respect loom even larger as principles of survival. There must be cooperation and equality or there will be instability, injustice, and war.

This is the situation that prevailed in the early predawn of the Space Age. The astropolitical age was ushered in as a military arena, with all the dangers attendant on the calculation of attack and defense. Yet elaborate, if rudimentary, systems of public order also existed from the international to the civic level. These systems were based, at least to some extent, on the values of cooperation and equality and were designed to reduce the expectation of violence.

Thus we see two distinct and dissonant sets of values at work in the modern social arena. They are the ancient, territorial, military, survival strategies versus the modern, cooperative,libertarian, social-transitional values. These paradoxical, competing values are important both within and among countries. Totalitarian states, of course, adhere to military techniques both for survival and as the firmest foundation for loyalty and respect. They adhere to the atavistic view that the only true respect is born of fear. They fail to understand the random, self-organizing, irreversible, complexifying nature of reality.

The modern scientific view says that human diversity and sovereignty demand liberty both within and among states and that world peace will never be achieved otherwise. Surely Hitler convinced us of the utter insanity of the idea that the world could be dominated by force. Not only did he demonstrate the moral mindset of someone capable of attempting such a thing, but he also demonstrated the utter destructive futility of such an attempt, even with overwhelming forces. And need the much greater dangers of the nuclear age even be mentioned?

Yet many states do not seem to have learned this lesson fully. And since military tactics are to take by force, fire is fought with fire. All sides risk the incendiary consequences, because the chosen countertactic is counter-force. This same division of focus has thus invaded even the inside of the constitutional democracies, which have been compelled into the greatest military "advances" in history. And the countertactic is endless escalation, perhaps even conflagration.

And so we find ourselves in the young Space Age. The competition for dominance between the two sets of values is fierce. This is the true nature of the Cold War. It is a battle between consciousness and instinct, between cooperation and control, between peace and war. It is not really limited to the bilateral arena between the first two space powers, the United States of America, and the Union of Soviet Socialist Republics. It is characteristic, instead, of the entire human arena, both public and personal. It is still isolation, parochialism, and the expectation of violence versus convergence, cooperation, and social transition. These paradoxes and polarities are characteristic of the ecotone where consciousness and entropy interact.

5 Intelligence Agents

Mankind has been converting natural
energy into social organization at an ever
increasing pace. . . . Industry is the sum
total of human activities involved in the
process of converting natural energy into
social structure.

Carleton S. Coon
The Story of Man

The silver lining to social polarity and parochialism is individual human consciousness. Consciousness itself is transparochial. It is ecumenical, capable
of integrating many facts, perceptions, and feelings into integrated world
views, piercing visions of space and time, and timeless artistry of all types.
We are once again reminded that intelligence is another order of being.

So our explorers are not only the single-combat warriors of the nurturing, protecting, territorial, sovereign, social machine, not simply exemplars
of the right stuff. They are also intelligence agents, the nerve cells of the
machine. And as conscious, intelligent entities, they are more intimate with
the metaphysical-transcendental perspectives and the values of rectitude
and enlightenment than are any of their robot social organizations. The tendency to increasing mind capabilities is most strongly expressed in human
consciousness. The biotechnologies are useless without an intelligence to
apply them.

Behind the practical motives involved in large expeditions of any kind
are the imagination, insight, knowledge, and ideology of individual human
beings, the real envoys of mankind. The efforts of these explorers are crucial in helping us to discover the immutable laws of nature. They do this by
exposing us to more of reality, truth, and each other and by forcing us to
adapt our inner models and world views to new realities and more accurately discerned natures. Our envoys are thus the constituents of a more
enlightened awareness and better-informed consciousness.

There is a strong sense of infinite potential in Tom Wolfe's description of
the quest for the right stuff, a quest to be one of "that special few at the

very top, that elite who had the capacity to bring tears to men's eyes, the very Brotherhood of the Right Stuff itself." It is the quest for cosmic effect, for immortality. Such a perception demands respect, and it tends to make the social-transitional values of respect and loyalty dominate the physical-survival values. It helps us to understand that cooperation and liberty, among the highest expressions of the social-transitional realm, are essential to survival of the species and therefore to conscious survival.

This is because the ecological thread that runs through human consciousness is the desire to transcend the limitations of the material universe, to be immortal. It expresses itself in the human desire for recognition, to be special, to make a difference, to be a winner, a genius, a leader: to have the right stuff. It is a desire that needs to be accommodated, mediated, and integrated with the similar desires of others in such a way as to produce social resonance.

The desire is to move faster, to fly higher, and to achieve justice and higher intelligence, and to do it, as Wolfe said, in "a cause that means something to thousands, to a people, a nation, to humanity, to God." There seems to be an inner need in many people to have their species win against the horrendous odds of nature and the elements and perhaps, one day or some millenium, at least to have some distant progeny stand on the works of his countless ancestors, grab God by the lapels, and shout with the exultation of a victorious warrior, "At last, I found you!"

Not that the survival circuits of the nervous system have been turned off. Not at all! The territorial, ritualistic, militaristic, reptilian brain is still a substantial physical component of every human brain and is indispensable in human development. It still predominates in the highly unstable metabolizing environment of politics. It still controls in most socio-organisms. The mind-set of the high-flying envoy is still often parochial. It is to carry out the mission, to do what must be done. Nor have the envoys had it easy. Often, their only chance to create, innovate, and discover has been to fulfill the role of organizational envoy, of single-combat warrior.

Nevertheless, the underlying intelligence is still at work in the envoys. We all know that there were conscious underlying motivations in countless great achievements and discoveries. The same sort of debate that followed the voyages of Columbus and preceded the colonizing of the New World is now centered on the way to open up the new frontier of space. And the debate is centered within, among, and between Earth's largest societies.

In that debate the highest aspirations and hidden agendas of humanity are being purveyed by our individual envoys of mankind. These envoys are going to use the social ships of the great organizations; but the purpose, the style, and above all the necessary freedom will not come from the social machines, but rather from their human passengers and pilots. These passengers and pilots have been tampering with the design and function of the social machinery, refining it since the very beginning of history. They are the programmers of the system. And, where possible, they are designing against overcentralization and unchecked social or political power.

Thomas Jefferson also believed in tampering with the system and refining it. In one sense, such thinkers and activists as Jefferson, Patrick Henry, Madison, Rousseau, and Locke were some of the earliest systems thinkers. The American founders were students of the classics and of all the old utopian texts. They saw that any social organization was infinitely more powerful than the individual human being. They foresaw correctly that structural mechanisms are needed in the design of the system to protect the individual from the overwhelming power of group sovereignty. They felt that the design of the state should conform as far as possible to the natural order of the cosmos. And this is why they were emboldened to describe their new republic as the *novus ordo seclorum,* "the new order of the ages."

These early natural jurists designed against parochial institutional tendencies. President Kennedy called the fight against these tendencies "a twilight struggle, day in and day out, to secure the blessings of liberty to ourselves and our posterity." It is a battle being fought in every corner of the globe, with champion envoys such as Ghandi, Martin Luther King, and Lech Walesa.

There are several new studies in jurisprudence that are focused on this battle. One, called jurimetrics, is both the jurisprudence of science and technology and the science and technology of jurisprudence. A good example of the latter can be found in modern designs based on the American tradition of decentralization and limited powers, such as the sunset laws. These laws rest on the proposition that social systems have predictable structural and conscious qualities and that legal adjustments can be designed to minimize their adverse effects.

There is a proposition that an organization, for instance, like an organism, is primarily motivated by the instinct for self-preservation. If the organization is insulated from market demands it has little incentive to accomplish its assigned task, for to do so would be tantamount to suicide. A sunset law would therefore set a date for the termination of both the task and the existence of the organization, as an incentive to accomplish the task.

The example is simplistic, of course, and the effort has not always succeeded in practice. But it is indicative of new types of research now being conducted in schools of law, business, administration, psychology, sociology, and political science, under such names as "the legal environment," "organizational behavior," "public administration," "social psychology," and "systems management." This search for synthesis is also the preoccupation of many natural scientists who wish to discover the ecological bases of our cultural forms and our social behavior. They are searching for synthesis in the laboratory of the past, looking for embryonic clues to the underlying laws of hierarchy and state formation.

What they are all seeking, in one way or another, is the attributes of organizational operation that can be identified and should be taken into account in the constitution of social systems. The search is for ways to make the biotechnology coexist and cooperate with its human constituents efficiently, symbiotically, and at arm's length. The attempt is to manage the entropy and to increase choice and freedom. Even despots often claim to be pursuing such a goal for the systems they preside over. It is a goal so basic to human ecology that even the mightiest tyrants dare not forget to pay at least lip service to it!

So what is really at risk on the new frontier is the freedom and growth potential of the people who go there and the people who send them there, because we are dependent upon our machines, both social and technological. And we have seen that these machines have predictable, conscious, territorial qualities, which, if unchecked in a nuclear and scientific world, could threaten individual intelligence, the species, and conscious survival.

Of course it may be that many of the "fighter jocks" who made up the first American astronaut corps did not perceive their function in quite this way. One does not aspire to the royal brotherhood of single-combat warfare through social-scientific analysis of organizational checking functions. One lives the piloting experience, both physically and emotionally. But the astronauts were nevertheless fulfilling the intelligence function of the envoys from the moment they entered the space program. Recall that they were top-flight test pilots, possessing some of the highest, most refined physical, emotional, and mental skills. Yet they were recruited to be "Spam in a can," passengers in a capsule that would be piloted in its first flight by a monkey.

But the Mercury Seven would have none of it. They demanded piloting controls, windows, self-ejection, and involvement in the design of tasks and of future vehicles. They were products, not only of the military, but also of an intelligent, endlessly striving species and a scientifically designed, constitutional nation-state. They were the spear throwers in a game that had the most complex, sophisticated rules in history. And they were intent upon tampering with the machinery.

6 Astropolitics

There can be no thought of finishing, for
aiming at the stars, both literally and figuratively, is the work of generations; but no
matter how much progress one makes
there is always the thrill of just beginning.

Robert H. Goddard to H. G. Wells
April 20, 1932

Civilization is a movement and not a condition, a voyage and not a harbor.

Arnold Toynbee

The aerospace game didn't really begin with the Wright brothers or the
1783 balloon. As we have seen, the history of space exploration appropriately begins in the conscious realm, with the legend of Icarus, the stories of
Lucian of Samosata, and the notebooks of Leonardo da Vinci. But from a
cultural point of view the real game began with the interest and involvement
of social organizations, with the accumulation of "hive energy."

Although the first institutional attempts to "explore space" may have
been by someone like Jason and his argonauts, the first institutionalized
attempt to study Earth on a large scale came just before the aviation conventions of the early 1900s. It was called the International Polar Year and
took place from August 1882 through August 1883. Eleven countries participated in this first polar year. Their concern was the exploration of the virgin territory of both the Arctic and the Antarctic, for the purpose of studying
the magnetism, meteorology, auroras, and geology of the Earth.

This is a hopeful place to begin our examination, for despite the continuing militarism of most countries, the polar year was a product of the desire
for enlightenment and information and used the social tactics of cooperation. It was an extraterritorial event, with the planet as the parochial unit.

Great changes were afoot on the planet Earth at this time. The Western
world was in the grips of the First Industrial Revolution, which essentially

was the substitution of machines for human or animal labor. This great revolution reached its peak in Europe and America between 1875 and 1910, but it has yet to peak in many of the developing countries of the world. In some sense, of course, an industrial evolution had begun with the invention of stone tools, fire, the wheel, and the plow. But we have finally arrived at a point of significant, revolutionary acceleration of the drive for discovery and invention in the social order.

In *The Third Industrial Revolution,* an examination of the potential for a third, new, space-based industrial revolution, G. Harry Stine noted,

A revolution is a rapid and radical change in the way of doing things, of social organization, of life style. If industry is the sum total of Human activities involved in the process of converting natural energy into social structure in accordance with Coon's hypothesis; [then] . . . an industrial revolution is a drastic change in the work operations, products, and manual-mental output of Human beings.

The aerospace enterprise was born into just such a revolutionary environment. Economics, science, technology, and geopolitical interests were all beginning to assume global dimensions. It was the generation of the world wars. The social dimensions of the "twilight struggle" were being redefined in the direction of our modern version of the Cold War.

It is not just idle curiosity to seek out the historical beginnings and organizational foundations of our current space enterprises and of our cultural genesis into the outer space environment. The growing pervasiveness of culture and collective consciousness is particularly apparent at the level of the socio-organism. The grand internal models discussed earlier have discernible, concrete external manifestations.

One such manifestation is physical—the how-to level, the familiar terrestrial skills, the necessary acquisition of knowledge, and the establishment of organization. We need to understand the social and political nature and origins of humanity and its astronaut or cosmonaut envoys just as much as we need to understand their cosmic and evolutionary nature and origins. In this chapter, therefore, we shall begin to examine these biosurvival and social-transitional aspects of humanity's new yeoman efforts in space.

Although national and ethnic identities remained dominant at the advent of the Space Age, global society had been forced into different forms of interaction, cooperation, and conflict and thus into a growing necessity to recognize and accept the principles, aspirations, needs, and perspectives that are common to all people. There had already been a rapid growth of new international organizations, both public and private.

There were private international professional organizations such as the

International Council of Scientific Unions (ICSU) and the International Astronautical Federation (IAF), the latter including most of the early rocket societies, which were formed to promote human interplanetary travel. There
were international religious institutions, university programs, corporations,
and other arrangements, both public and private.

There was also a growing number of official, public organizations to
which governments belonged, such as the International Telecommunications Union (ITU) and the World Meteorological Organization (WMO). A Second International Polar Year was held, fifty years after the first, in 1932 and
1933. Scientists from forty-four countries participated; twenty-two countries sent out field expeditions. The community of interests began to transcend geopolitical borders and ethnic barriers. Most notable in this respect,
of course, was the United Nations and its Universal Declaration of Human
Rights.

The groundwork was being laid for the conception of space as the common heritage of humankind—a keystone of all the space treaties that would
follow the launching of Sputnik. Astronauts and cosmonauts would be designated envoys of mankind in the first instance and of particular nation-
states only secondarily.

Again we are seeing a redefinition of parochial cultural and nationalistic
attitudes as a result of ecumenical forces. We are seeing a reconsideration
of the values that are essential to the universal priority of survival. And the
resultant redefinitions are tending in the direction of social cooperation.

Information, imagination, and insight, the metaphysical, transcendental
elements, are growing in importance, just for basic survival. They were
already becoming more important by the time of Sputnik. In fact, if we look
closely enough, we can see that the real resources of the Space Age are
information, enlightenment, intelligence, and higher consciousness. Call it
what you will. It is the simple interaction of the mind with different arrangements of matter—that is, physical experience. Information is both the subject and the product.

Nor is this simply the optimism that flows from an undisciplined accentuation of the positive. Rather, it is the empirical conclusion of late
twentieth-century content analysis of widespread sources of local information, such as hometown newspapers. In *Megatrends* John Naisbitt explains
how content analysis arose within the military intelligence community during World War II and is still a preferred tool of the intelligence community.

Trends can be revealed by looking at continuities and discontinuities in
the various sources of information—essentially the approach of computer
intelligence. Relative concerns can thus be examined empirically. Naisbitt's
first contemporary Megatrend reveals the second industrial revolution—a

movement from an industrial society to an information society, characterized by Toffler as a third wave of global civilization—a society based on consciousness and intelligence.

Of course, by Coon's strict definition of the word *industry*—"the sum
total of human activities involved in the process of converting natural
energy into social structure"—information and industry are indistinguishable. That is why we have called this information revolution the Second
Industrial Revolution. By whatever name, of course, it is a physical, cultural,
conscious process that is incapable of precise definition.

Since the early 1950s, the pivotal period of final labor just preceding
the birth of the Space Age, the percentage of the U.S. population in occupations in which the creation, processing, and distribution of information is the
job has increased from 17 to 65. After the shock of Sputnik there was an
even stronger push toward an information-intensive society, with the
emphasis on public education and the explosive effect of the communications satellite and the computer. The birth of the Second Industrial Revolution is closely related to the birth of the Space Age.

The effects of the information and communications revolution on societies with freedom of information were truly staggering. Communications
satellites began to turn the world inward upon itself, thus transforming it
into Marshall McLuhan's global village. And, as we have seen, the revolutions, wars, and myriad other interactions—information exchanges—of the
modern era had already begun the process of global parochialism before satellites even arrived. Both the potential and the horrors of modern events and
discoveries were affecting the social ideologies of humanity. Experience
was driving humanity to search for survival in the direction of more conscious, transcending awareness.

The growing strength of such a universal awareness is demonstrated
by the fact that the fledgling Space Age was not to have an entirely military
face. The participation of many people and organizations interested in the
increase of knowledge and the benefit of all mankind had a civilizing effect
on the Western space effort. The concrete result was significant involvement of groups other than the military in the actual physical and organizational components of early American space exploration.

This civilian involvement was heightened by the proposal for an International Geophysical Year (IGY). In April 1950, twenty-five years after the
Second International Polar Year, a group of scientists met at the home of
James Van Allen to discuss important scientific problems that required
investigation. Lloyd V. Berkener suggested that because science had made
such progress during and since World War II, another international scientific
year was in order, without waiting for the end of the fifty-year interval pro-

posed at the time of the First International Polar Year. He urged further that the event not be limited to the poles but be expanded to include the entire geophysical environment of the planet. Such an event would typify the social ecumenism necessary for global parochialism.

By 1952 Berkener's suggestion was being studied by the International Council of Scientific Unions (ICSU). He continued to urge the world scientific community to broaden the purview of the project to include the study of the properties of the ionosphere through the use of both satellites and sounding rockets. For this reason, he suggested 1957 as the best year for the IGY, since, according to astronomers, sunspot activity would be at its peak.

The reaction of countries, organizations, and scientific communities brought into being one of the first important transnational cooperative efforts since the establishment of the United Nations. In October 1954 the ICSU formally agreed to hold the IGY from 1 July 1957 through 31 December 1958 in order to observe the entire period of maximum sunspot activity. A series of World Data Centers was established, with collection of complete data in the United States and the Soviet Union and subcenters in eight other countries. Sixty-six countries, 20,000 to 40,000 scientists, and tens of thousands of volunteer observers finally participated.

It was Berkener who drew up the proposal for U.S. participation in the IGY in 1954 and, through Alan Waterman, director of the National Science Foundation, presented it to President Eisenhower in March 1955. Naturally, the question of possible interference with military ICBM efforts was raised almost immediately, but when Eisenhower turned to his defense advisers for guidance they indicated that such a program need not delay important military programs. Eisenhower then gave his full support to the IGY effort, including the go-ahead for civilian development of a satellite as part of the U.S. contribution to the IGY. This set the stage for two important initial realities of the Space Age.

First, the American space effort would be organized under civilian authority. Careful attention was given to the coordination of the American announcement concerning the nature of its commitment to the IGY. Despite concern over the possibility that deliberation might cause a delay that would allow the Russians to announce their program first and gain a propaganda advantage, the decision nevertheless was made to arrange for the simultaneous release of the satellite announcement by the IGY Secretariat in Brussels and the White House in Washington on 29 July 1955.

And second, as might be expected in our paradoxical world, the shock of Sputnik would once again heighten the interest and participation of the military — the security apparatus — in astronautics, bringing renewed emphasis, even within the nominally civilian American program, to the importance of the single-combat warrior, the astronaut.

Although President Eisenhower may have initially believed those who professed the military inapplicability of space technology, as the 1950s wore on he became more fearful that space activities might extend aggressive militarism beyond the surface of Earth. Eisenhower had been a direct witness to the grotesque nature and wastefulness of modern warfare. He had a keen appreciation of the risks associated with the institutional momentum of "the military-industrial complex," which he warned against in his farewell address. Eisenhower said, "the people of the world want peace so strongly that one day the governments are going to have to get out of their way and let them have it!"

His concern was manifested in the civilian nature of the American IGY project and also in the presentation of his dramatic "Open Skies" proposal in Geneva, Switzerland, on 21 July 1955. The proposal offered the Soviet Union and other countries reciprocation of "a complete blueprint of our military establishments . . . [and] a comprehensive and effective system of inspection and disarmament."

This extraordinary proposal, in addition to the announcement of a civilian satellite as a goal of the United States for the IGY, expressed two basic principles related to space activities that were ultimately to pervade many significant developments in international space law and several other international agreements of the Space Age. These principles were that the objectives of the activities of man in space should be scientific rather than military and that such activities are for the benefit of all countries through cooperation and sharing of data.

In fact, the International Astronautical Federation (IAF), which would soon establish the first International Institute of Space Law, sent a message to President Eisenhower expressing pleasure about "the announcement that the scientific data obtained . . . will be available to all nations as testimony of the peaceful application of rocket technology for the benefit of all mankind."

Unfortunately, the Soviet IGY satellite announcement, just one day after the announcement by the United States, contained much less detail and fewer promises of international participation. Later, the Soviet Union rejected Eisenhower's Open Skies proposal with a counterproposal. They would agree to an international space authority to conduct cooperative launches if the United States and all the countries of the world agreed to the total and outright abolition of all overseas military bases.

Eisenhower was thus forced to nurture the survival aspects of his divided sentiments and, for reasons of national security, to forge the weakest link in his developing "peaceful uses of space" policy. Despite his persistent public insistence on the compelling need to avoid the militarization of space, in private conversation he emphasized to Deputy Secretary of Defense Donald Quarles that although information gathered in connection with the IGY would be made freely available, "many defense secrets will be jealously guarded." National defense was still to have top priority. Eisenhower indicated that "to keep the satellite effort from interfering with the high priority work of ballistic missiles—it seemed mandatory to separate the programs."

Since Stalin and Khruschev both saw large ICBMs as the way to compete with American military supremacy, the real nature of the missile gap lay not simply in the chronological primacy of Sputnik or the boast of Khruschev that the Soviet Union intended to turn out rockets "like sausages," but rather in the size of the Soviet rockets and their ability to carry nuclear weapons. Because of the need to hedge U.S. bets on the militarization of space, the Army, or Wernher von Braun's Huntsville group, had also been assigned to develop a backup contribution to the American IGY satellite program.

So it was that the easy perception of space as just another place to send military equipment and military personnel as the initial couriers of Earth's cultural values was relied upon and exploited by both of the world's superpowers. Thus, the evolving pattern of future spacekind as star wars militarists found its roots in the cold-war politics emanating from Moscow and Washington long before President Ronald Reagan accepted the military importance of space as the high ground.

III

From the Right Stuff
to the Appropriate Stuff

7 NASA and the Space Race

I wonder whether [the astronauts] do not instinctively adopt a "jock" style and a wry slang in order to be able to live with such a monstrous enterprise without becoming pompous. Many of them have returned from space quite changed, and some of them have turned to careers in public service, ecology, or religion. Perhaps Earthmen will in time be as affected by the discovery of space as Europeans were by the discovery of America.

Mauricio Obregon
Argonauts to Astronauts

Obregon may be making a valid point with his description of the reason the early astronauts adopted a "jock" style. But as we have seen, a more detailed evaluation of the early astronauts shows that another good part of the reason was that they *were* jocks—fighter jocks, military test pilots—in a space program that had its origins in the highly charged competition between two powerful countries deeply involved in the geopolitics of the Cold War.

The new NASA was actually to choose the first astronauts of the Western world, those destined to be among the world's first legally designated "envoys of mankind." NASA was to carry out a feat that, through the milennia, had inflamed the imagination of humankind: to "break the surly bonds of Earth!" NASA thus had a decisive voice in determining just how and by whom those surly bonds would be broken. In some sense, NASA would become the arbiter of Olympus.

Yet despite its shiny new title, it was the legatee and recipient of many old traits and trends. First, and perhaps most hopeful, was President Eisenhower's unbending insistence that the space effort have a rigorously civilian character, with a primary emphasis on original research, development, and exploration. This was clearly reflected in the 1958 National Aeronautics and Space Act.

This act, the new NASA charter, made dissemination of information a duty of the agency, and despite a grant of considerable authority, the purview of the agency was specifically limited to those developments necessary for research and exploration. To insulate the program from what Eisenhower feared would be perceptions of involvement with the military-industrial complex, the space act, in its Declaration of Policy, specified that NASA was to be responsible primarily for "research and development associated with aeronautical and space activities, *except* for those activities peculiar to or primarily associated with defense." It was also required that the administrator of NASA be a civilian. In several respects, the United States took a courageous step in July 1958, when President Eisenhower signed the space act, which charged the space agency of the U.S. government to lead a strictly civilian, peaceful exploration of space, "for the benefit of all mankind."

These were not the words of parochial nationalism and sociobiological territoriality. They were not the words of conquest. They were precisely the words that would turn up almost ten years later in the unique Outer Space Treaty of 1967, sometimes affectionately referred to by practitioners of space law as the mother treaty.

The U.S. space act seemed to strike an unorthodox and elevated philosophical and political posture usually witnessed only in extraordinary times. NASA's entire legal and organizational environment was formulated to cultivate a broad spectrum of constituencies for its programs, even if those constituencies were comparatively small. NASA was deliberately connected to other important constituencies outside the president's office and cabinet. Integrated high-level consideration of space policy and an institutional memory, moreover, were assured by the creation, in the space act, of a broadly based National Aeronautics and Space Council in the Executive Office of the President.

Still, the old dual military-civilian program remained. Significant early acquisitions of NASA included the Vanguard program of the Navy, the Lunar Probe Project of the Air Force, the Jet Propulsion Laboratory of California Institute of Technology, *and* the five Army satellite projects at the prestigious Army Ballistic Missile Agency at Huntsville, Alabama.

The continuing nature of this military-industrial-civilian symbiosis, despite the organizational philosophy and extraterritorial nature of the new NASA, was once again apparent in the actions and words of President Eisenhower. Although he insisted, in a news conference on 4 November 1959, that nonmilitary space exploration was a "sort of doctrine in America," he had laid the groundwork in 1958 for the new, second version of the "dual" space program. Six months before the creation of NASA, in February 1958, the Congress had passed the administration's bill creating the Defense Advanced Research Projects Agency (DARPA), which had its own director of guided missiles.

The next month, pending the formation of NASA, the president gave his approval to the plans advanced by DARPA, making it, in a real sense, the first U.S. space agency. When NASA was finally formed, the accompanying Space Council was directed to provide a civilian-military liaison committee composed of an equal number of representatives from the military departments and NASA—which meant that the military predominated over civilians on the committee three to one. Also, despite the requirement that the administrator of NASA be a civilian, the space act did not require NASA to be managed by civilians in the ranks. NASA was heavily staffed at high levels with retired or borrowed military personnel.

In the May 1958 congressional hearings on the space act, DARPA Administrator Roy Johnson stated the Eisenhower administration's approved position on the proposed space legislation. His testimony included this statement:

The legislation setting up a civilian group should not be so worded that it may be construed to mean that the military uses of space are to be limited by a civilian agency. . . . For example, if DOD decides that it is militarily desirable to program for putting man into space, it should not have to justify this activity to this civilian agency. . . . The [NASA] authorization act should be amended to provide that insofar as such [space] activities may be peculiar to, or primarily associated with, weapons systems or military operations, in the case of which activity, the DOD will be responsible.

So it is interesting to note that even the limitation of NASA by its charter purely to peaceful, nonmilitary activities was not motivated strictly by altruism. It was as much to keep NASA out of the military's business as it was to keep the military out of NASA's business. The fact that peaceful research and development by NASA also fulfilled nonhostile military needs simply made it easier for the civilian effort in space to be undertaken hand in glove with the military. The space act made the intent of the relationship quite clear when it indicated that a primary objective in establishing NASA was to achieve, "the most effective utilization of the scientific and engineering resources of the United States with close cooperation among all interested agencies . . . in order to avoid unnecessary duplication of effort, facilities and equipment."

Still, though the intent may not really have been to accomplish a full division of efforts, a striking degree of division remained. It was undeniable that an open civilian program was created for the exploration and exploitation of space on an internationally cooperative basis for the benefit of all mankind, with accompanying "man-in-space" publicity hype and space extravaganzas that convinced most of the United States population, as well as most of the world, that it was the *only* U.S. program. There was also an almost secret commitment to a secret space program, the highest priority having been given to space research with a military application, and there was significant military involvement and interest in the new civilian space program.

Nowhere was the place of the military in NASA programs better illustrated than in the selection of the original astronaut corps. In addition to its general research and development mission, President Eisenhower gave NASA a specific twofold mission in manned space flight. The mission was given high national priority, second only to national defense. NASA was, at the earliest feasible time, to launch a man into space, provide him with an environment in which he could perform effectively, and recover him safely. This was Project Mercury. NASA was also to use the support of leading life scientists to develop the capability for extended manned space flight.

The original civil service job specifications for Mercury astronauts did not require that an applicant be a pilot. It was felt that the astronaut would simply be a passenger in a cannonball capsule with no controls and no windows. After all, the whole point was to get the man into space as fast as possible. The government was unwilling to wait for three or four more years of rocket developments so that the Air Force might be able to orbit a *real* pilot in a *real* rocket-plane—some version of the X-15. Such a feat would be a purely military one. And everyone was mindful of what the Russians were doing.

The Russians were launching a virtual menagerie of mice, rats, insects, dogs, guinea pigs, frogs, and mannequins. They were clearly testing the feasibility of manned flight. So, for reasons of international strategic posture and national prestige, NASA was directed to take the quick-and-dirty approach. It was essential to launch a man in a can on top of a Von Braun rocket.

NASA's civil servants thus initially chose the more or less logical solution of simply putting out a call for qualified volunteers, essentially any young male college graduate with experience in a physically dangerous pursuit. Test pilots were mentioned in the general description, but so were members of submarine crews, parachute jumpers, arctic explorers, mountain climbers, deep-sea divers, scuba divers, and veterans of either combat or combat training. Although the astronaut would not be expected to do anything during flight, he would have to be able to withstand the conditions of spaceflight. He simply needed to be five feet eleven or shorter in order to fit into the Mercury capsule.

Eisenhower was aghast. He stepped in before the regulations could even be officially issued. The idea had been to do things as quickly and simply as possible. He saw potential chaos and a political hotbed that could divert attention from the prime objective of competing with the Soviets, both literally and figuratively.

Should women be allowed to go? How about noncitizens? Will there be pressure to appoint members of other interest or ethnic groups? It was even feared that every lunatic in the country might volunteer. Powerful members of Congress might tout favorite sons. The selection process could take months, not to mention the time necessary for security clearances. Eisenhower thus simply directed that the original astronaut corps be chosen from among the 540 test pilots then on active military duty.

8 The Selection of Astronauts

Intelligence without genius; knowledge
without inflexibility; bravery without fool-
hardiness; self-confidence without ego-
tism; physical fitness without being
muscle-bound; a preference for participatory over spectator sports; frankness without blabbermouthing, enjoyment of life
without excess, humor without dispropor-
tion, fast reflexes without panic in a crisis.

*Portrait of the most desirable astronaut candi-
date by Robert Voas, psychologist, Training
Director for the Mercury Astronauts*

Michael Collins, Major General, USAF, born 31 October 1930, Rome, Italy,
married, three children, U.S. Military Academy, test pilot, public official, corporate executive, and locker-room jock. He is in tune with the military line of
command, but he, like most fighter pilots and test pilots, has a love affair
with the shiny silver airborne stallions. He'll do almost anything to fly. He's
an astronaut, a single-combat warrior. In his own words, Michael Collins
was *Carrying the Fire.*

*Then the shrinks take over. . . . Thrust and parry. . . . How can I
describe the blank, white piece of paper this year? Last year I said it was
nineteen polar bears fornicating in a snowbank . . . interviewer's face tight-
ened . . . my lack of reverence for his precious cards. Hostile, they said I
was. But not this year. This year I want to fly to the moon, badly I want it,
and I will describe that white card in any way that will please them. . . .
Second-guessing the shrinks is not easy.*

This vignette from the life of Astronaut Michael Collins illustrates several important aspects of the natures of our initial American envoys of mankind:
—They were military and comfortable with the rules of command.

—They were usually uncomfortable with and distrustful of those who dealt with the nonquantifiable aspects of being human.

—They were human experiments, guinea pigs in one of the most fantastic experiments in history.

—Though privately rebellious, with a sort of wild ruffian mode of conduct and a tendency to subvert the system to their own liking, like Von Braun and Korolev before them, they were nevertheless subservient to, and complied with, any game rules that were essential to their personal objectives and dreams of spaceflight.

This description, it must be admitted, bears little resemblance to Voas's profile of the ideal astronaut. But if the candidates in the first several astronaut groups had fitted all or most of Voas's profile there would not have been very much entertainment value in the right-stuff metaphor.

These first astronauts were getting ready to conduct a very expensive, slightly premature stunt for the benefit of international political perceptions of power. They could easily become human sacrifices. On that basis alone, it was not surprising that test pilots were chosen. Their records were readily available. They had the highest mortality rate in the service. People with their particular attributes were necessary if the space program was to be infused with sufficient honor and if the degree of daring that would be necessary was to be justified.

Yet, apart from Eisenhower's insistence on the use of military test pilots, the real screening, the critical choice, was made not simply on the basis of social caste or perfunctory training. The real choice was psychological and medical. Like it or not, NASA was confronted with the unavoidable necessity of constructing a workable man-machine symbiont that would be capable of sustaining human life off Earth in apparently lifeless and environmentally hostile regions.

Thus, the fifty-six initial finalists were subjected to interviews, psychiatric examinations, and a complete medical evaluation, including medical stress tests, such as measurement of blood pressure and heart rates immediately after immersion of an arm in ice water. So there was clearly more to being selected than just being the hottest test pilot and graduate engineer under forty and five feet eleven.

Yet, despite Eisenhower's stated reasons for choosing only test pilots and despite the rigor of the selection process, there were still complaints that the process was not open enough or flexible enough, particularly because it did not allow for equivalent qualifications. Imagine the disappointment and resentment felt by many parachutists, skydivers, scuba divers, and others who, because of other career training or military service, might have been equally well qualified to fly. The limitation to military test pilots even disfranchised the great civilian X-15 test pilot Scott Crossfield, who became the world's first official astronaut when he piloted the X-15 up to more than fifty miles above the surface of the Earth, the military line of demarcation for the official issuance of astronaut wings.

Yet it would be misleading to portray the original selection of astronauts as controversial. The man-in-space furor and the "missile gap" made the choice seem entirely logical to the vast majority of the American public. After all, why not select bona fide heroes for such a heroic task?

The right stuff of the Edwards test pilots was evident long before Tom Wolfe's popularization. Remember the ancient origin of the single-combat warrior idea. The late 1950s was a time of traditional values and strong patriotism in the United States. Therein lies one of the most important ingredients in the success of the early American space program.

That ingredient was the participation of the new astronauts in shaping, or even altering, the nature of the man-machine entity that NASA had begun to construct. Had individuals been chosen who did not have the stature, the heroic aura, and the personal determination of these first test-pilot astronauts, they probably could not have influenced the program nearly so much.

Also, had they not been astronauts in the United States, a pluralistic representative democracy with free speech and a free press, they could not have threatened to blow the whistle on ill-conceived parts of the program. They were able to use their constitutionally guaranteed access to the new Space Age extensions of their senses, the electronic media, to threaten contact with the commonweal or the collective consciousness.

Although the Soviet cosmonauts have also significantly affected the evolution of their space systems, they have not done so nearly as much or as quickly as their American counterparts. The American astronauts achieved, within the system, an informal authority that came to be called astropower.

Still, President Kennedy's emphasis on a commitment to the moon landing by "every citizen of this country," coupled with his broad emphasis on civil rights and equal opportunity, eventually led to a reevaluation of the qualifications for becoming an astronaut and flying into space. In 1962, in anticipation of forming the second group of astronauts for the Gemini program, NASA decided to ease the selection criteria somewhat.

The educational requirement was liberalized to consider applicants with degrees representing the physical and biological sciences, not just engineering or its equivalent. The heavy dependence upon military test pilots diminished somewhat, although only slightly, by requiring "experience as a jet test pilot, having attained experimental flight test status through the military services, the aircraft industry, or NASA, or having graduated from a military test pilot school." So, someone like Scott Crossfield might qualify if he was of suitable age.

During the 1960s a tidal wave of cultural change hit the American scene, part of which was a growing social insistence on equal access to opportunities and freedom from arbitrary and stereotypical social categorizations. As early as 1959, after the selection of the first group of astronauts, the Lovelace Clinic and General Donald Flickinger, an Air Force physician, began to act as a result of the public clamor for wider access to the new frontier of space. On their own authority they asked Jerrie Cobb, already a noted woman pilot, to undergo physical tests similar to those given the Mercury astronauts in order to determine the potential fitness of female applicants for future selection.

Cobb, daughter of an Air Corps captain, had been flying since she was twelve years old. She had a DC-3 captain's rating, was a flight instructor, had several single and multiengine ratings, and was highly trained in navigation and meteorology. She had piloted more than sixty-four different types of aircraft, mostly in general aviation but including a jet fighter and a four-engine turbo prop. By the time of the abrupt termination of the experimental testing program in 1962 Cobb had successfully completed three separate batteries of tests, one of which, a nine-hour and forty-minute "profound sensory isolation test," had not even been required of the Mercury astronauts.

As a result of Cobb's success, twenty-five additional women pilots were chosen early in 1961 to undergo the testing program for astronauts. The tests were still unofficial and were not conducted under the auspices of NASA. They were conducted through the cooperation of the Lovelace Foundation, the U.S. Navy, and the Veterans Administration, for some of the women were ferry pilot veterans. Of the twenty-five, twelve passed phase one of the testing—essentially the tests endured by the original Mercury astronauts—and along with Cobb were shown to be medically qualified as suitable candidates for space flight.

The profound sensory isolation test is a good example of the second mile the female subjects were scheduled to endure in order to prove beyond a reasonable doubt that they were medically and psychologically qualified for spaceflight. In the test, the subject is placed in a soundproof and light-proof tank of water at body temperature for more than nine hours. The simulated weightlessness and total lack of sensory input can cause a person to retreat inward and begin to hallucinate. The point of the test was to endure the isolation and sensory deprivation—all the while hooked up to biomedical sensors—without hallucinating.

Despite Cobb's successful endurance of the isolation test, and despite the successful completion of phase one by twelve additional women pilots, the testing partnership was abruptly broken by the Navy because of NASA's refusal to participate in and state a "requirement" for the testing. These events provided the women pilots with a potent argument for congressional hearings. Behind-the-scenes pressure by these enterprising women was a prime factor in the establishment of the 1962 Special Subcommittee on the Selection of Astronauts, Committee on Science and Astronautics, of the U.S. House of Representatives.

The hearings revealed the strong emphasis on security and survival in the early American space program. The testimony showed that the problem with broadening the selection criteria was not based on biomedical or psychological criteria of the women or other groups that may have been excluded, but on the necessity for military discretion. Until the implications of the new experiment could be better understood, there would be tight control. Despite Kennedy's assertion that we were not just in a race, we really were in a race in many ways. The voyagers were being preselected by the nature of the voyage, and the overriding need was still for single-combat warriors.

It has been observed that the swashbuckling argonaut-astronaut caste always forms the first wave of exploration. Once the mysterious frontier has been demonstrated to be safe and inhabitable, then the engineers, doctors, lawyers, and social and economic bureaucrats move in. But nothing really develops until the women arrive. The real importance of the hearings on the selection of astronauts was that concerned voices were recorded and made public, and the women were activated.

Perhaps even a little consciousness was heightened, as exhibited in the statement of Congressman James Fulton of Pennsylvania. He spoke in response to the testimony of George M. Low, Director of Spacecraft and Flight Missions, Office of Manned Space Flight, NASA. Low had indicated that the logistics of selecting and training women might diminish America's ability to be the first to accomplish a lunar landing. Fulton said:

I disagree basically on your approach, because I believe that space is not [merely] an experiment or adventure . . . it is a new area where everybody will operate. . . . When women are paying the taxes, as much or more than the men, I don't think they should be kept out of space because of rigid requirements.

The real evolution of the selection of astronauts had begun, despite contrary appearances. There was a significant ripple effect from the seemingly parochial congressional hearings and the issues raised there. Later that same summer a startled chain of command at the elite U.S. Aerospace Research Pilot School at Edwards Air Force Base, California, received an order directly from Commander-in-Chief Kennedy. A black fighter pilot was to be selected for the next astronaut class.

The national debate was now centered on access to and use of space. Who is going to go? Why are we going? Can machines go for us? Would we want them to? Can we gain economically from space? What are the social ramifications of increasing extraterrestrial activity? Might the knowledge to be gained, alone, justify the presence of human beings in space? Meanwhile, the astronaut program and the Astronaut Office underwent significant and continual change after 1963 as a result of the shift in public attitudes and changes in public policy already described.

Although both were former military fighter pilots, the first two civilian scientist-astronauts, Russell L. Schweickart and R. Walter Cunningham, were chosen in the Apollo class of 1963. In 1964 applications were invited on the basis of educational background alone. Required was an earned doctorate in one of the natural sciences, medicine, or engineering. This fourth group would consist of six new scientist-astronauts, chosen by NASA from among sixteen recommended by the National Academy of Sciences.

Essentially, this selection round was forced on NASA. The Apollo class of 1963 was the first class that could not be promised that each of its members would fly in space. An intense desire to fly in space was the one factor uniting the astronauts. Morale problems were foreseen. The Astronaut Office maintained that a highly experimental test flight program required specialists trained in the most closely related equipment, test jet aircraft.

The Astronaut Office also maintained that additional astronauts meant more astronauts who would never fly—*un*astronauts. Astronaut John Young set the tone for this category of astronaut upon his return from the first Gemini flight. "You're not an astronaut until you've flown in space," he said.

The 1964 class was selected in spite of the astronaut's arguments. It consisted of three former pilots and three pure scientists, including Harrison Schmitt, a lunar geologist. Some of these astronauts would serve as more outspoken dissenters regarding the military complexion of the civilian space program. They were people who had prepared themselves to be scientists, not test pilots. They had not tailored their lives and careers to be astronauts. In some ways the status of astronaut was only incidental to their scientific objectives.

As noted in later years by Astronaut Robert L. Crippen, there was great difference in the atmosphere surrounding the astronaut corps caused by the classes of new recruits who grew up intending to be scientists rather than pilots. Spaceflight was still a specialized world of engineering projects, and it was often easier to train an engineer to be a satisfied scientist on occasion than to train a scientist to be a true utilitarian every day. The methodologies and underlying philosophical constructs are somewhat antithetical.

In *The All-American Boys,* Apollo astronaut Walter Cunningham, recalling his experience as one of the first scientist-astronauts, said "Even though NASA was a civilian agency, the Astronaut Office had a definite military cast. I felt as though I had been recalled to active duty with a fighter squadron. . . . [It] operated on a 'rank has its privileges' philosophy."

Cunningham indicated further that both he and Schweickart suspected they had been chosen merely as "sops to the scientific community." Still, he says, "we were just like the rest of the 'dumb fighter jocks.' Flying was much more attractive than working out a problem in physics." He and Schweickart were in agreement with the Astronaut Office in its assessment of what qualifications best suited a man for a trip into space:

[All the astronauts] were cheering like mad [for the position of the Astronaut Office]. This was no time for unselfishness. The National Academy of Sciences was just as provincial as we were. Space was such an appealing and unexploited area of investigation that the subject simply precluded objectivity. The Academy's position seemed to be that anyone with a yen for adventure could be a pilot, but only God could make a scientist.

A real clash developed within the astronaut corps between the pilots and the scientists and between the goals of technology and those of science. The question of access to space, still something of a parlor exercise in the Congress and the public at large, had become a highly charged issue within the astronaut community itself. Scientist-astronauts such as Cunningham, Schweickart, and Schmitt began to concentrate on and highlight their aviation skills in order to increase their chances to fly. The military hierarchy either enveloped or suppressed the worst dissent. The good-old-boy network for flight opportunities was kept firmly in place. Cunningham put it this way:

The pecking order . . . was primarily related to the hierarchy of selection. If one were a Mercury astronaut presumably only God and James Webb held higher positions. . . . Then came the Gemini group, whose members outranked and overruled all the weenies and plebes underneath them . . . the Apollo astronauts. . . . At the very bottom of the pile were the hyphenated astronauts, the scientists, who the pros simply assumed would be unable to cut the mustard. . . . That pecking order prevailed throughout the system. In fact, it was the system.

Still, the change in the astronaut corps had begun. Although many of the scientists would never go into space and would expend many dedicated and frustrating years in not getting to go, both the system and its mission were undergoing subtle changes. In 1966 the fifth group of astronauts was selected on the same basis as the third — Apollo — group. Out of nineteen selected four were civilians, and eleven of the nineteen held advanced degrees.

In 1967, the sixth group consisted of all civilians again, another group of eleven scientist-astronauts chosen from National Academy of Sciences nominees. The academy nominated them on the basis of scientific competence. NASA evaluated them on the basis of medical and psychological suitability. It didn't take long for this highly intelligent group to catch on to the realities of the astronaut corps. They quickly dubbed themselves the XS-11 (excess eleven) in a premonition of their bleak spaceflight future. The first flight of a member of this class would not come until 1982 and the advent of the space shuttle program.

9 The Changing Nature of Astronauts

We are not all cut of the same cloth any
more. . . . The Astronaut Office is much
less sharply and strongly competitive à la
the right stuff than it was in the right stuff
era. . . . There are many avenues, many
areas of human endeavor, where you're
tested for the right stuff. It's not something
astronauts alone have. It's just a certain
amount of discipline and focus and ability
to keep cool and react properly when you
need to.

Kathy Sullivan, Mission Specialist Astronaut
Member, National Commission On Space
and Member, First Official Group
of NASA Women Astronauts

By the 1980s even the concept of star wars was no longer limited to the
realm of fantasy. A growing number of people around the world feared that
an unimpeded military mindset so early in the Space Age might become self-
perpetuating as the primary philosophical conception of the human occupation of space and the exploitation of its resources. As the 1990s
approached, NASA was still a military-industrial-civilian symbiont. The
world was still polarized into opposing military camps. For the first time in
American space history the budget of the military component of the dual
United States space program exceeded the budget of the civilian component (NASA).

Yet, paradoxically, it continued to be evident to interested civilians that,
even if the military should have its way, it was possible, and might even
become essential, to hitch a ride on the military wagons. It was seen as necessary for humankind to be well established in space. Even if Armageddon
were perhaps the likely result of the planet's problems, there would be an
even greater need to know ourselves in the new biotechnical ambience of

space, so that we could vouchsafe the future of our progeny and the rightful odyssey of our genus, if not our species.

The new necessity for survival might very well become the presence of a large number of human beings living and working in the ecumenical environment of orbital space. Such space communities might even help to prevent a global holocaust. Though there was very little consensus among Americans on whether prevention would be made more or less likely by Reagan's "star wars" initiative, there was a high degree of consensus that building the space station was a wise undertaking. The station was to be entirely civilian—an orbiting NACA-style laboratory—available for lease by international industries and governments. Many felt that one of the best guarantees of the peaceful uses of space would be the presence of private civilian projects such as the station.

Still, the evolution of a military complexion for the civilian manned space program continued. This could be seen in the authorization for appointments of command pilots, pilots, and mission specialists for NASA's Space Shuttle Astronaut Program. It came in the form of a Presidential Executive Order in 1977.

NASA first announced the Astronaut (Pilot) Candidate Program and gave a brief description of the duties and responsibilities of astronaut pilots. Shuttle pilot astronauts were to serve as both shuttle commanders and pilots. During flight, the shuttle commander would have onboard responsibility for the space vehicle, the success of the mission, and the safety of the flight. The shuttle pilot would assist the commander in controlling and operating the shuttle.

The nonpilot mission-specialist astronauts were described as having overall responsibility for the activities of the crew, the use of consumables, and shuttle activities that affect the operation of experiments. They were also authorized to assist in specific experimental tasks at the discretion of the sponsor of the experiment, whether government, military, or private industry.

It was clear that the mission specialist would be involved in many activities whereby he, or now she, might simultaneously serve many masters and be subject to a variety of jurisdictions and legal regimes. Mission specialists might be responsible for handling two or more payloads involving different sponsors, for example, or owners of different nationality, whose interests might be diametrically opposed in the event that damage, death, or injury should occur. This would be particularly true aboard the new Space-lab, a fuselage module developed by the multinational European Space Agency.

The Spacelab would be the first experiment to require the presence of a so-called nonastronaut in space — truly a private civilian. Known as a payload specialist, this position was emphatically described as that of a passenger by George Abbey, NASA Director of Flight Operations. The payload specialist is expected to have some indispensable connection to an onboard experiment, something so technical that it would not be cost-effective to train a mission specialist to do it.

The payload specialists have been resented somewhat by some astronauts. They have been seen as interlopers who have not paid their dues for the valuable flight time for which some full-service astronauts have been waiting years. The payload specialist is not subject to NASA sanctions or career controls and is subject to the line of command only during ninety days' training and during the flight and postflight activities. The sensitivity of the Astronaut Office to the existence of this new nonastronaut position is perfectly understandable as an example of the same sort of social parochialism and turf protection that occurred at the time of the selection of the first scientist-astronauts.

Another important jurisdictional aspect of the selection of shuttle astronauts arose under a 1976 agreement between NASA and the Department of Defense (DOD). It was NASA's stated policy, despite the developments of the preceding twenty years, that of the thirty new shuttle astronauts to be selected, "a substantial number . . . be selected from the DOD." The Memorandum of Understanding provided that lists of candidates for the space shuttle program would be prepared by the Army, Navy, Air Force, and Marine Corps and that "NASA will select potential crew members from these lists." The vast majority of pilot-astronauts ultimately selected came from the lists.

Although the NASA-DOD agreement provided that a military member assigned to NASA shall not be subject to direction or control by his service or any of its officers, either directly or indirectly, the separation of jurisdiction and control was limited to those situations in which the military member is exercising responsibilities as an employee of NASA, "in the position to which detailed." He is still working for the commander-in-chief, the president of the United States, and he is still subject to instant recall to duty when operating a civilian space vehicle capable of functioning as a tactical or logistical military weapon. The space shuttle is the first American manned vehicle to fly classified military missions. There is no open dissemination of the results of such missions, despite the mandate of the NASA charter.

The NASA-DOD agreement characterized military astronauts in such terms as to leave little doubt that their work in fulfillment of military objectives was equal in importance to their work in fulfillment of civilian NASA objectives. Three provisions from the agreement are of particular interest.

First, the detail of military members to NASA shall in no way affect the status, office, rank, or grade they may occupy or hold. Second, while detailed to NASA, military members will be subject not only to appropriate NASA regulations, but also to that of the Department of Defense. Third, military personnel detailed to NASA will remain subject to the Uniform Code of Military Justice and to the policies and directives of their military departments, both with regard to military discipline and also to circumstances that do not affect NASA responsibilities.

The provision that "NASA will prepare each military member's fitness, efficiency or effectiveness report in accordance with the regulations of the member's service" further commits NASA to the military component and the influence of the military in space shuttle operations. For this reason, even some otherwise dovish observers have welcomed the prospect of a separate military shuttle organization operating out of Vandenburg Air Force Base in California. They have welcomed it because it would once again make the division between the activities of DOD and NASA more stark, as they were in NASA's earlier years.

NASA established separate rosters for civilian and military applicants, with requirements for shuttle pilots nearly as strict as those in the 1963 selection. NASA justified continuation of strict criteria for pilots by opening a civilian roster for the new category of Mission Specialist Astronaut. It was a fancy new name for the old scientist-astronaut. But with the configuration of the new shuttle missions, larger numbers of in-flight support personnel would be needed. Half the new shuttle astronauts would be mission specialists, and NASA took steps to ensure that a large proportion of them would be women or members of minority groups. If the corps was to be split into two rosters, it would be necessary to choose a large number of civilians to assert the peaceful face of the civilian space program.

In 1978, the eighth group of astronauts was selected on the basis of criteria substantially different from those used in the selection of previous groups. Of the 659 pilot applicants, 147 were military, 512 were civilians, 8 were women, and 10 represented minority groups. Fifteen pilot-astronauts were selected. There were 5,680 mission-specialist applicants, 161 from the military, 5,519 civilians. Of these applicants, 1,251 were women and 338 were members of minority groups. Fifteen were selected.

The educational backgrounds were infinitely more varied than those of earlier groups had been, with subject matter of speciality ranging from aeronautical and astronautical engineering through mathematics, physics, administration of science and technology, nuclear engineering, medicine, and biochemistry to electrical engineering and astrophysics. And for years not a word from the poets, at least not until after the fact, when astronaut Alfred M. Worden broke the silence of the ancient medium to characterize his unique perspectives from space in *Hello Earth* (1970).

Seventy of the first 108 persons selected as astronauts were reassigned to the corps from the military. Of the 38 civilian astronauts, 18 had been in the military before their selection as astronauts. Twenty, all of whom were selected as mission specialists, had never served in the military. Selection factors embraced a progressively greater reliance on academic degrees in lieu of flying and test-pilot experience. But most of the degrees, and all the advanced academic degrees, still represented engineering and the hard sciences, not the interpretive disciplines or social sciences.

There was some logic to this emphasis, of course. Scientist-astronauts soon learned that work on specialized engineering projects was a critical part of training for new astronauts and they became less and less involved in their own special academic interests — from Harrison Schmitt's interest in geology to Sally Ride's interest in free electron laser physics. Training was startlingly like beginning graduate school all over: endless hours of lectures on engineering and computer sciences. By and large, it took a special sort of personality to accommodate the adjustment successfully.

NASA's concern was that the new astronauts should not have to undergo the same types of tension and professional frustration experienced by the early scientist-astronauts, many of whom had dropped out of the manned space program. According to a *Washington Post* interview with Carolyn L. Huntoon, deputy chief for personnel development at the Johnson Space Center (9 May 1983), NASA was interested in trying a new approach to the selection of scientist-astronauts, the last group of whom had been selected more than ten years earlier.

This time the selection committee was looking for candidates who were willing to commit themselves and their careers to the space program. They had to be very good at what they were doing, yet they had to be willing to give it up to do more general things. They had to understand that they would be "Indians, not chiefs," as Flight Director Abbey put it. He said, "You're not going to be winning the Nobel Prize yourself. You're going to be an implementor for somebody else."

Since mission specialists would have to work closely with clients of NASA, such as research, communications, and defense industries contracting to use the space shuttle, their social skills and patience were as important as their scientific and technical skills. There was no ranking of the candidates with respect to the physical or psychological tests. They either passed or failed.

Consistent with much of the nondiscriminatory social legislation and employment regulations that appeared during the 1970s, women astronaut candidates were not queried about their personal lives in any way different from the way the men were questioned; they were not asked their personal views on childbearing, travel, and moving to Houston. According to Huntoon, the selection committee "looked for poise and self-confidence in the women they chose, knowing that they would be subjected to the pressures of intense public scrutiny and an overwhelmingly male environment at NASA."

In 1978, the pilot applicants were required to satisfy many of the same phase one psychological and biological tests given the earlier classes. By 1978 they were referred to as Class I physical examinations. The real difference was that mission-specialist applicants were required to pass only a Class II physical examination with a set of standards for sight, hearing, and endurance less stringent than that required for the pilots.

The symbiotic nature of the dual American space program had eventually promoted the presence of civilians in space and the development of permanent industrial facilities in space. By the 1980s industrial study teams, university research teams, venture capitalists, and science fiction fans were discussing a generation of transitional space habitats: those that would house the first permanent communities; from Gerard O'Neill's huge, rotating, *High Frontier* communities of thousands to those that would come before the first O'Neill colonies or lunar bases; those that would be built by the beginning of the twenty-first century.

Even before Reagan's decision to have NASA build a space station, there was a surge of private studies on inflatable stations, stations made from the shuttle's external tank, stations made out of modules that could be put in the shuttle's bay, and so on. The proposed new NASA station would initially carry only six to ten people, but there were designs for stations that could carry from fifty to two hundred people.

Support for these visions came in the form of increasing interest in new alternative modes of transportation. A number of engineers designed passenger modules for the fuselages of existing and predicted shuttles. The boldest designers were even attempting to create interest in new shuttles — with new and exotic propulsion systems that might reduce the cost to orbit by a factor of ten. Entirely private shuttles were proposed primarily for tourist travel to commercial space-station resorts. Hard money has been spent on such preliminary studies by both public and private organizations.

The first private rocket was launched into space in 1982. The small Conestoga I, launched by Space Services, Inc., of Houston, Texas, was suitable only for launching small satellite payloads. But private space transportation had begun. In the same year the first International Conference on Doing Business in Space was held under the auspices of the Smithsonian Institution and the American Law Institute.

In 1984, President Reagan established the Office of Commercial Space Transportation in the Department of Transportation. It was to facilitate and promote a private space transportation industry. Meanwhile, civilian jet pilots across the country had banded together to form the American Society of Aerospace Pilots (ASAP). ASAP was formed not merely to complain that civilian pilots had not been given serious consideration by NASA. ASAP was also an attempt to bypass NASA. With more than 300 members from among the ranks of commercial jet pilots, and with Apollo 11 Astronaut Edwin E. Aldrin, Jr., as an advisor, ASAP set out to create a private ground school for astronaut pilots, complete with a shuttle simulator. It was time to prepare for the near-term advent of commercial space transportation, they said, and they were doing something about it.

Even NASA itself joined the game. In 1984 NASA announced its Civilian Observer program. Approximately one seat a year would be set aside for members of the government, educators, journalists, artists, social scientists, and other members of the general public, who would finally be designated Space Flight Participants. It was suggested in commentary on the proposed regulations for this new category of passenger that the designation Civilian Observer should be replaced by the designation Citizen Astronaut/Participants. But NASA was not yet ready to let go of the holy "astro" title. As stated in the final announcement of regulations: "NASA reserves the title Astronaut for professional flight crew."

The findings of a special NASA Advisory Council of prominent citizens led to the new regulations. The council suggested that those selected should have proven or promising ability to communicate their experiences to their compatriots. Yet NASA would also require them to enter into a contract requiring preclearance of certain subsequent publications concerning the experience. "Whatever the arrangement," said NASA, "it will be by mutual agreement of both parties, and will cover participants' rights to publish, as well as the rights of NASA and its employees (including the right to privacy of other crew members)."

The participant-observer program was not purely a public relations gimmick, however. Any person selected would have to survive some sort of peer-review system and would have to show how the flight would advance the understanding of his or her discipline. Yet the focus was clearly on public relations. The people chosen would be passengers, like the payload specialists. They would have to accept NASA employment for the duration of their training and flight, undergo the Class II physical examinations, and be subjected to a background investigation by the FBI. The media were particularly concerned about the potential effect of this approach on freedom of the press in space.

More and more it became evident that the greatest obstacles to be overcome by the space migration were not technical or economic, but social, political, psychological, and medical. Estimates of the number of those who would like to go into space or visit space have ranged into the millions, starting with Walter Cronkite and not ending with Senator Jake Garn. Apollo 17 astronaut and former United States Senator Harrison Schmitt noted that especially the young wanted to go and that they were especially interested in Mars.

Yet no conceivable NASA program could provide so vast a number of opportunities. If more people wanted the opportunity to visit or live in space, it would not only be necessary to go along with the government, but it would also be necessary to go in addition to, or alongside, the various governments — to go as free men and women and free new enterprises in service to the planet.

As we have examined the developing political and organizational nature of our early space endeavors, we have seen that space migration is measurably different from other migrations, at least in the degree of social sophistication needed to accomplish biosurvival objectives. It requires complex, complementary physical interrelations. It requires scientifically designed organization — an intricate machine for communal work — a socio-organism. Increasing amounts of energy are being converted into social structure.

Earthly civilizations are naturally and organically growing and changing in complexion and character. They are now in the process of creating new civilizations off Earth, with numerous intricate cultural filaments running between progenitor and progeny. We are presented with a unique formulation and growth pattern because of the tightly controlled planning required of the earth-sitting builders of this space civilization.

An early venturist with Hudson's Bay Company may have received a pat on the back and whimsical good wishes for a safe voyage, but the embryonic settler in space, because of the awesome technological requirements for human survival and successful completion of missions, will require highly integrated, interdependent relations with those who stay behind. In the electromagnetic information age there will be constant interaction. Unlike previous migrations, migration into space will not entail long-term or total loss of contact with the departed territory and its matrix of requirements, support, and interrelations.

In addition, space migration, and the concomitant sophistication of intelligence necessary to bring it about, may be unique in its effect on

human behavior, perception, and consciousness. The environment and outlook offered by space are unique. The artificial life-support requirement
imposes a high degree of biotechnological integration. The degree of sophistication required even necessitates the use of thinking machines —
computers.

How is this radical change in survival requirements, cultural norms,
social expectations, knowledge, and point of view going to affect the space
settler? How can the social system here on Earth adapt so as to permit and
symbiotically interact with these new requirements, expectations, and perspectives? How can the new migration be facilitated — made beneficial for
both earthkind and, ultimately, spacekind? These are the questions of the
adolescent space age. These concerns underlie the success or failure of the
newly developing space law.

IV

Spacekind: The Transition Species

10 Biofeedback

The medium is the message. . . . Any new
technology gradually creates a totally new
human environment. Environments are not
passive wrappings, but active processes.
. . . Any extension, whether of skin, hand,
or foot, affects the whole psychic and
social complex.

Marshall McLuhan
Understanding Media

New frontiers are the harbingers of things to come. The Old World was itself
radically changed by the migration to the New World. The first tentative
attempts at colonization began only four hundred years ago. There had been
nearly a hundred years of probes and expeditions before attempts at settlement began. After the Renaissance—and years of advancing knowledge
and advancing populations—Europeans needed a new frontier. The Old
World needed a New World.

The frontier of the New World decreased limits, expanded the system,
created new wealth, and brought about the evolution of more libertarian
legal structures. All these were felt as much in the Old World as the new.
Most of the men who built and sailed the boats that brought the first settlers
to the New World had no idea of the visionary sociological and democratic
possibilities of freedom. Yet among them were visionaries—restless rebels,
the migratory, the intelligent—who knew that the future lay in the open
spaces of America.

Migration is an escape valve. It rids the home hive of restless outcasts
and eccentrics. It allows for new experiments—technological, political, and
social—in a new ecological niche far from point of origin. Those left behind
inevitably benefit from the fallout of the frontier experiments. In the new
genetic, electric, atomic, global village no one will be unaffected by space
migration. The Second Industrial Revolution has provided the integrated
energy, communication, and information technologies necessary to expand
the system once again, into infinite spacetime.

Now that mortals are capable of navigating the endless ocean of space, they must attempt to understand the effects of traversing that ocean. They need to understand how they are affected by their specialized new vessels, their synthetic life-support environments that include media such as computers, robots, satellites, chemicals, increased radiation, and electronic communication. We already have seen the psychological and biomedical nature of the early selection criteria. With the ultimate freedom of space travel comes the ultimate responsibility of complete preparation and thorough understanding of oneself, of each other, of the structure of space, and of the interrelated nature of one's biotechnological body, which, in space, is the human body and nervous system and its surrounding medium, the spaceship or space habitat.

Nor are these considerations limited to the prospective space traveler. We are again reminded that the new technologies, views, and knowledge of the space environment are also remote extensions of earthkind. Millions of people, from the comfort and security of their own terrestrial habitats, have watched live television pictures from the moon, Mars, Jupiter, Saturn, and newsworthy locations around Earth.

Up-to-the-minute satellite pictures are seen on televised weathercasts around the clock. Children pilot spaceships through three-dimensional space in video arcades. We are bathed in an artificial ocean of electromagnetic radiation. Satellites tell oil companies where to drill and fishermen where to fish. Our eyes and ears have already been extended into space. Computers have come into homes and schools.

Just as in earlier migrations, terrestrial humanity will be as much affected by the new environment of space, albeit somewhat differently, as will the new space inhabitants themselves. Earthkind will be dependent on the new production and energy of the space economy and on the global and ecological awareness of the space perspective. There will be a parent-child relation between earthkind and spacekind that should be recognized now in order to plan properly for the symbiotic, but independent, cultural evolution of spacekind.

Yet such a recognition may not come easily. Throughout the history of civilized societies, the cultural evolution of humankind has suffered the deadly aristocratic habits of anthropocentric and ethnocentric chauvinism. Those habits are now recognized, in so-called open societies, to include the familiar blandishments of nationalism, religious persecution, and unmerited discrimination by birth, unearned wealth, racism, sexism, and institutionalized bigotry.

The resistance of civilizations to change is obvious and natural, just as it is predictable down to the simplest biological specimen. Anthropologist

Carleton S. Coon, in *The Story of Man,* indicated the existence of three sociobiological laws which seem to be recognized and understood primarily by the life scientists and which reveal some causes of the resistance to change:

—*The Law of Least Effort:* Any organism or organization of organisms will select the survival solutions that require the least effort to sustain and achieve.

—*The Law of Evolution:* Any organism, or organization of organisms, that has evolved into a successful, surviving entity, will not undergo further noticeable evolutionary physical changes for a very long time.

—*The Law of Acceleration:* Biological parameters always exhibit an exponential, cumulative increase up to the moment that a physical climax occurs, which may be caused by direct physical limitations or by damping from other factors.

Marshall McLuhan called such a physical climax, or reformulation of matrices, a break boundary. Pattern reversals and exponential changes are characteristic of these break boundaries, which are identified in communication, the sciences, law, and philosophy by paradigm shifts in patterns of basic assumptions and practices, as well as general perception and belief. The Law of Acceleration reminds us that resistance to change is not necessarily immunity from change. It forecasts Ilya Prigogine's discoveries concerning open systems—energy-dissipative structures.

We are reminded of the relevance of the new theory of self-organization to the evolution of humankind in space. What will be the result of the new fluctuations in the biorhythms and biochemistry of people in space? What will be the result of perturbation of earthly social systems by new space industries and civilizations? What will be the result of the acceleration of the technological extensions of humanity? Prigogine's description of dissipative structures is instructive:

The form or pattern is self-organization, maintained by a continuous dynamic flow [of outside energy]. The more complex such a structure, the more energy it must dissipate to maintain all that complexity. This flux of energy makes the system highly unstable, subject to internal fluctuations — and sudden change. If these fluctuations or perturbations reach a critical size, they are amplified by the system's many connections, and can drive the whole system into a new state—even more ordered, coherent, and connected. With each new level there is greater potential for change . . . new rules. There is a change in the nature of the laws of nature.

If there is something unique about the developing biological and neurological underpinnings of human envoys functioning in the synthetic and alien life-support environment of space, the destructive characteristics of parochial, chauvinistic human attitudes should not be allowed to cloak the self-knowledge and the evolutionary information that are necessary for survival. Old earthbound attitudes should not mislead the scientists, engineers, policymakers, legislators, and jurisprudents who have been and will be charged with developing a sensitive and responsive set of norms for social order among spacekind and between spacekind and earthkind.

Except for a comparatively few individuals committed to a realistic search for evidence of earth-alien extraterrestrial intelligence, as that term is now defined, just about every disciplined proposition and argument that would shift *Homo sapiens* away from center stage in the cosmos has been resisted. History teaches that the resistance has frequently been characterized by intense and widespread violence.

The critical issue of whether bioecological evolution of *Homo sapiens* has even taken place continues to be fought in the trenches of Western cultures, particularly in the United States, where some Christian fundamentalists are refining and retuning their logic and presentations to refute the notion of change throughout the ages. Perhaps they merely wish, as Niels Bohr said of Einstein, "to tell God what to do," or how to do it. But the intensity and furor of this and related debates involve a deep cultural, perhaps genetically coded, fear that humankind, collectively and individually, will lose its central position in the universe, perhaps somehow forfeiting the promise of paradise.

Thus we stand in the late twentieth century, on the threshold of extending old civilizations into space, perhaps even of creating new ones, in which our own sons and daughters may be extraterrestrials from every point of view. We quiver at the calamity such a reality will create in the ageless security of our traditional anthropocentric world. Not only are our sons and daughters pioneers in the firmament, they could also become biologically, if not taxonomically, different. If that is true, are earthkind citizens preparing properly, sensitively, and adequately for contact and lasting relationships with the extraterrestrials they are creating?

What is the evidence that our original human space envoys are in any way different from their Earth-sitting counterparts or that both earthkind and spacekind might become different in the course of generations? Are we really suggesting the possibility of a new subspecies in space—*Homo sapiens spatialis,* space human beings, extraterrestrial spacekind—or even on Earth—*Homo sapiens alterius,* changed human beings, postterrestrial earthkind?

In its initial stages, the changes we are suggesting are not necessarily taxonomic or phylogenetic, although those principles are helpful in making comparisons, drawing analogies, and establishing anticipatory juridical codes. Indeed, taxonomic and phylogenetic change has been much discussed in the future tense. Most of us have seen drawings or illustrations of future humanity with large craniums and diminished bodies, or in some other form. Still, such changes are not our immediate preoccupation.

The types of change that we need to be aware of in our time are the transitional changes, the traumatic initial stages of metamorphosis, which will probably not have morphological or taxonomic effects, at least at first. The initial effects of the changes would be more of a medical, social, political, philosophical, or psychological nature. They might interest philosophers, jurists, psychologists, anthropologists, and project managers more than systematists or taxonomists.

This is not to say that systematic metamorphosis is not possible in the course of hundreds of years of change as rapid as that of the twentieth century. *Homo sapiens* has already passed through a number of types such as Neanderthal man and Cro-Magnon man. The passage from Cro-Magnon, now extinct—or transformed—to *Homo sapiens sapiens,* the modern human being, took only 30,000 years under the natural, unaltered bioecological dictates of the earlier, less conscious, pretechnological Earth. *Homo sapiens sapiens* has been subjected not only to the accelerated change of technology, classical philosophy, the Renaissanse, science, migrations to the New World, and the first and second industrial revolutions, but also to 12,000 years of evolutionary time.

We can see the rapid acceleration in every discipline, in our ancestors and even in our children. Why can we not see it in our species and expect it in our distant progeny? With the growth of genetic knowledge and microtechnology and with the advent of the biotechnologically integrated space habitat, great biological and psychological change may possibly come about in the next few generations.

In the sociobiology of today it is already perceived that individual development recapitulates, to some extent, the development of the species. The human embryo, for example, repeats the evolutionary cycle by existing as a single-celled organism in the womb of the mother. Neurologists know that our brain is layered, the deeper, inner, lower layers being essentially the ancient brain—the autonomic brain. Reptilian and early mammalian vestiges remain, with the higher orders of thought left to the most frontal and outer lobes, the cerebrum, a comparatively recent evolutionary innovation.

According to the new discipline of sociobiology the human gene pool is a complex molecule that builds on new elements as it evolves. Each generation is seen as a wave moving through the gene pool—contributing to its locomotion through time. From this perspective the migrations of life from the water to land, or of human beings from one part of the world to another, or from Earth to outer space, can be seen as a type of evolutionary swarming phenomenon.

In sociobiology even the general tendencies of human nature, such as altruism and cooperation, are seen as genetic predispositions to survival. Certain universal social taboos, such as incest, have been identified. Apes smile to curry favor with their fellows. The human organism is seen as a biological spaceship of a sort, given the task to develop sufficient fecundity, mobility, and intelligence to assure the perpetuation and continued upward evolution of the gene pool and of its evolving consciousness.

Some see in this new view a frightening new determinism. Yet we are reminded of the magnificent trend discussed in chapter 1. Polymerization, complexification, ordered association, transformation, cooperation, random experimentation, and free interaction represent the ingredients of acceleration, the exploring edge of the magnificent trend, and the fundamental expression of evolution, even at the energetic level, ever since the big bang.

Physics tells us that information is simply organized or ordered energy. As we have seen, consciousness feeds on energy and entropy to create ever higher states of ordered complexity or interiority—that is, intelligence. It creates resonance. The design is cosmic, energetic, genetic.

Edward O. Wilson, the Harvard sociologist generally credited with starting the sociobiological revolution, defined the new discipline most concisely in his book *On Human Nature.* He defined sociobiology as a hybrid discipline that incorporates knowledge from ethology, ecology, and genetics. It extracts the most important facts about social organization from their traditional matrix of ethology and psychology and reassembles them on a foundation of ecology and genetics studied at the population, rather than the individual, level. The purpose is to show how social groups adapt to the environment by evolution, through a genetic selecting out and selecting in of characteristics compatible with specific environmental dictates.

What knowledge could be more helpful for space migration? What knowledge could be more necessary for the construction of intelligent and symbiotic new extensions of humanity—the auto-mobile, biotechnological bodies of outer space—the new space habitats?

11 Transitional Changes

The Earth is merely the starting place on our
journey to the stars.

S. Dillon Ripley
Former Secretary of
the Smithsonian Institution

It is essential to the growth of any new and
high civilization that small groups of people
can escape from their neighbors and from
their governments. . . . A truly isolated,
small, and creative society will never again
be possible on this planet.

Freeman Dyson
A Space Traveler's Manifesto

Human productivity. Human productivity of spacekind for the consumer satisfaction of earthkind. Cost-effective principles of financing for business as
usual in outer space. The human being is finally in the center of the loop—
finally an interdisciplinary concern of habitat designers. Still, the initial
attempts are a roundabout melding of social considerations, designed primarily to serve not the principal members of society within the space habitat, but rather the distant and physically uninvolved consumers of their
services.

Yet the market mechanism has had a salutary effect, forcing a government bureaucracy to consider space habitation from a point of view other
than that of the military test pilot, the mission scientist, or the technocratic
specialist. Productivity means a laboratory compatible with transient passengers in space. In an effort to spur private enterprise to exploit near and
deep space capabilities, the Reagan administration adopted a policy of a
permanent space presence and a blue-collar space labor force to serve a
supporting Earth-indigenous society and economy.

While the shuttle remains both experimental and routinely operational, the space station is justified primarily as a site of manufacturing and service to paying customers. "This shift in emphasis," says B. J. Bluth, project sociologist, human productivity program, NASA, "represents an important modification in the place and importance of the role of human systems in the design, development, and operation of a space station. Human productivity is now a far more significant factor."

To determine what constitutes a productive human being for the purpose of designing the most effective interface between space-station crew and space-station technology, NASA established the 1983–84 Space Station Task Force. One of its first priorities was the human productivity program, created to offer the magic key to a technocrat's heart—a design for error-free operation.

Productivity, as defined by Bluth, is "cost effective, basically error free, timely results" of an astronaut crew providing commercial services or products to paying customers. The space and weightlessness interface must be as natural as possible. Not all the paying guests will necessarily be adventurous, strong-willed types. They will not be as highly trained or as extensively prepared for the space environment as were the early astronauts. At a training cost of $20,000 to $30,000 an hour per astronaut, the emphasis in NASA's study is on cultivating space station crew members who are "alert, attentive, motivated, flexible, aware of the goals and objectives, skilled, knowledgeable, and able to operate the equipment with a minimum of undue stress."

One way of doing this is to design an environment that reduces stress to the greatest extent possible. The design and life-support ambience of a space habitat of any sort helps shape the astronaut's behavior and sensory reactions. As Bluth says, "it impinges on the individual." The external environment of the life-support structure is filtered by internal, physical, and psychological factors—the result, as NASA regards the equation, being the degree of health and productivity of the astronaut.

The medium is truly the message in space. The passengers and crew will be impinged upon, affected by, and totally involved with an environment the nature of which is within their own power to create and manipulate. A space habitat is a prime example of intelligent self-control. The task of the NASA human productivity program was to identify those areas of the human biotechnological interface that were critical to making the first permanent settlement, according to Bluth, "user friendly, hassle free, and worth the money." Still, NASA's method of identifying commercially productive astronauts did not yet include factors of individual freedom and legal or social structures that are peculiar to space-station societies.

What do we already know about the differentness of humankind operating in a space ambience — about spacekind? Much of our knowledge about life-support systems in space habitats, whether in a tiny Mercury capsule, Skylab, Space Shuttle, or the record-holding Soviet manned space stations, is supported by ground-based research involving both human beings and the lower orders of animals. A highly sophisticated interdisciplinary approach, embracing the medical sciences, engineering, and the social sciences, has been needed to sustain something like normal human physiology and psychology in space.

Much of the biomedical effort so far has been focused on the prevention of health problems and disease before the start of a manned mission. But with the establishment of a U.S. space station, and with the rather spectacular Soviet accomplishments toward a permanently manned habitat, new gravity-free therapeutic techniques and procedures will be required to support human life in space permanently.

During the late 1950s, courses in U.S. aviation medicine began to include biomedical aspects of space flight, even though the medical profession in general had some substantial reservations about attempting to support human life in space. Many of the hypothesized biomedical problems turned out to be real, some did not. Thirty potential biomedical problems were initially investigated by the National Research Council Committee on Bioastronautics of the U.S. National Academy of Sciences.

The important point to remember, however, was that manned missions were going full steam ahead, regardless of the incomplete knowledge available about human life-support systems in space. The engineering technology required for getting human beings into space and ensuring their safe return dictated the efforts and directions of space medicine. Mission objectives, rather than the most favorable conditions for the human passengers, determined the kind of life-support system that would be established. To be sure, astronauts were to survive at all costs, but that was all that was expected. Space medicine had to catch up. Not only did short-term mission objectives dictate the limitations and characteristics of life-support systems, but President Eisenhower's mandate that all original astronaut candidates for the one-man Mercury project should be military test pilots also helped limit the area of consideration by those involved in designing life-support systems and in the practice of space medicine.

The Mercury program showed that the astronauts suffered an orthostatic intolerance upon return to Earth — that is, they had difficulty standing and moving in an upright position, as well as dizziness and pooling of blood in the lower body. Still, there were no behavioral difficulties, probably because of the short duration of these missions.

The two-man Gemini project showed a number of changes in the physiology of the astronaut, such as loss of red cell mass, postflight orthostatic intolerance, loss of some exercise capacity, loss of bone density, sustained loss of bone calcium and muscle nitrogen, and a higher physiological metabolism than had been predicted for extravehicular activity. None of these changes was considered unacceptable for missions of about two weeks' duration. But the physiological changes were cumulatively beginning to create subtle changes in the basic organic value-forming processes and conceptualization characteristics of a biotechnologically integrated organism — the astronaut.

The three-man Apollo project focused attention for the first time on prevention and care of in-flight illnesses. It was far more difficult, if not impossible, to order an early recall of a flight to the moon or to bring astronauts back from the lunar surface prematurely than it was to recover the Earth-orbiting Mercury or Gemini astronauts who might become ill.

Although there was the possibility of some exotic biovector being brought back from the moon and introduced into the atmosphere or life-support ecosystem of Earth, it was a remote possibility, but one specifically addressed in 1967 in the first UN Outer Space Treaty. As a result of this concern, back-contamination procedures and elaborate quarantine protocols were established and adhered to for the first few lunar missions. Considerable analysis was even given to the prospect, in longer-duration or permanent habitats, of earthborn microbes being sufficiently irradiated in the space environment to mutate and, therefore, necessitate continuing in-flight or habitat quarantine protocols.

The Apollo program focused study on the problems of cardiovascular deconditioning, bone demineralization, metabolic balance, vestibular or inner ear disturbances, inadequate consumption of food, cardiac arrhythmias, decreased red cell mass, and increased postflight orthostatic intolerance. Perhaps most important was the first real indication that the duration of the mission, architectural confinement, physiological anomalies caused by the life-support systems, and the physical and psychological distancing from Earth were having an effect on normal patterns of behavior among crew members and between the crew and support personnel on Earth. Unique ways of looking at things emerged. Feistiness and short tempers increased. The line of command between those in space or on the lunar surface and those directing the mission from Earth became a hot, at times negotiable, topic.

In the multiman Skylab project, astronauts were no longer simply piloting a spaceship. They were living in a habitat and working in a space laboratory. There was more of a sense of going to stay than of simply getting there and getting back. Skylab was designed to support three astronauts for an uninterrupted period of at least three months. Although preflight and in-flight procedures and precautions were taken against space-motion sickness, it remained an unpredictable problem. Cardiovascular deconditioning was found to stabilize after four to six weeks with no apparent effects on long-term health or behavior. The loss of urinary calcium and bone mineral, however, was found to be continuing and not self-stabilizing.

In general, the biomedical efforts undertaken with the Skylab missions helped distinguish those physiological changes that were self-limiting from those that appear to continue during the longer missions. Again, little effective consideration was being given to the cumulative effects of these physiological abnormalities on ultimate in-space value-forming processes, judgment characteristics, and consequent behavior patterns. The biomedical tests and studies were still limited to the short-term problems of life-support requirements as defined by the specific mission rules and chain of command.

The Soviet manned program has also provided some significant data on human physiological adaptations, and failures to adapt, to a space habitat. Although the Soviet life-support technology may not be as sophisticated as that employed in the U.S. manned space program, the biomedical research in the Soviet Union and the Soviet-bloc countries has been extensive and perhaps more comprehensive in regard to sustaining human life and *societies* in space for long periods, even permanently.

Biomedical research is a critical underpinning of a scientifically managed society, and a political and ideological commitment to such research continues in the Soviet manned program, largely because of the Soviet ideological commitment to space dominance as part of its own manifest destiny, not unlike the commitment of the United States to westward expansion in the 1800s. Although life-science efforts of the Soviets have spread into areas of clinical interest usually associated with a scientifically managed society, such as psychological and behavioral control, many of the critical biomedical findings have tended to confirm those of the U.S. manned program. Ever since the 108-minute, single-orbit flight of Yuri Gagarin, the Soviets have focused on the psychological and physiological stability, or normative behavior, of their cosmonauts in space.

Biomedical and other researchers of human factors in the Soviet Union have concluded that most physiological changes in a space ambience are self-limiting—that is, they level out and stabilize within an acceptable spectrum of dysfunctional tolerance. With proper exercise and controlled diet the problems of cardiovascular deconditioning and loss of muscle mass can be controlled within acceptable limits. Although changes in the production and shape of red blood cells and in water-salt metabolism appear to level off and even reverse, there are some processes, such as loss of bone calcium, which, though slowed with time, do not level off even after six months in space.

Even so, with certain exceptions still under study, during missions of longer duration, cosmonauts seem to make a more thorough, efficient psychological and physiological adaptation to the space habitat than they had achieved in missions of shorter duration such as those of Skylab. The Soviets may have discovered some effective interim measures to assist in psychological adaptation to the long-duration missions of Salyut 6.

Aboard Salyut 6 they instituted a sleep-wake-work cycle keyed to normal Moscow time, with a five-day work week and a two-day weekend. A comprehensive psychological support program, including frequent two-way communication with families, access to radio and television, and delivery of gifts, letters, and news was also undertaken. Thus was the stress of long-term sensory deprivation, with intermittent sensory overloads, made tolerable.

At the present stages of both the U.S. and Soviet manned programs, almost all the engineering and biomedical techniques employed to solve the problems of life-support requirements are, in the final analysis, aimed at ensuring postflight readaptation to the environment on Earth. This is particularly true of the pharmaceutical and psychological measures designed to assist astronauts and cosmonauts in physiological readaptation and in identifying with the familiar routines, distractions, and people left behind on Earth.

Much of this effort is designed around relatively short-duration crew rotation, although the Soviet program is in the forefront of pushing long-duration and permanently manned facilities. Some of their long-duration biomedical prophylactic and remedial support techniques may become more characteristic of the way to deal with psychological needs, values, and expectations of astronauts and settlers in the future. The underlying shift to different psychological or neurophysiological behavior patterns in space will begin rather subtly to mold the principles requiring new, perhaps unique, social requirements in a space habitat.

12 Biojuridics

An individual born in weightlessness could
never effectively visit Earth with its one-G
gravity. An anatomist might not even recognize the fetus as human. Genetics is only
one part of the complex understanding of
body growth and development. Gravity
shapes and molds the bones, organs, vas-
cular system . . . all of the body systems.
. . . A child may well be irreversibly changed
if born in space. . . . Re-entry by a space-
child into the Earth's strong gravity fields
might even prove fatal.

Astronaut-Physician William Thornton

If people are born in space, they will adapt
themselves to the environment in which
they live. This is another futurological tendency to diversion. Evolution doesn't work
that fast; but within one or two generations
it will become effective.

Krafft Ericke, Space Scientist

Not all life scientists share William Thornton's views of the effects of
weightlessness on the developing fetus. Others feel that the simulated
weightlessness of the amniotic environment may minimize any prebirth
changes. Embryologic studies are already being conducted on animals by
the Soviets, NASA's Ames Research Center, and several graduate schools.
Still, regardless of the effect on the fetus, it is widely assumed that the
effect of weightlessness on the development of a human child would be
enormous.

Most observers share Thornton's concerns that some comprehensive or
cumbersome training, rehabilitation, and life-support mechanisms might at

least be needed to facilitate a visit to a planetary surface by a true member of spacekind, or to train the development of terrestrial locomotor skill with high skeletal-muscular stress and coordination. To what extent is the existence of that stress necessary for the development of healthy physical coordination of muscle groups and neural pathways even in spacekind? Neurological faculties, motor skills, self-image, and overall psychology could be significantly affected. "I assure you," says Dr. Thornton, "Superman would very quickly become Clark Kent in a weightless environment."

It therefore seems inevitable that serious thought will be given to rotating environments, such as those envisaged by Gerard O'Neill, that produce artificial gravity through centrifugal force. Yet, even the rotating environments produce perceptual conflicts. Whenever the head is moved perpendicular to the direction of rotation there is a dizzying and disorienting effect from the Coriolis force that accompanies rotation. One might become desensitized to this effect after a time, but one revolution a minute seems the minimum tolerable speed. At that speed, one Earth gravity would require a spinning station with a minimum diameter of one mile.

Even in habitats with gravity the broad-ranging concerns of space habitation remain. What is the sensitivity of human physiology to changes in design? Recall Marshall McLuhan's statement that every new invention creates a wholly new psychic and social complex. What level of gravity is necessary? Can we get away with 0.2 G or 0.5 G? What level will stop decalcification? Or is decalcification caused by different gases or a higher level of ionizing radiation? What sensitivities are there to greater population density, the inverted perspective, faster rotation, higher overall levels of radiation, higher levels of carbon dioxide, and lower levels of nitrogen?

So far, in both American and Soviet planning for human habitation in space, consideration has been given to the laws of gravity — weightlessness in orbit. The total dynamic interplay of physiology, morphology, and psychology, forming what we would call the human experience, responds ever so sensitively to Earth's one-gravity force. Every conscious movement is made in a manner that takes gravity into account — which is one of the most important underpinnings of civil, criminal, and evidentiary law in every legal system of the world.

All facets of law and legal regimes are promulgated and learned as an articulation of human behavior in the one-gravity environment of Earth. The rules for the space jurisprudent, legislator, judiciary, and sanction enforcer, have changed significantly, perhaps drastically, by alteration of the most critical factor that has shaped human evolution on Earth. So, the life scientists working on the design and biological support systems of space habitats must also number among themselves the jurisprudent and the practitioner of the law, who, in turn, must become equally familiar with the physical laws and nature of Earth-orbital space.

What do space stations have to do with law and jurisprudence? Aside from the unavoidable administrative matters of modern technocracy, there will be a need for mediators, counselors, interpreters, and advocates. There will also be a need for political philosophers. Historically, jurisprudence has tended to be a synthesizing influence in the shaping of civilizations, from the smallest tribal units to the most sophisticated societies. Empirically tested legal regimes have given organization to the physical and cultural evolution of those civilizations. This will continue, in some form, for extra-terrestrial societies.

Unfortunately, jurisprudence has become enmeshed in the sterile trappings of its innumerable definitions. One result has been to obscure the function of jurisprudence by elevating the discipline above its biological origins into an area of mystique safeguarded by jurists and practicing members of the legal profession — the secular clergy. The tendency has been to enshroud jurisprudence with the protection of parochial, constantly fluctuating, moral and ethical characterizations. This parochial jurisprudential elitism has been one of the principal barriers to human progress. It was the basis of the American forefathers' fear of the state.

We must approach the new frontier of space, and the changes it brings to social and legal theory, with an updated awareness of the pitfalls for freedom in the operation of systems. What do law and jurisprudence have to do with space stations? Assume for a moment that the biochemical, bioelectrical, neurophysiological, endocrinological, and psychological characteristics of a space station society or lunar community produce individuals with significantly different perceptual and value-forming processes from those of persons living on Earth. Further, assume that patterns of judgment and behavior are so significantly affected in the course of long periods that space inhabitants evolve who are ethologically and sociobiologically distinct from *Homo sapiens.*

Again, the change is not necessarily phylogenetic, at least in the structural sense. At first, it is a behavioral, psychological, and cultural transformation — an ethnogenesis. There will be new ethologies, psychologies, and sociologies, even in the near term. The possibility of conscious advancement, of temporal advancement of the species, may not be far away.

The initial manifestations of the transformation will be conscious and social. They will be manifested in values, behavior, and perception. Ethnography, neurology, psychology, and sociobiology now become the tools of jurisprudence. They join physics, chemistry, political science and the philosophy of classical humanity as the primary tools with which to fashion Thomas Jefferson's natural state, his ecologically based law — a sensitively articulated interrelationship among cosmos, ecology, and community — a true biojuridical system, on Earth and in space.

A good example of this type of interplay between science and jurisprudence can be found in necessary institutional responses to fields of charged particles which include the electrons and protons of the solar wind. Inhabitants of Earth are largely shielded from the effects of these particles, which become trapped by the magnetic field of the Earth and oscillate backward and forward in space completely around the Earth. These trapped particles form the well-known Van Allen belt. It is of primary importance not to conduct extravehicular activities, or spacewalks, while in a low Earth orbit, such as those used in the shuttle missions, through what is referred to as the South Atlantic Anomaly of the Van Allen belt. The intensity of trapped protons there is unsafe.

The lack of gravity and the presence of energized particles in an Earth-orbit environment indicate that life-style and activities will be molded or constrained by factors totally alien in source to those found in a biologically Earth-normative ambience at sea level. Galactic cosmic radiation consists of high-energy particles originating from previous cataclysmic cosmic events outside our solar system. These particles are highly dangerous to biological integrity and are virtually unshieldable by passive technology.

The engineers, therefore, have passed the problem for the time being to the biomedical researchers and the economists, policymakers, business managers, lawyers, and, indeed, labor unions. Why? Because at present our principal interest is in determining the extent to which periodic or continuous exposure to this radiation might affect career limits for space workers.

Even for high-altitude supersonic flights of the Concorde, the existence of solar flare radiation is always of concern, just as it is for military flights. It is even truer for shuttle missions and low Earth-orbiting space stations, where solar flares are a serious hazard to health. These flares, or solar magnetic storms, occur in a ten-to-eleven-year cycle and produce highly dangerous amounts of high-energy, high-flux protons. Passive shielding in habitats, along with effective scheduling of operations, appears so far to be adequate. Any extravehicular activities during a period of solar magnetic storms, however, could very likely cause astronauts or cosmonauts to be exposed to lethal doses of irradiation.

This characteristic of space habitation not only has a bearing on short-term considerations of human health and consequent formulation of protective health laws, but also on the protracted view of such mundane matters as space construction contracts incorporating "time is of the essence" clauses based on solar cycles, not to mention complicated union contracts involving collective bargaining over working conditions and health benefits, which, in turn, invites the pivotal considerations of the risk managers and underwriters, ad infinitum. Here again is a mixture of unfamiliar physical factors with cultural institutional responses that help mold value-forming processes and behavior patterns of space inhabitants that are alien to the familiar traditions of social order for Earth-sitters.

Imagine trying to apply the Environmental Protection Act and the Occupational Safety and Health Act to the manned space program without shutting it down. Imagine the burgeoning discipline of labor and employment law waiting to be practiced by labor lawyers and union representatives!

Not only should space biomedical researchers and other life-support scientists and engineers know the factors that affect human systems, they should also have an expert grasp of the very nature and forces of space itself. This knowledge is necessary if they are to design the most effective biological protective systems, habitat work and living quarters, cycles of work, rest, and leisure, and all other facets of supporting both the best survival and performance capabilities and the highest quality of life for human beings living in space.

For all those involved in the space life sciences, including the jurisprudent and the legal engineer, the understanding of the nature of space has, as its primary objective, the understanding of human nature in space and on Earth. That understanding must initially include a firm grasp of the human rights that must be critical components of any biomedical and design engineering studies for space habitats, certainly for permanent space habitats.

If occupancy of space habitats with a predominantly alien, synthetic ambience, produces significant, measurable physiological abnormalities, then conscious and behavioral consequences must be expected as well. Despite the extensive biomedically telemetered data we continue to collect on the physiology of astronauts in a synthetic, weightless environment, our knowledge is still sketchy about abnormal physiological processes and their direct effects on individual and societal patterns of behavior.

It should be emphasized at this point that just because certain aspects of a person's physiology in a space habitat are not Earth-normative does not mean they are abnormal or unnatural responses to the Earth-alien influences of a synthetic life-support environment necessary for living in space. It does not mean that these responses are not necessarily better adapted to the physical and temporal influences of space itself. The primary consideration is to determine and understand the consequences of these influences. Are the consequences within the spectrum of human survivability? Are they consistent with underlying political or legal values? How can they be mediated by architectural, biomedical, psychosociological, and legal invention and creativity?

So far, physiological self-regulation, or biofeedback, continues to be one of the more promising areas of individual adjustment to such tenacious problems as motion or space sickness, control of gastric motility, stomach pressure, cardiovascular perturbations, olfactory, tactile, and auditory reactions to a strange gaseous ambience or source of noise, headaches, cardiovascular self-regulation, blood pressure, and other stress-related disorders. Other areas of concern, not so readily sensitive to the panacea of biofeedback, are the loss of blood volume and bone mass, deterioration of the heart muscle, reduction of the number of red blood cells, and changes in fluid and electrolyte balance. In these instances, biofeedback is supplanted by behavioral intervention, a fancy way for the emerging field of "behavioral medicine" to say "making changes in habits."

In space habitats, some of these physiological aberrations have been controlled by establishing, maintaining, or modifying behavioral interactions related to the health status of both individuals and groups. Examples are controlled use of drugs, exercise, diet, and even termination of such habits as the use of tobacco and alcohol, although allowances may be possible for some forms of personal practice similar to the last-mentioned examples.

Another area of investigation into unique behavior patterns possible in a space habitat involves the chemistry and physics of biorhythms and the overall behavior patterns produced by biorhythmic entrainment.*Entrainment* is defined as the determination or modification of a biological phase or period, such as the effect of light on circadian rhythms.

Biorhythms and environmentally conditioned variations have significant effects on interactive behavior, from the major rhythms, such as the menstrual cycle and the circadian or commonly recognized twenty-four-hour cycle, to the molecular cycles in individual cells. The biorhythmic lag of jet travel between time zones is a good example. It makes one feel out of sorts, sometimes unable to sleep or concentrate. During space missions of long duration there are even more varied and drastic effects on the biorhythms.

The use of drugs for bioecological or psychological adaptation is an area of biomedical investigation that is growing in importance. The extent to which drug interventions can assist in the control or management of space-related psychological and neurophysiological alterations requires substantially more empirical investigation. According to the NASA publication *Space Physiology and Medicine,* the developing data base "suggests that judicious applications of selected drug-performance . . . may have considerable potential for stabilizing adjustment levels under a range of difficult environmental circumstances" in space, relating both to required skill performance levels and social interactions or cohesiveness.

Nor is such therapy necessarily limited to prescribed drugs. Despite the almost overwhelming desire of cosmonauts for fresh foods during a long mission, a desire gratified rather expensively by the Soviet Intercosmos program and one that caused strawberries to become currency aboard the Soyuz 6, Cosmonaut Valery Ryumin still once said, "I would give up all my strawberries for *all* of this mission for just *one* cigarette." The sensitive integration, therefore, of psychological, biological, engineering, and cultural needs will prove to be one of the most challenging tasks of space migration.

13 Astronautical Jurimetrics

> Man is still the best computer that we can
> put aboard a spacecraft—and the only one
> that can be mass-produced with unskilled
> labor.
>
> *Wernher von Braun*

> Behold, I tell you a mystery; We shall not all
> sleep, but we shall all be changed, in a
> moment, in the twinkling of an eye.
>
> *1 Corinthians 15.51, 52*

We have looked at some of the inanimate external influences that shape human physiological and neurological characteristics in space. But when we discuss drugs, nutrition, or neurological function, we are crossing the boundary to internal influences. Indeed, beyond being one of the primary internal influences, food and its preparation even figure significantly in the social symbolism of astronauts.

A satisfying sense of taste and food-sharing rituals are just as important in space as they are among societies on Earth, perhaps even more so because of fewer distractions in the daily routine of a space habitat. The physiological requirement, of course, is for nutrients, the necessary chemical conversions to produce body energy. But one simply cannot take the gross chemical specifications necessary for an acceptable diet in an Earth environment and apply them to astronauts with satisfactory results.

The rate of energy use, for example, during the first month of Skylab missions was measurably lower than that of the astronauts one month before the mission, while there was a statistically significant linear increase of the use of energy over Earth-based counterparts through the second and third months. Paul C. Rambault of NASA indicated that this may be the result of a metabolic inefficiency in space, which may be "attributable to the fact that . . . more work was being demanded of a diminishing muscle mass."

Indeed, good nutrition and prescribed exercise may not only become the subjects of civil rights but also of civil sanctions for failure to meet established requirements. Like everything else in the microcosmic society of a space habitat, precise nutritional supply and consumption becomes a critical issue for societal survival, although there may be a diminishing juridical significance in larger space societies.

If we are to rely on normal bulky foods as sources of calories, we shall quickly have a weight problem and a logistics problem in supplying space inhabitants with adequate calories. As noted by Rambault, however, "foods can be selected to provide more or less energy from the three sources [protein, carbohydrates, and fats], and specially prepared food mixtures can be designed to incorporate any desired balance among these sources."

The real problem arises when long-duration habitats require self-regenerating sources of nutrition that "could cause extreme departures from the normal mixture." At this point, providing fats for the astronaut's diet becomes more psychological than logistical since taste and the form in which fats are offered in the diet would differ significantly from the norms. Further, the problem of the type of fat to be included in the diet is accentuated by the need to consider dietary fat and its effect on cardiovascular disease, particularly where exercise is at a minimum.

Because carbohydrates in normal diets come in a number of different chemical structures they have been found to produce different levels and characteristics of work output in humans. They also affect the central nervous system differently, depending upon the chemical structure, and have the potential to elevate serum tryptophan and, through some form of entrainment, the concentrations of serotonin.

Studies have shown that while serotonin is produced in the body to help in blood-clotting and various muscular functions, it is also produced by the pineal gland and serves as a biochemical regulator in the brain for what we call traditional normative thought. In essence, it is a neuroinhibitor. Too much of it can limit cognition, just as too little can cause accelerated neural function and unconventional or nonsymbolic thoughts, such as may occur with the use of some kinds of psychoactive drugs, such as LSD, when the chemoelectrical activity and neural structure of the brain are prevented from interacting with normal amounts of serotonin.

It seems that high-protein diets are preferred in most Earth societies. The psychophysiological reasons for this are important, but not yet known. The types and amounts of protein are important in determining acceptable taste and satisfaction of the appetite. These characteristics, in turn, significantly influence the general sense of well-being and happiness of all those in space habitats. It is therefore important to determine the effects of a low-protein diet on the psychophysiology of the inhabitants of a space community.

As part of planning for a closed-loop food system the Soviet cosmonauts grow vegetables on their long missions. These supplement the fresh fruits and vegetables routinely delivered by the robot *Progress* resupply ships. As reported by B. J. Bluth, "the Soviet position is that the nutrition process goes beyond the bounds of physiology and hygiene. Here the social psychology of man becomes dominant." Consequently, visiting cosmonaut crews bring along feasts of ethnic foods, and ways are found to have a pantry to raid on occasion.

In discussing the development of currency in a space habitat, Bluth reports an interesting 1983 conversation with an unnamed American Skylab astronaut. He told her that butter cookies were used as space money. They were traded for doing chores or using facilities and other kinds of food and drink. This is another example from the initial, small habitats that all factors, all systems and subsystems, affect human health, satisfaction, and productivity in some way.

Although significant advances have been made in recent years regarding human nutrients and their functions in human neurophysiology, no tests have actually been undertaken in the Western world wherein a person is fed for a long period on highly purified or synthetic nutrients and related materials, such as elements and trace elements. We do not know all the trace elements or organic compounds that are essential to normal life functions and socially interactive behavior. There is frequently an imperceptible measure between the absolute minimum level of a certain nutrient for effectiveness and the level at which it becomes toxic or causes significant aberrant behavior. Even with substances whose thresholds are known, the metabolic differences in space may call for a cautious approach.

Until serious design studies began on the proposed space station the focus of the nutritional program of NASA was on design engineering for comparatively limited mission objectives. The emphasis in nutrition was on minimizing bulk and weight, preservatives, taste satisfaction, and reduction of the likelihood of flatulence. Except for the Skylab program, missions have been so short that the primary emphasis was on a last meal, before departure, of steak, eggs, and potatoes.

Virtually no systematic study of the effects of trace elements, synthetic foods, and allergies on crew physiology and behavior patterns has been undertaken. Mental disturbances are treated with megadoses of vitamins and trace minerals under the new discipline of orthomolecular psychiatry, where the focus is on the effect of these nutrients on the bioelectrical activity of the brain. So far, however, this narrow, specialized discipline is beyond the ambit of the space program and does not address the effect of such substances in the normal diets of well-adjusted people. Although perhaps somewhat shortsighted, the reasons for this neglect are understandable:

—Nutrition has been treated primarily as an engineering and not a biomedical factor. The questions emphasized have been, How is it possible to get food into an astronaut in a weightless ambience? and, How can it be made reasonably palatable to ensure that it is consumed with at least minimum regularity until the end of the mission?

—The discipline of environmental medicine, and the study of allergies that appear in a highly technological environment, is embryonic.

Space habitats incorporate and intensify almost every irritant to normal human biological processes that can be found in a highly industrial or technological society on Earth. These irritants range from intense electromagnetic energy fields beyond the normal wavelengths and frequencies experienced on the surface of Earth, through problems of psychological identification with a totally engineered environment, to artificially produced and preserved foods and antibiotic medicines. Western societies and astronaut societies have relied heavily on the so-called wonder drugs to yield quick, short-term results. But this is a symptom-treating approach that often masks the real cause of an illness or aberrant behavior and ignores the causative sequence.

In the past few years, medical literature that deals with the pathological, physiological, and psychological abnormalities or apparent side effects of modern medical treatment involving the so-called wonder drugs, irradiation treatment, chemotherapy, and the like has increased voluminously. These nonspecific effects of modern technological treatment are referred to as iatrogenic diseases.

Frequently, the resolution of one medical problem with modern medical treatment will create other, or indeed a series of other, biological dysfunctions that are difficult to identify, expensive to treat, and often impossible to treat effectively. Nowhere will this be truer than in the very long-duration or permanently manned habitats in deep-space exploratory missions or in a near-Earth orbiting mode.

Even more prevalent in space habitats may be the continuation of old, and the emergence of new, symptoms related to a general malaise, a sick-all-over or half-well feeling, now referred to by many practicing physicians as "functional disorder." This is simply another way of saying that the person is suffering from all the cumulative effects of a modern, technological society.

Into this category are lumped alcoholics and other drug abusers, people suffering from high-stress environments, and the average office worker who spends less than an hour a day in the natural electromagnetic energy fields of sunlight, totally bathed instead in a synthetically created energy spectrum that is alien in many critical respects to the spectrum in which the species evolved and survived. These are the people who, through an extended period, manifest ambiguous emotional illnesses, which themselves are frequently defined vaguely as disturbances of thought, feeling, and behavior and are observable as migraine headaches, fluctuating blood pressure, attacks of angina, allergies, dizziness, and skin and bowel disorders.

Frequently, we become too much used to these symptoms to recognize them as something abnormal. When we do recognize the symptoms, more often than not they are evaluated individually and not seen as a matrix of disorders related to the modern pace or synthetic environment and are not treated accordingly. This matrix of malaise, if not recognized and prepared for, could become a critical factor in the survivability of life in a small, completely technologized space habitat in which interdependency among the technological components and the human participants is complete.

In one form or another, the earliest medical records in history have included relations between physical or chemical stimuli and reactions in body tissue, internal as well as external. In 1906, a Viennese physician by the name of Clemens von Pirquet first used the term *allergy* to describe these reactions. Despite this early recognition of allergic reactions, the causes of many of the common allergies are still not well understood.

Unfortunately, what might be referred to as ecological illness is such a new area of public health that few statistical studies have been undertaken regarding the relations among environmental factors — chemicals, electronics, radiation, gravity, synthetic nutrients, and the like — and their effects on allergies and behavior. It is known that allergies cover reactions to a multitude of incompatible stimuli, ranging from certain nutritional complexes to industrial and natural pollutants. One source of stimuli not often considered is synthetically derived electromagnetic energy fields. Some of the forms of the electromagnetic spectrum that are used frequently by industry and found frequently in space are X rays, microwaves, and radio waves.

A fair amount of research has been conducted in the Soviet Union on the effects of low-energy, nonthermal microwave radiation, and the results show definite behavioral changes in animal subjects. The Soviet scientists assert that the central nervous system is particularly sensitive to this form of invading energy. Some of the physiological aberrations noted are endocrinological disruption, thyroid hyperactivity, olfactory desensitization, progressive hypertension, and a quantifiable surge in the histamine content of the blood.

Some of the frequent complaints of the 525 individuals studied by the Soviets were chronic fatigue, headache, and acute irritability. Curiously, American researchers have not been able to replicate precisely the correlation shown by the Soviets, although some instances of protracted hyperactivity, irritability, diminishment of learning thresholds and neurotic syndrome have occasionally been related to high electromagnetic flux. Indeed, there has been research on both sides of the Iron Curtain on the potential of electromagnetic weapons, including radio-frequency weapons that are intended to interfere with normal patterns of thought.

The critical nature of such biomedical dysfunctions can be especially apparent in a space inhabitant. Less than peak performance in a space habitat will quickly draw attention from fellow inhabitants. Thus, design engineering and architecture are among the most important long-term means either of dissipating or accentuating these dysfunctional symptoms and their socially interactive consequences.

Architects are sometimes heard claiming that they can ensure, within six months of living in a specially designed house, the embittered divorce of otherwise compatible newlyweds. Metaphorically, at least, the same may be true of the designers of space habitats, who are burdened with having to design sane habitability in a totally synthetic life-support environment.

The unique biomedical, psychological, and social demands of an alien and synthetic life-support environment in space clearly indicate the need for disciplined artistic, architectural, biomedical, psychological, social and legal evaluations of the effects of these demands on the values and standards of living and working in space. Legal positivisms that have evolved on Earth's surface simply are not sufficiently responsive, if at all, to the biological changes in space that manifest themselves in different value-forming processes and behavior patterns. Changes need to take place in the perspective of the traditional jurisprudent in order to facilitate the inevitable "Restatements of Law in Space"—a kind of astronautical jurimetrics.

14 Biocultural Transition

Clearly any extraterrestrial community will
be a planned experiment, just as all space
exploration, manned or unmanned, has
been to date. Thus culture becomes part of
the input variables, instead of the matrix
itself. It is important, in any consideration
of extraterrestrial communities, that this
distinction between culture as a given . . .
and culture as a manipulatable variable, be
kept in mind. Otherwise, we shall confuse
community with experiment.

Philip Singer and Carl R. Vann
Cultures beyond the Earth

Biological humanity is not simply a race of "mucilids," as they are contemp-
tuously called by a renegade electronic brain in *Memoirs of a Space Traveler*
by Polish author Stanislaw Lem. Humanity is a hierarchy of structures and
systems based organically on atomic and molecular interaction and complexification. It is not somehow ugly or slimy to be biological creatures with
biological origins and potentials. We are trying to limit the capacities of the
creator again if we forget the basis of our biology, which is the marvelous
structural transformation and dissipation of energy in nature.

We are trying to step outside nature or the cosmos if we try to elevate
ourselves above—or lower ourselves beneath—our biological origins. We
are originally star children. Each of us is a more or less coherent arrangement of a basic energy that emerged at creation, star dust.

Our cultural interpretations, our scientific and psychosocial beliefs and
points of view, should be open to growth and change. Our viewpoints are
not designed to be coveted. They are not property to be defended and maintained. They are only interpretations, mediators of our experience. The nervous system is our internal medium. It experiences what it encounters. The
encoding for this characteristic is genetic, and genetic memory is very old.
Genes, of course, are megamolecules, masses of interrelated atomic inter-

actions, the complexity and dynamism of which have given rise to conscious nature.

In examining both specifics and patterns of humankind adapting to environmental changes of all types, three kinds of fundamental question, which are closely related to the three-tiered Jeffersonian model of values and needs that we described in our earlier chapter on the philosophy of space, come immediately to mind.

—*Life*—Survival: What are the biological limits of the species to adaptation? Are there any?

—*Liberty*—Society, culture: Is technology an integral biological extension of human adaptation?

—*Pursuit of Happiness*—Consciousness, transcendence: How do we protect the sanctity of individual personality, creativity, privacy, autonomy, diversity, choice, spontaneity, love, compassion, empathy, piety, and other highly evolved traits—the need for which will only be heightened by the planned nature of foreseeable extraterrestrial communities?

Donald J. Ortner, an anthropologist at the Smithsonian Institution, offers a workable definition of human adaptation as "a process by which a group of people achieve an optimum interaction with their bio-cultural environment." This definition avoids implications of values inherent in more conventional definitions of human adaptation that incorporate such concepts as good and bad, accommodation, adjustment, plasticity, and even acquiescence. But what is meant by *biocultural*?

Biocultural can be defined in several ways, each describing the same phenomenon. Biocultural has been defined as indicating the intellectual articulation of bioecological dictates. A house, for example, is such an intellectual articulation of the need for shelter from the elements. Biocultural has also been defined as characteristic of an intellectually expressed set of relations between biology and culture that produce a specific set or sets of individual and group behavior patterns and possibilities. Space programs and legal systems are good examples.

Yet such definitions are deceptively simple. Culture and ecology are infinitely complex in interaction and ultimate expressions. Most surveys of the history of philosophic thought disclose at least nine major concerns in every human cultural ecology:

—*Origins*: When, where, and how did life arise?

—*Politics*: What is necessary to survive? Answers cover questions of power, security, and territory.

—*Epistemology*: What are knowledge, understanding, and consciousness? What is the capacity of human beings to conceive reality and make artifacts?

—*Ethics*: What are good and evil, right and wrong? How do human beings differ in their moral beliefs and systems?

—*Aesthetics*: What is the difference between feeling and knowing, between beauty and pleasure? What is balance?

—*Ontology*: What is being, existence? What is the difference between perception and reality? What is real?

—*Teleology*: What are the purpose and destiny of creation and evolution? Is there a purpose or a destiny?

—*Cosmology*: What is the basic energy? What is the basic structure? What holds the universe together?

—*Theology*: Is there a cosmic consciousness, a higher intelligence, a universal creator-designer—God?

These are the basic inquiries that compose the grand internal models discussed earlier. They form the basis of healthy human biocultural or socioecological growth. The cause of much of the suffering and scarcity that still afflict humanity today is biocultural or neuropolitical. Much of it arises from wrong answers to these questions.

Unfortunately, most of the people in the world have precious little time to ponder such questions, and rote institutional answers are too often substituted for real inquiry and intuition. Even in the affluent industrial countries there are so many things that distract us, demand our attention, divert us from what pleases or perfects us or the systems and relations within which we exist. The present dilemmas of the affluent countries demonstrate that even ample material rewards are not enough. The crisis the human race now faces can best be described as navigational. Humanity has somehow lost the compass, misplaced the maps, misunderstood the guidebooks.

From this point of view René Dubos asserted that perhaps human beings have the capacity to adapt too easily to undesirable conditions. Such adaptations can be destructive in the long run, at great cost to biological, psychological, and social quality. This has certainly been observed in some of the ecological disasters of the twentieth century and the threat of a nuclear Armageddon. Is it possible that the human movement into near and deep space is creating bioculturally hostile circumstances that may be destructive of the quality of life—either of earthkind or spacekind?

Philip Singer and Carl Vann seem to think so. In *Cultures beyond the Earth,* they foresaw Big Brother in space in controlled, militaristic-bureaucratic societies. They proposed that space stations are military expressions of an anthropocentric and geocentric utopianism and suggested that

Ecological analogies, biological models, physical science metaphors and ethological speculations are not adequate to describe or explain cultural behavior. The political and economic aspects of human experimentation within a vivarium (for that is what an extraterrestrial community would be) are directly related to man's theoretical and practical attempts to construct ideal societies. . . . The utopian tradition from Plato to our own time hypothesizes that the external manipulation of the environment can bring society to a static perfection with fixed and clear human relationships and functions. No matter how idealistic or seemingly desirable . . . to succeed there must be an element of coercion. . . . It appears that the only type of authority structure which can be used must involve the military model. . . . Any other structure . . . would conflict with the basic technological assumptions of the community. . . . [Still] hierarchical command does not in itself guarantee compliance, and the entire extraterrestrial community experiment could come to a rapid halt in the event of any appreciable amount of deviant behavior. The cultural-political system of the vivarium community would thus be based on some type of group theory of organization involving subordination of the individual to the collective good.

We cannot agree. In focusing on the static perfection of Apollonian democracy, Singer and Vann overlook the more dynamic and evolutionary Dionysian models. Of course, it would be foolish not to admit that technology can be used coercively to reduce individual freedom and to enhance the power of politicians and technocrats who control centralized governments — and perhaps, soon, even more centralized space habitats. The collective good is a seductive theme, particularly if it offers the quickest road to life-sustaining benefits. Even the imaginative H. G. Wells, who dreamed of space travel and world government, saw such a government as an authoritarian technocracy.

B. F. Skinner spoke for the authoritarian technocrats when he advocated a form of operant conditioning, systematic and sometimes secretive behavioral sanctions and rewards for behavior control as a means of inducing "normative patterns" of behavior in docile, dependent, Soviet-style workers. Pavlov was able to obtain the same sort of conditioned responses in dogs. It is the same conditioning theory graphically demonstrated in Ken Kesey's *One Flew over the Cuckoo's Nest.*

The purpose of such conditioning, of course, would be to ensure loyal, predictable, habitual, robotoid, and insectoid service to the sovereign hierarchy — or, in the case of outer space, the sovereign space habitat. Such a subjugation of individual growth, adaptation, and psychology is a degree of control beyond human freedom and dignity. This is now widely realized by most modern schools of psychology and sociology, which recognize self-actualization, human potential, and mutual support as the new survival paradigms.

As we approach a cultural change of the magnitude possible in space settlements — controlled, experimental, biocultural change — are we prepared to say what this new change must *not* become? Are we prepared to challenge the self-doubts of our own earthbound ethnocentricity and affirm strongly that it was diversity, freedom, individuality, and innovation that brought us to these new ecumenical capabilities?

The vulnerability of any technological system of totalitarian mind control is its prerequisite of parochialism, secrecy, and unanimity. As Singer and Vann admitted, hierarchical control doesn't guarantee compliance. One dissident electronic-media expert, one libertarian philosopher, can disrupt the system. Studies of isolated communities in Antarctica or the North Slope of Alaska, or in deep-sea habitat experiments such as the *Tektite* and *Ben Franklin* Gulf Stream Drift missions, show that established hierarchies can lose their meaning, even in societies that require a high degree of coordination for survival.

Most researchers and observers of isolated societies now feel that the most effective social system in such environments is some form of participatory egalitarianism, with a hierarchical protocol available for emergency situations only. Even the Soviets went to a less hierarchical form of "participatocracy" for management of the leisure time and personal affairs of their cosmonauts on missions of long duration. Nor should this be particularly surprising to Americans experiencing the current megatrends from centralization to decentralization, from representative to participatory democracy, and from hierarchies to networking.

Even Singer and Vann admit that the military hierarchy would apply only to the service member or space worker. It would not apply to their accompanying dependents or families. "We would expect," they said, "that the most important cultural-legal problems relating to human community experimentation would arise with respect to private persons."

In addition to the new evolutionary forcing factors of science and technology, there will be new ideologies, religions, and philosophies that will have to be dealt with in creative and adaptive ways. Methods must be found to avoid the conflicts that inevitably arise from such new formulations, and we must avoid the development of political and economic imperialism, colonialism, and violent revolution between and among earthkind and spacekind.

How could we have failed to learn our lesson? We are blessed with the relatively recent example of a previous New World migration. A thousand years before Columbus, Vikings and other Celts and Norsemen returned from sea voyages to the New World. But the exploration alone was not enough to open up visionary new possibilities to the communities who heard stories of the exploits. The adventures were more akin to Jason's skirting of the Infinite Ocean. The real possibilities came with migration.

The appropriate technology for substantial migration had not yet emerged at the time of the Vikings. The great ships were needed, for only a society of self-actualized families, democratically linked together, was capable of pushing civilizations through the stormy latitudes of the North Atlantic and into the New World.

It wasn't easy. The boats were still Spartan technologies, largely alien to the needs of family life. No studies of optimum biotechnological integration were being undertaken. As recounted by Isaac Asimov, those European families made dangerous six-week journeys across the Atlantic in scarcely seaworthy cockleshells to land in an uncharted and sometimes hostile wilderness. Many crossed the same ocean in "stench filled and confined steerage space to land in city slums and work in sweatshops. Millions . . . were seeking something that to them was worth any hardship and danger. And so it will be when the space colonies are established. More will wish to go than can be carried."

Although marauding conquistadores and single-combat warriors are the beginning envoys, nothing really develops until the family units move together. Such a view may be mildly disturbing to NASA, as they are forced to fight perennial budget battles over a modest space station, the mere stepping stone to high orbital bases, lunar settlements, and the exploration of Mars.

NASA visions of the foreseeable future still do not include free social structures or self-actualizing permanent space inhabitants or domiciliaries. NASA's plans only marginally take into account, with the Space Flight Observor/Participant Program, that civilian Americans and their families might insist on getting into the frontier action.

Astronaut John Young seemed to understand this during an airport conversation with author White. When questioned as to the way he foresaw the future of humanity in space he replied, "You're asking the wrong guy. I just fly to and from. These are the people [with a gesture to the huge Los Angeles airport waiting area] you should be asking. They'll be the ones who will decide, and whose children may be living there." This response was from a veteran of Gemini, two lunar flights, and the first flight of the space shuttle.

We should hold no illusions. Space migration will produce some of the most intense genetic, political, epistemological, ethical, aesthetic, ontological, teleological, cosmological, and theological struggles the planet has ever seen. This is because space migration offers our young, unfinished species the opportunity to create new realities, new habitats, new neurological perspectives, and new worlds unlimited by planetary chauvinisms. It is also because the early space infrastructure is a governmental, military, industrial bureaucracy, which is not much concerned with pluralism or poetic vision.

We may do well to listen to the shrewd advice of Astronaut Russell Schweickart, who said that we must keep government bureaucracies out of space colonization. *Colonization* itself has historically been the buzz word for political, economic, and military imperialism. Schweickart's preference was to rely instead, as far as possible, on private initiative and personal investment and vision. There are those who say that such a thing is not possible, of course. Authoritarian technocrats will say that it's all going to be a serious business, unpleasant and difficult to adjust to. Such an accentuation of the negative, of course, often means that someone wants control, for whatever reason. Fear is often a psychological weapon used to gain control.

Yet, while care is called for, fear is not. One of the primary reasons most of the migrants will want to make the trip is to get as far away from old conventions and obsolete controls and limitations as possible, to leave them behind. The history of migrations is replete with examples of this motivation. If we really are in a position to affect our own natures through the necessary technological manipulation of our total ecology, then we can do so by anticipating what is necessary in our new communities to encourage and do justice to the full potential of every community member.

René Dubos noted that one of the prime reasons human beings are biologically geared for such facile adaptation is "because our bodily and mental mechanisms can be activated by the process of imagination." It seems logical that more nearly ideal social systems would preserve and promote the existence of, and social access to, this imagination. Isn't this a likely way to conform law to human nature?

Genetic coding in human beings should manifest itself in extraordinary imaginations, capabilities, or temperaments, such as those of Einstein or even Daniel Boone. It only makes sense that new frontiers attract the eccentric, the adventurous, the intelligent, the courageous, the reckless, all full of imagination and potential. There is a self-selection process of sorts. As socialist equality and cyborg insensitivity become dogmas in the old hive centers, sensitivity and individuality reappear among the temporally advanced frontier outcasts.

Most settlers on a new frontier are self-selected for frontier behavior.

The newest ecological niche is usually filled by those genetically templated for mobility, independence, and change. America is still one of the principal agents of change for the world. This is no secret. In relation to other places in the world America is full of ambitious, recent migrants, true volunteers.

The fabrication of new miniworlds in outer space should therefore be voluntary. No government bureau should decide all by itself who goes into space. Those that want to go can try. Perhaps some system of licensing, similar to pilot training, might ultimately be negotiated. Short of clear and present danger to the health, safety, and welfare of the society, however, self-selection, not bureaucratic selection, should be the preferred mode. Some will be impelled, compelled, obsessed, and driven to move into space. Others will be bone-deep, heartfelt horrified by the idea.

Naturally, the former will inevitably tend to become the ones who will go into space. Like their frontier forefathers, they will have the necessary attributes to make the move a successful one. Even the early government astronauts are good examples. It was entirely proper and predictable that they would possess an individualistic bravado, a sort of death-defying right stuff. Their apparently acquiescent bureaucratic subservience was misleading. The astro game was not difficult for the thrill-seeking fighter jocks who were inculcated with a "can-do" attitude about accomplishing missions.

Oh, there will inevitably be regulations even for the most private and libertarian of enterprises—regulations for launch safety, orbital location, traffic patterns, defense arrangements, commercial relations, mediating authorities, individual community structure, and the like. Not everybody who wants to go is going to get to go, even with multiple public and private opportunities. Still, motivated people in reasonably good physical and psychological health should have many types of community arrangements and ways of living from which to choose. Even those who are unable to live in space will be able to visit space and its spacekind communities as tourists.

Nor are we saying that the government should not be going into space. Government resources are necessary to force the collective technology to the point of mass availability. Space exploration, experiment, and enterprise are precisely what a progressive government should encourage to the maximum extent possible, as nothing short of a moral imperative. In addition to its duty to protect the physical safety and integrity of its constituent members, the purpose of the system is to increase individual choice and increase intelligence structurally through peaceful, cooperative arrangements.

If we have learned anything in our look at the evolving space enterprise, we should know now that effective intellectual and biological self-awareness and self-control are absolute prerequistes for seizing the opportunity to go into space. But when the requirements for space travel are refined and more widely shared, the adventurous space inhabitant will add his or her own style of right stuff for a continuing and more diverse migration into space.

As human beings, we adjust to the future through informed anticipation of events likely to occur, given an awareness of history, the present, and the foreseeable future. We cope and create on the basis of deliberate individual and social choices through human free will. Prospective space societies will come into being through free will in relation to cultural circumstances.

Individuals shape their cultures and environments through free will — informed, intelligent, conscious self-awareness operating cooperatively and deliberately to satisfy basic human needs. The real importance to astronauts of anticipatory decisions based on models of free will is that they show that survivable space habitats can be designed for technological and cultural success. They can even be designed to maximize individual potential, privacy, and cultural freedoms.

The social scientists, therefore, should be acutely aware of the necessarily scientifically controlled nature of space habitats and should come closer to the goal of generating social environments in which the development of personality can achieve greater harmony between one person's inclinations and the needs of the rest of society. This could possibly be the greatest gift our envoys of mankind could give in return to their Earth-sitting progenitors. Indeed, since social innovations could be critical to the salvation of human society, both on Earth and in space, social conditions should be encouraged in which individual creativity can flourish.

Unfortunately, the predominant attitude among many leading scientists, engineers, and makers of public policy is that we have made such a mess of the planet Earth that we should not rush to expand the mess into space and onto other planets. Yet this is simplistic, even atavistic. We grow or we die. It is simple evolutionary history.

The problem is not simply the mess we have created, the perhaps natural and too often unavoidable fouling of our nest. The problem includes our degree of willingness to learn from our messes and establish long-term philosophical constructs — new global paradigms — new objectives for humankind.

What options do we want for humankind, for the next stage of the human odyssey, for our children's children's children? Are we prepared to make the future really possible, to lay the necessary foundations, no matter how amorphous the initial paradigms may be? We must look carefully and often at the direction of the human experience as a whole in order to understand the developing nature and peculiar needs of spacekind, most of which find their origins in the groping works of progenitor earthkind.

One thing does seem clear: Diversity is necessary to healthy transformative survival; and diversity is also one of the underlying sources of social conflict on this hair-trigger nuclear stockpile we call Earth. It should be seen universally that the loss of cultural diversity is as threatening as the loss of genetic diversity to the maintenance and salvation of humanity on Earth and in space. Diversity allows the kinds of specialization and interdependence characteristic of a complex and highly evolved culture. Delight in difference will thus become necessary, like oxygen, if humanity is to survive. Infinite diversity in infinite combinations is a key to survival.

Yet again it is possible to become enmeshed in a paradox. How is true free will possible in a totally planned ecological system? How do we design social structures and reflective legal regimes for human societies in space on the basis of empirical data generated by Earth-sitters, especially if the physiological underpinnings of the manifestations of free will in space are measurably different from those of earthkind?

Somewhere, the answer to this paradox lies in the answer to humanity's basic questions. It lies in the determination of the nature of free will and consciousness itself. What is consciousness in a complexifying, genetically determined, highly sophisticated, integrative system like a human being?

V

Spacekind:
A New Definition of Humankind

15 Conscious Transformation

> We are in the midst of a knowledge revolu-
> tion that shows signs of breakthrough. . . .
> Researchers in the human sciences are
> moving independently in converging lines
> toward common targets. . . . They are dis-
> carding traditional models of the cosmos
> and ourselves . . . and reaching for new
> ones. . . . They have been spurred on by
> recent work on the brain hemispheres, on
> molecular biology, and biochemistry, on the
> genetic code, on primatology and ethology,
> on biofeedback and altered states of con-
> sciousness, on medicine and psychothera-
> pies, on archaeology and astronomy, on the
> evolutionary process, on the structure of
> language and the nature of meaning, on
> leadership and power, and on the gover-
> nance of peoples and nations. Thus, the
> startling fact is that for the first time an
> American renaissance is taking place in all
> the disciplines, breaking the boundaries
> between them, transforming them at their
> farthest reaches — where they all converge.
>
> *Max Lerner*
> *Foreword to* The Aquarian Conspiracy,
> *by Marilyn Ferguson*

One of the most interesting places to start looking for intelligent consciousness and free will is at the heart of the substance that makes up the
system — that is, elemental energy, atomic and subatomic particles. Scientists have discovered, through the use of quantum mechanics, that these
bits of energy-matter manifest a kind of free will in movement and direction
beyond mere randomness, the latter a term regarded by physicist Freeman

Dyson as "a cover for ignorance." Dyson also believes that "it would seem likely that brains have evolved in order to take advantage of this elementary freedom."

Apparently, it is not possible to know both the direction and the location of these constantly shifting patterns of vibratory energy simultaneously. Cause and effect are more illusory at this dynamic level than they were formerly thought to be. It seems that in some high-energy processes, effect may actually precede cause. Niels Bohr, the discoverer of the quantum theory, said that "anyone who is not shocked by quantum theory has not understood it."

The quantum theory suggests that human beings can influence the structure and evolving nature of the universe simply by observing or experiencing it. Subatomic experiments can be affected by observation in various ways. Subatomic particles show evidence of communication with each other—the ability to affect each other's behavior—across seemingly impenetrable light-speed barriers.

This integration of observation and outcome, this evidence for the melding of mind and matter, has tended to support the concept of free will. This new conscious view of physics has been the subject of such commentaries as *The Tao of Physics,* by Fritjof Capra, and *God and the New Physics,* by Paul Davies. The philosophical implications have been thoughtfully discussed by many physicists, such as J. A. Wheeler, "the universe is preselected by consciousness"; Nobel laureates Eugene Wigner and Brian Josephson, "consciousness is at the root of the quantum principle, from which space-time-mass arise as secondary structures"; and Jack Sarfatti, "the physicist is an artist who molds atomic reality with the aesthetic integrity of his intention."

In many ways, the most up-to-date concepts of holistic body consciousness, biofeedback, neuroelectronics, and quantum physics were anticipated, however metaphorically, by the religious revelations and occult systems of ancient history. For that reason the question of consciousness is, to many, indivisible from the question of the sacred, of the higher consciousness, of God.

Here is where the very indispensable principle of true religious freedom, the right to believe and perceive as you please, shows itself also to be indispensable in space. Here is where a fully conscious, transcendent point of view may prove to be crucial for survival. Both quantum theory of microstructures and the Prigogine theory of dissipative structures indicate that the fundamental basis of existence, complexification, organization, and growth is nonequilibrium.

Humanity has grown enough during the past 2500 years to discover, even in the realms of society and culture, that utopia, or something meta-phorically approximating it, is not spelled equilibrium, not spelled "static perfection," but is rather spelled nonequilibrium, a constant groping evolution, a constant state of becoming. This state of being or becoming is more properly described as dynamic equilibrium or dynamic process, shifting balance. It is vibrant interaction, infinite diversity in infinite combinations, intelligent self-control, free will.

Human beings tend overwhelmingly to want to be determining factors in their own environments, captains of their souls, masters of their fates. As observed by theoretical physicist Paul Davies,

Certainly our desire for freedom includes the requirement that what we decide may actually be caused by us to happen. In a completely deterministic (Newtonian) universe the decision is itself predetermined. In such a universe, though we might perhaps do as we please, what we please is beyond our control.

Recent breakthroughs in such disciplines as physics, genetics, and neurophysiology are eliminating impersonal change and blind accident from the philosophy of science and substituting personal choice. These discoveries have provided the gifts of relativity, singularity, multiple realities, mental choice, and quantum indeterminacy. Perhaps the subtle interplay of these factors in the altered physiology of spacekind might even change or advance consciousness sufficiently to surmount the paradoxical conflict between an unconscious cybernetic, biotechnological integration on one side and human divinity and free will on the other.

Surely we are not deciphering all the evidence and studying all the master guidebooks just so we can be uniformly preselected and psychoconditioned for the service of space cyborgs — conditioned without our conscious and informed consent, without involvement in the design of the program, without awareness of possible outcomes, and without the right to withdraw from the community. Does this sound like the promised new migration? Does it sound like the kind of inviting stimulus that could spark a swarming phenomenon?

A better clue to the cultural and juridical forms of spacekind lies in the transformed consciousness and intelligence of spacekind. With a new, emergent, holistic, ecological awareness it will be possible to personalize, subjectify, neurologize, philosophize, eroticize, and humanize the engineered environments, the high orbital miniearths that spacekind will call home. This effort has already begun on terra firma. It is the "high tech to high touch" megatrend coined by John Naisbitt. "The more high tech in our society," he wrote, "the more we will want to create high touch environments, with soft edges balancing the hard edges of technology."

Part of the high-touch response in space can be egalitarian community structures based on mutual rights, responsibilities, respect, personal integrity, and free will or personal choice. Again, this is only made more necessary by the very high degree of unavoidable biotechnological integration in a space habitat. Astronaut Kathy Sullivan talked of the absolute, unavoidable necessities of early space habitation. She pointed out the unavoidable responsibility of biotechnical awareness and symbiosis:

There is a certain sense of personal integrity to it. You owe it to yourself to always do the best that you can do. You also owe it to everybody else you work with who is dependent upon what you are doing. Space is not a forgiving environment. You have to do things right. Every little tiny thing, even on days you don't feel like doing it right — you've got to do it right. . . . It's not a situation where someone can be nice and generous and say it's all right, that it doesn't matter. It does matter.

Undoubtedly there will be accidents in space habitats. There will be unfit or negligent actors. There will be unique and heretical philosophers. There will be laws and community structure. Mark Hopkins of the Rand Corporation has already made an interesting study of the possibility for, and management of, labor strikes in space. But legal articulations only facilitate or hinder natural attributes. Laws cannot guarantee peak performance and responsibility. The sanction and enforcement functions of the law do not even come into play until the system has already broken down. True justice is also self-selected. The Old Testament described the justice of God: "He who honors Me, I also will honor." The more recent description in the New Testament reads, "As you sow, even so shall you reap."

The real answer to community success probably lies in motivated, self-actualized, strong, adventurous, unconventional, yet disciplined and well-trained human beings. Such people are more likely to be self-selected for the trip. Most will feel the same sense of personal integrity that Kathy Sullivan expressed when she said

Space activity should change our view of ourselves. In a very idealistic sense I would hope that the kind of integrity and respect for yourself, and the people you work with, would continually rise to the fore and urge people to take each other honestly and straightforwardly, with a little less of the garbage that sometimes surrounds human interactions.

The ancient revelations, religions, and occult systems also foretold alternatives to authoritarian technocracy, alternatives similar to those suggested by Sullivan. The secret of success for the new electronic, biotechnological village is the emerging view that society can no longer allow anyone to feel abused, persecuted, or ignored. There is a great need for access and opportunity for all.

Our new global village cannot function with optimum human productivity as long as one person is in pain or even believes that he is in pain. We have no rational alternative other than to stop games as usual, pay attention to the wounded member, strive for balance, and increase opportunity. Life on this planet is one living organism. The pain of even the smallest cluster of cells can affect the whole. Hijackings, electronic sabotage, crime waves, terrorism, and warfare are all symptoms of the absence of resonance that affects everyone everywhere.

Lack of resonance may be even more noticeable and destructive in the confined environment of a space habitat, where the ordinary communal expectation is more likely to be of expert performance at all times. In contemplating the adaptability of humankind to its self-made environments, scholars seem to be evenly split as to whether humanity is headed toward its own extinction through its various technologies and evolving cultural values or whether those technologies and values will keep us one step ahead of the annihilation of the species.

As we have seen, part of the conscious change of dealing with the space environment is imparted to us even here on Earth. The technology that allowed a whole planet to watch—live—one of the greatest events of human history, the Apollo moon landing, is really as remarkable as the landing itself. Millions have directly experienced something of what actually being is space is like. Media analysts have suggested that the moon broadcasts were the finest use of television ever made and that the shots of Earth from the moon were a powerful unifying force for humanity. Neil Armstrong said it: "We came in peace for all mankind."

From a long-term economic and scientific point of view, a number of scholars firmly believe that the healthy growth and survival of *Homo sapiens* through the ages depends upon our technological capabilities to support human germ plasm permanently off Earth. Some feel that the destructive capabilities we have created on the planet may be evolutionary forcing factors for the expansion of the species into the solar system and the forced transformation to a higher agenda, a higher consciousness.

The industrializing New World civilizations have been facilitated and motivated by a manifest destiny of geographic expansion and human progress. After World War II, they perceived themselves in some ways as the annointed of the natural order. This strong sense of destiny and personal mission has been marked in Western civilization since the Renaissance. Following World War II there was a perception of victory in the evolutionary contest. The new United Nations of Earth would charge full speed ahead in the newly perceived contest of intellectual perfection through the awe-inspiring wonders of technology and democracy.

But then came Korea, the Iron Curtain, the Cold War, Vietnam, ecological deterioration, economic polarization, energy crises, the Club of Rome, and nuclear overkill. Western civilizations began to perceive themselves as having fallen from grace for having misspelled progress and for having been caged on this planet with Neolithic social orders that thrive on xenophobia.

Yet there is a manifest arena within which all can safely and profitably cooperate and compete. It is not necessary to club ourselves to death over the limited resources on the surface of Earth. Is it not obvious that the major powers have essentially the territory and popular allegiances that they want or need? As the Chinese have warned, intuitively understanding the rule of disequilibrium, hegemony is suicide. Static perfection is inanimate. The cosmos is animate. Throughout the past fifty years we have been teaching ourselves that we can and should adopt systems of international law that will be needed to mediate access to resources without planetary holocaust.

The next manifest destiny is space settlement and the Third Industrial Revolution. There is every evidence that the Soviets at least understand the potential and are preparing for such an eventuality. A 1983 report of the Congressional Office of Technology Assessment stated:

The Soviet space station program is the cornerstone of an official policy which looks not only toward a permanent Soviet human settlement of their people on the Moon and Mars. The Soviets take quite seriously the possibility that large numbers of their citizens will one day live in space.

We see, then, that any conflict over the future of space migration may well become a debate over the future of human evolution, a debate that is philosophical rather than strictly political and that finds its roots not in transient national rivalries but in an inevitable tension that has existed for at least the last several centuries.

That tension is best described as the old twilight struggle—that is, ceaseless entropy versus constantly complexifying and reorganizing conscious awareness. It is technology versus humanism, engineering versus ecology, poetry versus logic, freedom versus control, and consciousness versus instinct. Yet, are not all these attributes necessary for survival? Surely a way can be found to resonate these dissonances.

There is no empirical pattern of guarantees for survival in the history of any species. Humankind seems to be no exception. Yet no rational alternative to continuing human survival exists here on Earth or out in space. Nor do we have to give up our cherished religious insights or meditations in order to embrace the new discoveries and philosophies necessary for our postterrestrial survival. The new science is astounded by the revelations of the old myths and religions. Whatever our point of view, it would be helpful to concentrate on strengthening our hope of rising to new levels of collective intelligence, our hope for the ultimate survival of *Homo sapiens* and its evolutions to *Homo alterius, Homo spatialis,* and perhaps one day even *Homo universalis.*

The real question for our policy makers, engineers, scientists, and jurists is not whether *Homo sapiens* will find its continuing existence away from Earth, but how it will be prepared to do so beyond simple biological existence. Which values will be encouraged, which discouraged, which allowed? In what manner will earthkind permit spacekind to evolve its own value systems suited for the unique perceptual dictates of a space habitat?

Again, these questions should be asked from the point of view of parents, not authoritarian, imperial colonizers. Many of our problems on Earth arise from crowding, from inadequate resources, and from fouling of the nest. Yet we compound the difficulties with a massive arms race. The only value of an otherwise suicidal arms race may lie in the daring view that fouling of the nest and consequent imbalances are the natural evolutionary forcing factors in the environment. In this case they are forcing humanity to increase intelligence, advance consciousness, and begin intercourse with the entire cosmic environment. Humanity must get off and out of the womb planet for the outlet, vision, and resources that are available in space.

It has been suggested that twentieth-century earthbound civilizations approximate the toxic buildup and diminishing room in the mother's womb as the ninth month of pregnancy comes to an end. There is a metaphorical relation between the type of urgent question being asked about space migration and the labor spasms consequent to cervical dilation and the emergence of the infant. Perhaps a more parental outlook on the part of earthbound precursors of spacekind might cause the devotion of more time to the responsibility for preparation of these extraordinary offspring, our envoys of mankind, of humankind.

Nor should it be forgotten during this initial half century of inhabiting space that the value of the parental orientation is the recognition that earthkind, like good fathers and mothers, must accept, when the time arrives, the individuality and independence of their children. They must sever the political, legal, and cultural umbilicus and substitute for it a mutually understood, culturally determined, cooperative matrix for interaction and social order.

Certainly, human biological evolution did not sigh with satisfaction two million years ago and rest forever on the seventh day. All the religions speak of the continuing involvement with humanity of the father-mother God throughout history. We have evolved physiologically, morphologically, and bioculturally. And now, in long-duration, even permanent space habitats, our creative, adaptive technologies will become an ever more important component of the state of our biological evolution.

Biologists have observed that there are many all-or-nothing evolved characteristics. Evolution seems to involve true transformation, true reformation of the basic, dynamic, megamolecular structure of the genes—not mere adding on or isolated swapping of elements. In *The Aquarian Conspiracy,* Marilyn Ferguson pointed out that the new evolutionary paradigm involves transformation and punctuated equilibrium.

Punctuated equilibrium is a theory of Harvard biologist and geologist Stephen Jay Gould along with Niles Eldredge of the American Museum of Natural History. It is a theory akin to Carleton Coon's law of acceleration, Ilya Prigogine's theory of dissipative structures, Marshal McLuhan's description of break boundaries, and Teilhard's concept of complexification. Punctuated equilibrium suggests that the general equilibrium of life's systems is punctuated from time to time by severe stress. If the population is stressed intensely because of living near the edge of its tolerance, it may suddenly transform itself. Gould points out that new species arise suddenly in the geologic evidence, all at once and fully formed.

Ferguson observed that Albert Szent-Gyorgyi, the discoverer of vitamin C, proposed that a drive toward greater order may be a fundamental principle of nature:

He calls this characteristic syntropy—*the opposite of entropy. Living matter has an inherent drive to perfect itself. . . . Perhaps the cell periphery in a living organism actually feeds information back to the DNA at its core, changing the instructions. . . . We are oscillating fields within larger fields. Our brains respond to the rhythm of sounds, pulsations of light, specific colors, tiny changes of temperature. We even become biologically entrained to those close to us. . . . Couples who live together, for example, have been shown to share a monthly temperature cycle.*

Will all this new knowledge threaten or secure the survival of the human species? Can we be secure from species suicide or from the devastating effects on population of a lethal, mutant gene wrought by our self-made toxic ecosystem? It does little good to cry for abolition of genetic research. Abolition is at best impossible and at worst the surest way to cause a genetic accident. Expect DNA research to reap both scary and fantastic results and to necessitate a continuing involvement of the public in the integrity of the related needs for research and for public safety.

Homo sapiens is no longer simply a biological specimen. We are becoming a biotechnological specimen for the purposes of our own survival, and this trend will be heightened in space. Our dependence upon and interrelations with technology are already so great, our view of reality so much altered, that even George Washington might be culturally more closely related to Socrates or Justinian than to a late-twentieth-century astronaut.

16   Psychology in Space

Our problem is deeply human. We must
adjust to living together away from the rest
of the world. Robinson Crusoe . . . solved
problems by himself, accounting to himself.
We have to solve ours together, taking into
account the feelings of the other. True, we
had prepared for this long and hard
together, rehearsing every anticipated problem, but this was done in an environment of
other people. Here we are totally alone.
Each uttered word assumes added importance. One must bear in mind constantly
the other's good and bad sides, anticipate
his thinking, the ramifications of a wrong
utterance blown out of proportion.

Cosmonaut Valery Ryumin
Veteran of two six-month Salyut missions

We have been discussing the evolutionary odyssey of *Homo sapiens* in the
context of both biology and technology as a measure of cultural attainment,
and we have suggested that biology and technology are not really separa-
ble, in relation to either the requirements of physical survival or a genetically
coded toolmaking dictate. Can it be that technology is a result of biological
evolution, not only because increased brain capacity brought about its
development, but also because it contributes directly to the ability of the
brain to perceive and adjust the whole human organism for survival? It
would be difficult, for instance, to survive in space without the assistance
of computers.

In the totally synthetic life-support environment of a space habitat, is a
human being, culturally speaking, so bionically integrated for survival, with
significantly different patterns of behavior, that he or she might be considered a species variation in that environment from a colleague functioning in
a normal Earth environment where the species started its evolutionary odys-

sey and gave rise to the scientific methodologies of systematics and taxonomy? Pursuing the inquiry in a legal context, are we still dealing with *Homo sapiens* when we, earthkind, attempt to impose legal principles and systems indigenous to the surface of Earth on inhabitants of space communities? The question is intended to focus attention on whether earthly principles and systems are responsive to the social needs of space inhabitants.

Our basic tenet, as we understand the origin and function of culturally institutionalized laws, whether on Earth or in space, is that laws and legal systems are strictly intellectual articulations of the ecological needs and interactions of human beings. In turn, these legal articulations will either promote or deter human survival and growth. Laws are institutionalized ideas and values. They comprise the structure and reflect the underlying assumptions of civilized socio-organisms. In Coon's sense, laws can even be seen as the industrialization of ideas — whether the intended function of the product or tool be physical survival, knowledge, information, aesthetics, or altruism.

Perhaps the context of this discussion is dramatized most clearly in psychology — the conscious, holistic, and complex aspects of human behavior frequently generalized as perception, cognition, motivation, emotion, and so forth. We begin now to look at the critical aspects of social interactions and pattern. We become involved with the end product, the human mind.

Although reference is frequently made to traditional sources of data derived from earthbound situations that involve the isolation of small societies in, for example, submarines, arctic or antarctic stations, oil platforms, prisons, and the like, the fact remains that these data are of limited applicability to space habitat societies. The life-support technology, atmosphere, and energy spectra are significantly different from those experienced by astronauts.

Nevertheless, such research can create a new awareness that may lead to more such studies in the unique space environment, studies that may help diminish the unvarying, solipsistic nature of "life in a can." Some of the harsh and inflexible characteristics of early space habitation will gradually be eased by careful and effective variations in design for space habitats, which might be slowly rotating clusters with ample viewing ports. There can be environmental variety and a changing external scenery of fantastic dimensions.

Community purpose and coordination of interpersonal relations in missions of both short and long duration are critically important to the creation of effective social structure in a space habitat. Individual access to and involvement with essential life-support and decisionmaking processes are critical to a harmonious and successful space society. Such access and involvement are essential also for successful interaction with founding groups and support groups back on Earth.

Leisure time, recreation, and the need for privacy during a long stay in a confined habitat are critical to psychological health and a general sense of well-being, both of the group and of individual participants. As habitats are designed for longer occupancy and more permanent societies, the coordination of research, the design of the habitat, and the desired or even unexpected psychological and sociological characteristics of the inhabitants will become factors that control whether the community achieves success. Even mundane psychological considerations, such as each occupant's response to the waste-management system, are very important, particularly on long missions or in permanent manufacturing facilities, where all human waste products must be recycled repeatedly.

Included in both Earth-based and space-based psychological studies of microsocieties are traditional problems of decisionmaking, leadership styles, disciplinary models, and group processes, as well as differences in composition of the crews and shifts in the costs and rewards to participants in the space society. The shuttle now functions with disparity in the interests and vocational training of crew members, depending upon the specific tasks assigned to them for a given mission. By and large, however, the composite shuttle crews are highly educated, with broad interests and abilities beyond their specific areas of expertise.

People whose education is different in level and type from even that of the present astronaut corps, however, will be needed to work in space. Mix these types with highly trained scientists and technical personnel, then add different nationalities, political and religious commitments, races, sexes, and social classes, along with individual psychoneurophysiological variations in adjusting to the life-support environment of a space station, and the possibility of some intense and protracted social conflict arises. Fairly frequent rotation of crew members for biomedical readjustment to Earth may actually exacerbate conflict by not allowing the necessary time for new societies and their members to work out their differences and to settle down and adjust to the unique biosocial demands of a space habitat.

There is every reason to believe that an alert human intellect can avoid these pitfalls, can forge new affiliations, and can create new communities based on new types of relationship. Yet, in preparing to avoid the inevitable pitfalls, one must recognize that many of the psychological phenomena encountered during the early American and Soviet manned programs may be intensified in longer missions, particularly as work objectives in a station, manufacturing facility, or other form of space habitat begin to lose the pioneering and ground-breaking or space-breaking incentive.

Many of the discomforts and dangers of existence in a space habitat, which were largely ignored by astronauts in the pioneering phase, will continue to exist. Rewards for participation, once the pioneering euphoria that encourages self-sacrifice is past, will assume a variety of interesting and, perhaps, experimental characteristics. Perhaps the most realistic approach is to divert the values of astronauts from the traditional accumulation of material benefits to the psychological benefits of establishing new and independent societies that reflect the unique psychophysiological and socioeconomic values of a space habitat.

Again, reliance might well be on the strange mix of tangible and intangible rewards flowing from the pioneering spirit that underlies all the declarations of independence in history. Put another way, history is replete with examples of individuals and social groups that have endured horrendous physical conditions solely for the purpose of exploring, settling, and being masters of their own fate, with a few significant economic ties to the initially supporting homeland.

Because of the inherently confined nature of foreseeable space habitats, the need for privacy and social distance will continue to require creative solutions. Need for personal space ranges from a thin invisible layer around the body to a distance between two or more people that cannot be violated unilaterally without creating anxiety and stress from a sense of crowding and diminished well-being or security.

A number of internal strategies are available for coping with this crowding. One is the cultivation of psychological privacy and the protection of refuge and security in personal thoughts through heavily punitive sanctions against those who attempt to violate personal secrets or space. The violator might be deprived of his or her privacy, or of certain special foods, or even ostracized in some subtle way. Acknowledgment of the right to privacy and a well-developed standard of personal sovereignty will be among the necessary responses to the high-tech social ecology of the space habitat.

Some of the promising external engineering possibilities for helping space inhabitants cope are fascinating. A sense of crowding, for instance, seems to be as much a function of environment and surrounding activity as it is of interpersonal space. Individuals do not normally have a sense of being crowded, for example, in a football or basketball stadium that is filled to capacity. Psychological and physiological arousal from the excitement of the event mitigates the sense that one's personal space has been violated. This is already recognized in the common law of assault and battery; mild pushing and shoving in a stadium line, for instance, is not acceptable grounds for legal action.

An event or performance seems to evoke a much more positive sense of excitement when it is seen or experienced live than when it is read about or seen on television. This is precisely why the engineers of human factors for the Soviet habitats that are manned for long periods stress the development of holography, a sort of electronic audiovisual, wraparound ambience that can be programmed to change in response to the desires or needs of individuals or the group.

Changes in holographic programming may be the result of conscious decisions or in response to subliminal biological cues. At least in theory, it is likely that highly flexible environments would help accommodate the needs for both privacy and social intercourse in a physically confined habitat. Holography, adjustable screens and panels, and movable furniture can provide considerable flexibility in the use of space.

This way of coping with crowding and violation of privacy in a space habitat would be of significant help to participants who are, say, of different cultural origins, with different definitions of acceptable boundaries or limits to their personal zones. According to a recent government-sponsored study, "Women tend to have smaller and more permeable personal spaces and to adjust better to close social interactions [than do men]. . . . Therefore, work space and living arrangements should be flexible to allow for differences in the use of personal space."

In effect, the inhabitants of a space station would be involved in a reciprocal process whereby they would influence the environment, which in turn would affect the nature and quality of their responses. Here we see the critical need for artists and creative thinkers!

Within this context of unusual personal space requirements, there is an interesting additional twist. Psychological perceptions of space are no longer *up* and *down,* as they are on Earth, but rather *in* and *out.* In conditions of zero gravity, for example, various members of the Skylab crews stated that it was very difficult to adjust to an environment in which the vertical dimension was lacking—that is, in which up and down were not defined.

In 1980 Robert L. Helmreich and his colleagues reported on "psychological considerations in future space missions" in *Human Factors of Outer Space Production,* that "technical mistakes are likely to occur if an Astronaut is not sure from which side he approaches a switch or a panel, and mistakenly pushes the wrong button." A good designer can eliminate this problem by creating an artificial vertical dimension graphically, by using arrows and lines to denote a "floor," lights suspended from a "ceiling," graduated colors for up and down, and so on. Still, while these artificial surrogates are helpful for spatial orientation in a technological and passive environment, they may not be all that is needed to mediate the "in and out" problems of perceptual positioning for personal space among people in a zero-gravity environment.

As we shall see, this in-and-out perspective seems to enhance right-brain, interrelating, patterned, metaphorical intelligence. A 1976 Air Force journal article entitled "The Mind in Space," by Captain Stan Rosen, revealed that many of the highly trained, conservative astronauts still may have had what psychologist Abraham Maslow called peak experiences. Astronauts James Irwin and David Scott reported what have been described by some psychologists, sociologists, philosophers, and theologians as altered states of consciousness.

These shifts in consciousness often cause paradigm shifts—changes in philosophy or world view. Irwin has even pursued religion as a profession. Alfred M. Worden has published a book of poetry in which he offered insight into the shifts in his personal philosophy that have arisen from his experiences as an astronaut. Russell Schweickart has become involved in ecology and philosophy, and Alan Bean has expressed much of what he felt and perceived in space through his paintings, as have several of the Soviet cosmonauts, among them Alexei Leonov.

According to Robert L. Helmreich, a good example of social paradigm change, quite likely to be applicable to the inhabitants of a space community and their anticipated value-forming processes, judgments, and consequent behavior patterns, is found right here on Earth in the shift in the traditional assumption that masculinity and femininity are two antipodal ends of a psychological continuum and that the possession of one of these traits necessarily implies the absence of the other:

Psychological masculinity . . . [was] defined as a constellation of attributes denoting an instrumental, goal-seeking orientation, while femininity [was] defined as a set of characteristics reflecting psychological expressivity and sensitivity to the feelings and needs of others.

Apparently, masculine and feminine characteristics are not linked to traditional sex roles and sexual preferences, and the persons most likely to be able to adapt well to space habitation are the men and women who are androgynous—that is, "who score high in [both] masculinity and femininity," and exhibit the traditionally masculine goal-seeking drive, as well as the traditionally feminine traits of expressivity and interpersonal or social sensitivity.

Perhaps the dichotomy that developed between men and women over expression of the "softer" traits was artificially enhanced by the left-brain, linear, engineering, externalist bias of traditional Western culture. The enhancement of sensitivity in space may not only demand but also increase the need—not for either-or, but for both. An ecological, internalist, nurturing, holistic, artistic approach is needed just as much as a utilitarian, goal-seeking approach.

Helmreich also stated that the intensely competitive nature of the original groups of astronauts, although probably sublimated in flight to the requirements of a successful mission, can create unacceptably deleterious effects as the manned program matures, space habitation is prolonged, and the interpersonal relations of the crew or habitat society become of necessity more complex. Consistent with Earth-based studies involving lengthy undersea habitation, however, the most serious interpersonal conflicts have not been among crew members, but rather between crew members and ground-based or topside commanders or mission control authority. This has even been demonstrated by recalcitrant astronauts and cosmonauts, as was seen in the so-called Skylab revolt, in which the astronauts refused to perform an overload of experiments scheduled for them by ground controllers. Even the highly indoctrinated Soviet cosmonauts cut off their radios for a whole day during a long mission to protest ground actions.

Again, this points up the critical importance of the decisionmaking structure for space inhabitants and the philosophical authority underlying whatever legal structure is adopted. Helmreich believed that "on longer missions involving more nearly self-sufficient vehicles, vesting a higher degree of autonomy in the space crew [than has heretofore been permitted] would appear desirable from the standpoint of both morale and productivity."

Further, given the disparity in familiarity and degree of comfortableness with line-of-command authority shared by civilians and military personnel, Helmreich asserted that "with larger crews on long-duration missions, it may prove advantageous to have several command structures: a strong leadership for mission control and flight safety decisions and a more democratic structure for everyday life and leisure." This would certainly seem to be true of any potential American space stations. Americans are unlikely to adapt well to a highly bureaucratic command structure based on expectations that they be obedient soldiers and Soviet-style workers. Americans tend to be self-reliant, insistent on their civil rights. Our culture sets a premium on those values early in life, and if the lesson to be learned from the earliest astronauts is any guide, the first century of American space exploration will embody some dramatic extensions of those characteristics.

As noted earlier, even the Soviets have developed a highly sophisticated, even somewhat individualized, psychological support program, including an on-board "participatocracy" among Russian cosmonauts concerning personal affairs and apportionment of some tasks and the use of leisure time. Both the United States and the Soviet Union are recognizing that there are peculiarly human problems associated with space life, regardless of cultural or political origins, that must ultimately be dealt with in a way that is primarily responsive to the space inhabitants themselves.

The issue of sex and traditional perceptions of sex roles is a good example. According to Helmreich, it is better left to "benign neglect," meaning that there should be no social intervention in such essentially private matters. Helmreich indicated that this conclusion was a direct extrapolation of lessons learned from changes in current values in Western societies applied in theory to social structures in space habitats, where, as we have seen, invasions of privacy may be especially resisted. The fruit of adherence to any other theory in the midst of a highly individualistic, highly competitive, and confined community could even be violence.

The studies of psychology, physiology, and psychoneurophysiology in a space ambience are still incomplete, but their practitioners' approaches have already revealed much about the political and economic motivations and objectives of the social systems that are underwriting them. An excellent example is provided by the biomedical and political approaches to psychological problems in space habitats of the Soviet Union.

The human component of the Soviet manned space program is less involved in decisionmaking processes, more ground-dependent, and less critically interactive with technology for successful completion of a mission than is that of the United States. In a so-called scientifically managed—that is, Marxist—society political control over the social individual is essential. Consequently, the cosmonaut is subject to a strict line-of-command structure in which the ultimate authority over the mission is back home. This fact is the genesis of all Soviet biomedical and political planning for social order in space and between a space habitat and its supporting infrastructure on Earth.

Given the sensitivity and obedience of the cosmonaut to the line of command, much of the effort in Soviet space psychology is focused on off-duty occupations of crew members or others who work in a space habitat. This part of the Soviet program is still experimental and amorphous. So far, the leisure time of the cosmonaut continues to be organized around utilitarian planning—games, books, television, radio, and video movies.

According to the Soviets, the problem of leisure time on long flights or in permanent habitats remains substantial, since the overwhelming portion of the time spent by a cosmonaut in space will be free time. Except for the launching and landing phases, navigational corrections, routine maintenance of life-support systems, and scientific experiments, the amount of free time has been overwhelming on Soviet space stations.

The Soviets have expressed their preferences for the arts and scientific literature as sources of rest, recreation, and diversion in the work-rest-play cycle that has been established for cosmonauts. The problem seems to be that only so many books can be carried in a Soviet space habitat. Yet even in the American Skylab program, where living space was at less of a premium, not one astronaut finished more than a single book during the eighty-four-day mission of the third crew. A heavy work load caused most books to remain unread.

In any event, the Soviets shifted to telecommunications, microfiche, video movies, radio and television programs, and private communications with friends and family back on Earth. The Soviets talk about playing musical instruments during a lengthy stay in space. If cosmonaut A. S. Avanchenkov could play his guitar and sing from orbit, why not an ensemble of cosmonauts playing chamber music?

For the most part the Soviet manned program continues to deal with the issue of space psychology as requiring distraction from isolation and monotony, or sensory deprivation, in a short-term mission. Although the Soviets assert that the needs, tastes, and habits of the cosmonauts have been considered in the design of their psychological support system, it is clear that the primary emphasis is upon reinforcing the cosmonaut society's dependence upon Earth and, particularly, the homeland and the government. Both cosmonauts V. V. Kovalenko and A. S. Avanchenko gave high ratings to the filmscapes of Mother Russia projected in the cabin of their spacecraft.

The Soviets also use radio and television for meetings between the cosmonauts and other people, such as journalists, sports commentators, leading scientists and specialists, and theater and film personalities. The entire emphasis is to bring life in the space habitat closer to life under normal conditions on Earth. There is very little consideration, if any, given to the need of the cosmonauts to develop attitudes and support techniques that take advantage of the unique attributes of a space existence. Space societies are not encouraged to evolve their own individual and group psychologies.

In addition to extensive biological and clinical research into control factors that involve the individual psychology of cosmonauts, the Soviets also have given substantial time and thought to the questions of social psychology for long-term interplanetary missions and for the permanently manned Earth-orbiting habitat and likely settlements on the surface of the moon. Somewhat surprisingly, the members of the Soviet crews are not considered by their life-sciences support personnel to be the mechanical sum of the individuals. Soviet psychologists prefer that the crews or habitat societies of such long missions be composed of people who represent different ages, professions, and biocultural backgrounds and diverse life experiences.

Still, Soviet commentators have noted the inability to terminate or interrupt missions, no matter how urgent the personal, family, or psychological problem, and have thus mused that perhaps the cosmonauts for such missions should "be cholerics, sanquine persons, phlegmatic persons, and may even be melancholics." One of two basic approaches to the isolation, confinement, and social estrangement of early space habitation being pursued in the Soviet manned program is the development of small, economical devices for individual psychotherapy—specifically, the light-sound relaxer, which is designed to relieve psychological anxieties and abnormal behavior and to stimulate productivity.

The light-sound relaxer consists of a screen with a light filter of cool bluish-green tones thought to be particularly soothing and a special visual sleeve that focuses the cosmonaut's total attention—a kind of biotechnological integration that permits the individual to stabilize his or her emotions by "locking in and spacing out." A rhythmically widening and narrowing light spot that imitates the expansion and contraction of the rib cage during breathing appears on the screen, and at the same time the sound of ocean surf is played to the subject through headphones. Although the rhythmic changes in light and sound are synchronized, they do not remain constant; they change subtly, imperceptibly to the cosmonaut, from a frequent rhythmic repetition to a progressively smoother one that simulates the respiration of a sleeping person.

The objective is to remove psychological and physical tension. The economy of design means that the device can be used as needed at the cosmonaut's workplace, thereby diminishing the need for proportionately larger rest zones, which in foreseeable space habitats designed for long flights will be rigidly constrained by absolute requirements of size and mass. Despite this type of nonspecific psychological sensory soothing, using advanced state-of-the-art technology, the Soviet policy is still to tie space-habitat societies psychologically to Earth and politically supportive institutions. They consider the ships to be extensions of home and design them accordingly. This is the policy objective that requires emphasis on crew rotation rather than permanent habitation by the same individuals.

For ground control to yield to the evolution of the requirements for social survival articulated by the cosmonauts themselves, which flow from the unique physical and biological dictates of space habitation, would mean gradual loss of political control as psychological identity shifts from Earth to the habitat. With second and third generations in space, such a shift will inevitably grow in importance in earthkind-spacekind relations, particularly among their respective cultural institutions, regardless of any attempts to maintain identification with the ground. This challenge will face not only the Soviet and American space programs, but also the nations of the world.

17 Remote Management of Space Behavior

"Self actualization" as I have used it . . .
stresses "full-humanness," the development of the biologically based nature of
man, and therefore is empirically normative
for the whole species rather than for particular times and places, i.e., it is less culturally relative. It conforms to biological destiny, rather than to historically-arbitrary,
culturally-local value models.

Abraham Maslow
Toward a Psychology of Being

I expect that the sociological problems will
prove to be more difficult to solve than the
technological ones.

Astronaut Gerald Carr
Commander of the third (84-day)
Skylab mission

Joint existence cannot be serene.

Cosmonaut Sevastiyanov

Soviet research exceeds traditional forms of psychology and embraces
chemicals, hypnosis, biofeedback, and even the study of psychic phenomena. According to Soviet philosophy, a person quickly grows accustomed to
the surrounding environment. Therefore, any change in the environment,
even a change for the worse, such as reducing the illumination, is, at first, a
positive stimulus to keep cosmonauts from identifying too closely with their
space habitat.

Not only do the Soviets see a psychological need for techniques to
avoid monotony through the use of technology, crew rotation, and the like,

but they also see a political and ideological need to disrupt uniformity of environmental factors. They see a delicate balance of needs to keep societies in space habitats from identifying more closely with space than with Earth, thereby creating a definite we-they attitude of spacekind toward their progenitor earthkind.

Soviet life-scientist L. N. Melnikov suggested that the highest productivity and quality of life for cosmonauts can be established by designing the interior of a space habitat in such a way that various environmental factors, such as light, color, sound, pressure, temperature, and humidity, are kept in a constant state of flux. Not only would these factors respond sensitively to the unique psychological, physiological, and emotional states of each individual cosmonaut, they would be correlated with the season and time of day in, say, Moscow.

Melnikov says, "this, in turn, determines the temperature, humidity, pressure, and air movement in the room as applicable to the concrete time of day and time of year," as depicted on an ambient screen. The technology responds to changes in the physiological indicators, such as blood pressure, pulse rate, adrenalin flow, and skin-galvanic reaction of the particular individual, and "ultimately makes it possible to *influence the organism in the necessary direction*" (emphasis added). The Soviet belief is that "the interior of the space ship may *carry the imprint of the social order* characteristic for the country; the level of culture, national traits, style of the epoch" (emphasis added).

One of the tangible precedents for this type of psychological control over the behavior of cosmonauts and space societies is the Odessa Stroygidravlika industrial plant. Here was established a "psychological relief room," in which visual, audial, olfactory, and other sensate stimuli are put forth to relieve the detrimental effects of working in a monotonous industrial environment. It is a proven method, from the Soviet point of view, for mitigating visual fatigue, nervous-emotional overloads, and also the sensory deprivations that are expected in a small, isolated environment. "The method which we are proposing is directed at satisfying the higher social and aesthetic emotions, at creating the feeling of harmony and beauty."

With these techniques they have found a way to achieve a satisfied state of mind, and work capacity has been increased as much as 17 percent because of consequent focusing of attention and improvement in reaction time. In programming for natural distractions through these technological substitutes, Soviet literature stresses the need for the unexpected and unusual. The psychological costs to the individual cosmonaut and his or her space-habitat society, however, may include those required for an envisaged *system of programmed control of the condition of the organism [which] has become very widespread, with the utilization of measures for the regimentation of regimes of work, rest, food intake and physical activity . . . psychotherapeutic measures of influence, pharmacological regulation of psychology, neurophysiological intervention using biological adaptogens, use of psychotropic substances.*

Soviet literature is replete with such references, clearly reflecting efforts to plan for consciousness control, biological accommodation, and social order in space. Note that the means and techniques mentioned above are not indigenous personal explorations, psychological self-indulgences, or group recreational choices. They are not mere self-induced, consciousness-raising techniques. They are not even characterized as voluntary, victimless behavior being suppressed for the objective common good.

Rather, these are mandatory, externally imposed controls. While Americans are still arguing over which forms of psychotropic substances, from caffeine, nicotine, and alcohol on, are appropriate for voluntary, discreet, personal use and alteration of mood or consciousness, the Soviets are demonstrating that they have not learned a simple, self-evident metalaw: Thou shalt not change another's consciousness without his informed consent.

This is not to say, of course, that American agencies have never undertaken this kind of research on subjects, both voluntary and involuntary. But such research has not taken place within the ranks of the astronauts. The United States life-sciences approach to psychoneurophysiological support of astronauts and participants in space societies has in large part been based upon the type of biochemistry already examined, although some of the long-term planning has touched upon a number of the same psychological areas being explored by the Soviets.

For the most part the evolution or establishment of social order within the unique psychobiological environment and engineering constraints of a space habitat have not been topics of serious consideration in America, beyond rather parochial mission rules for each flight, which do not allow much flexibility for the unique social requirements of the space inhabitants. Of course, this is not particularly surprising, since most American missions have not lasted longer than ten days. There were some expressions of concern for social order and individual rights during the longer-duration Skylab missions, but the statements of concern originated from the astronauts themselves and were largely ignored by ground-support authorities. Any questioning of the line of command by the astronauts — usually the nonmilitary participants — was neither understood nor countenanced by NASA authority.

This again points up the fact that space migration necessitates a renewed naturalistic awareness that legal principles are intellectual articulations of human interactions with the ecological requirements of any given natural or cultural environment. Since these environments are ever changing and evolving, legal systems are ever changing and evolving as well. They must be responsive to the unique ecological dictates of any cultural environment that they reflect and to which they give structure. Legal systems are institutionalized matrices of social arrangements that represent social patterns. They are dissipative structures.

For these reasons, legal systems are subject to the same evolutionary tendencies we have been discussing — resistance to change, long periods of stability, then acceleration, perturbation, and either dissolution or complexification, and transformation. Such a transformation, however, requires that the very paradigms upon which the previous systems were based be superseded by new ones that are more holistic, more ecumenical, and more widely accepted.

Are we prepared to create our own extraterrestrial children in the context of "whither humankind?" Can we ask ourselves to imagine that we are members of a species far more mature than that of our forebears? Our navigation is improved by an awareness of the nature of biocultural adaptations and of evolution itself. We have already seen, for example, how the natural laws of acceleration, punctuated equilibrium, complexification, and self-organization all show that crises precede transformation. Incremental change, no matter how insignificant it may seem, does not add up or lead up to more of the same. Changes compound and become multidimensional and exponential.

The crises that precede transformation, however, do not guarantee transformation. There are two possible outcomes for any coherent or intelligent dissipative structure. One is disintegration. The other is transformation. These are the *only* two ultimate possibilities.

And so the solutions to the incredible flux of the Space Age and the global crises that hold us in their grip are creative transformations — changes that must be conceptual and perceptual, generated from within rather than imposed from without. There is a timeless, broad, global, cross-cultural affirmation that human beings are collectively like the cells of a greater body and that our individual consciousnesses are but components of a greater community of cosmic consciousness, such as the psychological concept of the collective unconscious, or even the philosophical and theological concepts of Compte's Great Being, Teilhard's Noosphere, or Christianity's Holy Spirit. Perhaps the human solution lies in an understanding of their roles.

We still do not have empirical proof of their existence, of course, but we have anticipated and intuited them across the ages. Could atoms have predicted molecules, molecules predicted cells, and cells predicted us? Perhaps not, but we are now able, logically, to anticipate and predict changes in response to crises—crises that we have often deliberately precipitated—and crises that inevitably call for a reconsideration and reaffirmation of evolutionary purpose and direction.

In this regard, it should be increasingly clear that the unavoidably planned and synthetic nature of space habitats and the scientific revolutions that led to them and will follow after them perturb all human social systems by accentuating and accelerating the search for a species-normative, ecological jurisprudence that will be mature enough and heterodox enough to accommodate and mediate new postterrestrial and extraterrestrial realities. It must be mature enough and heterodox enough to embrace and ensure the self-determination of individuals and societies.

In many ways this search was going on even before the classical period of ancient Greece, but it never had such a broad empirical base until the development of modern social science and such specialized disciplines as legal philosophy, jurimetrics, communications law, criminology, medical jurisprudence, psychiatry, psychoanalytic jurisprudence, environmental law, space law, and now a newly emerging neurological, psychological, and ecological jurisprudence that we might call biojuridics.

The importance of all this to jurisprudence and the social ecology of space is that it represents the disciplined sensitivity by means of which human beings understand themselves, communicate with each other, and understand what is ecologically and psychologically conscionable, and possible, in such omnifaceted social and jurisprudential realms. To enhance the likelihood of achieving this disciplined sensitivity was the reason for the ecological categories of values and demands offered by McDougal, Lasswell, and Vlasic in *Law and Public Order in Space.* It was also the reason for our somewhat Jeffersonian outline or simplified version of the categories of jurisprudential ecology: survival (life), social-transitional (liberty), and conscious-transcendental (pursuit of happiness).

Supreme Court Justice Oliver Wendell Holmes put it this way: "A law which punished conduct that would not be blame-worthy (generally so understood) in the average member of the community would be too severe for the community to bear." Yet how is a community defined? Who is the average member? Who is the mythical "ordinary, reasonable man" of the common law? Even our Newtonian, largely pre-Darwinian, storehouse of judicial precedents indicates that one is not always consciously the same person, or even the same sort of person.

The criminal law, for example, postpones the psychological accountability of children. The civil common law contains an inference that their psychological development earlier than certain ages is not sufficient for legal accountability. Under the traditional rule a child younger than seven was presumed incapable of criminal intent or negligence.

Another example might be the enraged witness of an unprovoked murder who reflexively strikes the murderer to death with no thought of mercy and beyond the degree of force necessary to subdue and secure the murderer for what we call due process under the law. Such a person is often found guilty, if at all, only of manslaughter or "negligent homicide." Under most homicide laws this person would probably not be considered psychologically culpable for the same degree of cold contempt for life and social order as is juridically required for him to be found guilty of the crime of murder itself.

The controversial insanity defense also recognizes various degrees of responsible, irresponsible, and unresponsible consciousness. The conviction of the assassin of the mayor of San Francisco in 1979 for homicide was mitigated to involuntary manslaughter on the basis of testimony that established a chemical neurosis aggravated by bad fortune, glycemia, and addiction to junk food. The press called it the Twinkie defense after a popular mass-produced confection, Hostess Twinkies.

The Twinkie defense exemplified the exploitability of a legal principle called diminished capacity, in this instance through the conjunction of the rapidly advancing science of neurochemistry and the peculiar judicial temperaments of the San Francisco jury. Nevertheless, the law has begun to recognize that certain states of consciousness can be measured. At an emergent, external level, we are all familiar with the still somewhat unreliable polygraph. The highway breathalyzer is another excellent, also occasionally unreliable example. We are familiar with attempts of the Olympic Committee and major league baseball to require chemical testing of athletes as a prerequisite for participation.

The issues of mind control, lack of due process, machine over man, self-incrimination, and scientific infallibility have already been raised. Several officers of the U.S. military were even disciplined for use of hard drugs on the basis of a test that inadvertently measured the poppy-seed-covered bagels they had eaten. So neurological jurisprudence is not only involved in micromeasuring, it is also involved in determining, from the macro laws we have been discussing, how to preserve the right to privacy, how to accommodate diversity, and how to assure justice.

Psychologist Gordon W. Allport resurrected the word *psychophysical,* a term first used in the mid 1800s by Gustave Fechner in his *Psychophysics. Psychophysical* is used to suggest that the personality and its stages and

types are based upon a body-mind nervous system. There are physical processes and structures underlying the mental stages. There is a neurological
connection to consciousness. Acupuncture is a well-known technique that
exemplifies this connection. Biofeedback, another example, is known to be
capable of affecting very small areas of the body in isolation.

The story of the assassination of the mayor of San Francisco is only one
isolated example of the growing importance of neurology to psychological
jurisprudence, based upon an assumption of the union of mind and body.
Neurology reveals the unique level of neurological development and function of the individual. Its subjects are measured on the basis not only of their
external behavior and their internal experience, but also of their internal
behavior—their electrochemical and psychophysical, or neurological, characteristics.

This is not an elitist point of view, despite its potentially negative implications for civil liberties. It does not scorn children, deny soul, or scoff at
cultures that are naturally at different stages of development. It is really just
a new, more scientific version of the old idea that no two persons are the
same, despite having been created *jurisprudentially* equal. The approach
becomes what Allport referred to as *idiographic,* or unique to the individual
case.

To look up or down, in or out, from any point on our multidimensional,
sentient, or psychological continuum without awe, appreciation, humility,
and a sense of proportion would be destructive of personal and social potentials. There is as much reason for humility as for scorn or elitism in considering the very near possibility of outer space humankind who, at least functionally or temporally, are neurologically distinct from earthkind.

The influence of this reality on interplanetary jurisprudence will prove to
be immense. The self-determination of spacekind will soon become vital,
even indispensable. The same is true for earthkind, of course, so that while
spacekind and earthkind will be physiologically, psychologically, and perhaps one day even taxonomically distinct from one another, exponentially
smaller examples of similar differences exist that will have to be recognized
both within and among earthkind and spacekind.

Not every habitat will be in the same region of space, for instance, generate or be exposed to the same radiation, have the same shielding, atmosphere, gravity, architecture, and so on. The phases of development in different regions of Earth will also be different in kind and pace. Advanced
communications, education, psychological and biomedical knowledge,
computer science, and counseling in eugenics will be available to some populations, perhaps not to others. The Information Age and the neurotechnol-
ogies are even accelerating the likely emergence of *Homo sapiens alterius*

right here on Earth through continuing advancement of the species by virtue of such technological capabilities as direct genetic intervention and alteration.

At the same time, within every population group, people will be passing through various stages of temporal development or coping with psychic imbalance or fluctuation. Our appreciation of the diversity, of the whole universe of conscious activity represented in this description, is the species-normative, sapient base of the ecological jurisprudence needed for survival of the species and the continuing hope and potential for social transformation and interplanetary culture.

The inevitability of diversity and growth indicates the need to establish early legal regimes for space communities based on conscious perceptions and cultural values peculiar or unique to dwellers in space habitats. There is also a critical need for a prerequisite reorientation of earthbound attitudes to the alien, possibly even repugnant—to those on the ground—values formulated by inhabitants of space in the light of their own unique perceptions and needs and despite their designation as envoys of mankind.

In addition to being envoys of mankind, they will properly and inevitably become their own envoys as they dwell for long periods or permanently in space habitats. They will become envoys of spacekind as surely as the founding fathers and mothers of the United States of America became patriots, radicals, and freedom fighters.

18 Mind in Space

We will get a different race in space eventually.

Stan Mohler, Director
Aerospace Medical Program
Wright State University

The right way . . . is . . . to look at the whole
structural interconnection of the thing . . .
not just the sciences but all the efforts of
intellectual kinds, [which] are an endeavor
to see the connections of the hierarchies, to
connect beauty to history, to connect history to man's psychology, man's psychology to the working of the brain, the brain to
the neural impulse, and the neural impulse
to the chemistry, and so forth, up and
down.

Paul Davies
God and the New Physics

We are beginning to see the mind as an electrochemical data-processing center with sophisticated neuron structures and hormone balances integrated with the entire psychophysical system. Individual cells have a definitive metabolism and all are hooked together, interrelated in amazingly sophisticated neurocircuits.

This image of the brain comes into sharper focus with the realization that every person has approximately 30 billion brain cells. Each cell is capable of relating to as many as 10,000 to 25,000 others. The number of associations is on the order of 30 billion to the twenty-five-thousandth power, a number larger than the number of atoms in the universe. This electrochemical complexity is the anatomical structure of consciousness.

It has been noted that the brain itself fires off about 5 billion signals a second. A fully functioning modern human being may be receiving as many as 100 million sensations a second. The brain consumes most of the body's energy as well. Although it composes only 2 percent of body weight, it uses 20 percent of the available oxygen. Still, as we have all been taught since childhood, we use only a small fraction of our mental potential.

Neurologically speaking, there are at least as many levels of consciousness as there are sensory, anatomical, cellular, molecular, and atomic structures within the human body. A primitive map of conscious intelligence that can be gleaned from present neurological studies involves at least eight structurally, ethologically, endocrinologically, or psychoactively identifiable stages or distinct neurological anatomies in human beings:

1. *The vital R-Complex,* which is the autonomic nervous system — the biosurvival structure or level of the nervous system. This basic psychic response may have been the first nervous system to evolve, perhaps a billion years ago in its most rudimentary single-cell form. Sometimes called the reptilian brain and associated with the fight-or-flight response, it is activated in human beings before birth and is closely related to the oral-sensory stage of infant development.

2. *The limbic midbrain,* a level of the nervous system that seems to mediate emotion, aggression, territorial instincts, and power and security. Its psychic capacity may have appeared first when land vertebrates appeared and began to compete for territory, perhaps as long ago as 500 million B.C.

3. *The left hemisphere of the neocortex,* which is the general region of the brain that seems to mediate empirical thinking, manual dexterity, language, symbolic learning, and the manufacture of objects. its psychic capacity may first have been actualized when hominids began to be differentiated from other primates, 4–5 million B.C.

4. *The cerebellum and corpus callosum,* which provide for holographic use of both hemispheres of the brain in comparison and unison. Here are the more complex areas of learning and enculturation, sex roles, moral and ethical behavior, career training, and so on. These are the tasks of childhood through late adolescence on contemporary Earth.

5. *The right hemisphere of the neocortex,* which seems to be connected to the sensory-somatic capacities of the psychic system, a neurosomatic level, circuit, or frequency of the nervous system that seems to mediate awareness of bodily function, rhythm, relationships, and aesthetics.

6. *The cellular structure and chemical nature of the neurons,* which allow the basic frequencies, catalysts, and rhythms of the brain to open consciousness to the reality of the brain as a bioelectric loom, fabricating realities — the observer influencing the nature of the observed, such as in biofeedback.

7. *The molecular structure of the neurons and neurotransmitters,* which encourage us to contemplate the genetic coding for human sentience. Why is there so much excess capacity? Are we genetically coded for a higher, better ordered, more transcendent consciousness?

8. *The atomic nature of the molecular genetic coding,* which offers surprisingly broad implications for evolution of awareness and complex sentience. The neuroatomic level allows maximum use of the increasing complexification of the frontal lobes of both hemispheres of the neocortex to permit direct awareness of and communication with electronic-atomic information. Examples would not exclude quantum theory, relativity, genetic engineering, biotechnological integration, linkups between brain and computer, or even so-called psychic or mystical phenomena and extrasensory perception.

The concept of incorporeal consciousness, which is closely identified with psychic phenomena, is still more a theological than a neurological concept, of course, although much empirical work on so-called psi phenomena is being carried out within universities and military and intelligence establishments on both sides of the Iron Curtain. It has even been suggested that historical figures, such as Buddha, the Enlightened One, and Christ, the Annointed One, may have been examples of the highest level of neurological attainment—complete neurological self-actualization.

The dangers to the social order contained in the latter notion are abundantly clear, of course, as are the implications for social order in habitats in which a more nearly complete actualization of neurological capability combines with a thoroughly altered psychophysical ecology to cause alien perceptions and philosophies and the behavior that follows from them. While it is safe to say that no one is going to be transformed into Buddha or Christ by either working or living in space, it is also safe to say that even our most cherished beliefs will begin to be framed in new contexts, interpreted within new realities and possibilities.

In his 1976 article "Mind in Space," in *USAF Medical Service Digest,* Stanley G. Rosen raised the possibility that the experience of being in space could have a significant effect on people—that is, that their consciousness could undergo radical change. Charles Berry, former Director of Life Sciences for NASA and at one time the personal physician to the astronauts, told Captain Rosen, "no one who went into space wasn't changed by his experience, although I think some of them really don't see what's happened to them." It was his feeling that they had all changed in some similar, inexplicable way, despite their disparate personalities or degree of recognition of the change. Technical and training personnel who worked regularly with the astronauts have made similar observations.

Apollo Astronaut Edgar D. Mitchell, one of those who experienced profound change, reacted this way:

Something happened to me during the flight that I didn't even recognize at the time. I would say it was a peak experience, if you will. I flipped out, or whatever, and the next two years I spent in resettling my entire thought process, because as a result of that experience virtually all of the philosophies, ideas, scientific truths, and so forth, that were dear to me and were a part of my scientific paradigm got tossed right up into the air and fell into a big heap like a bundle of pick-up sticks. Since that time I have been very carefully and slowly picking up those sticks and trying to put them into some sort of order again.

In a presentation to the Fourth Princeton/AIAA Conference on Space Manufacturing Facilities, entitled "Consciousness Alteration in Space," B. J. Bluth evaluated Captain Rosen's findings in the light of contemporary ethnomethodology and Abraham Maslow's lifelong experiments with peak experiences and altered states of consciousness. The focus of both Rosen's and Bluth's research had been on the potential for dangerous errors in transcendental states of awareness. The assumption was that if dangerous irrationality or undependability were to be exhibited, radical measures would have to be taken to control such states of awareness. No dangerous error or irrationality, however, was ever registered by any of the spacefarers who experienced different states of conscious awareness.

The only really earthshaking results of these experiences were such things as Apollo Astronaut James Irwin's formation of the High Flight Foundation as an interdenominational evangelistic organization to tell people that it is "God's plan to come back and tell people what a beautiful thing we have here on Earth, to take care of it, and to try to live in brotherhood, the way Jesus Christ would want us to." Bluth points out that Irwin was later joined by former astronauts Pogue and Worden, who shared his experience and his view.

Astronaut Edward White, despite his extensive military training, discipline, and experience and despite his knowledge of a limited safety margin of available oxygen, was so awed by the sights of America's first space walk that he had to be coaxed back into the Gemini 4 Command Module. A similar rapture is purported to have affected Scott Carpenter in Mercury's Aurora 7, possibly contributing to a risky and embarrassing result: he missed his landing zone by more than 200 miles. Apollo 11 Astronaut Edwin Aldrin had difficulty adjusting to his return to Earth, finding himself clinically depressed. Apollo Astronaut Russell Schweickart stated that he was, "quite a different person from what I was before I flew," although he hastens to add that the flight itself was probably less of a factor than the preparation for the flight and the fact that he opened himself to the experience.

Edgar Mitchell's experience is among those most thoroughly discussed, perhaps because he had a preexisting interest and knowledge of psychology and neurological studies. He even agreed to conduct an ESP experiment on the Apollo 14 flight. The experiment involved telepathy between the spacecraft and Earth, with the use of statistical controls—random choice of colors, and so on. It was on that flight that he had a peak experience, although the telepathy experiments were only modestly successful by statistical measures.

The metaphysical-transcendental realm of jurisprudential ecology had little empirical backing until the modern neurological discoveries, the self-actualization theories of Carl Rogers and Abraham Maslow, and the transpersonal theories of Aldous Huxley and others. There was some provision for the higher aspirations and potentials in Freud's concept of the superego, but Freud's general appraisal of human potential was quite pessimistic and deterministic.

As mentioned earlier, pre-Einsteinian science had an externalist, reductionist, micro bias. The post-Einsteinian paradigms tend to be more internalist, emergent, multidimensional, and macro biased. An example is modern Gestalt psychology, a paradigm of exponential conscious shifts from one neurological stage to another. Such shifts can be predicted to accompany the passage from one temporal stage of neurological development to another, for example, but may also be found to follow intense experience, such as physical stress, physical danger, death of a loved one, or a spiritual discipline. Many people have reported Gestalt or paradigm shifts as a result of watching the Apollo 8 Christmas Eve broadcast, which originated from above the terminator of the moon. People have also reported this type of shift when first looking at the Grand Canyon.

Psychologist Arnold M. Ludwig lists ten factors as commonly related to an altered state of consciousness:

1. Alterations in thinking
2. Disturbed time sense
3. Loss of control or an immersion in a cosmic consciousness
4. Change in emotional expression
5. Change in body image
6. Perceptual distortion
7. Change in meaning or significance
8. Sense of the ineffable

9. Feelings of rejuvenation
10. Hypersuggestibility

Abraham Maslow defined the peak experience as essentially a transcendent experience, a moment of great insight or vision. The person sees without the need for symbols or concepts for a moment, so that life is perceived in wholeness and unity. Such an experience, unless induced by sensory deprivation, psychoactive drugs, or intense and prolonged spiritual and physical discipline, is rare, is entirely unpredictable, and can cause disorientation, awe, and surprise.

Maslow described nineteen characteristics of the peak experience. Among them were the following observations:

The peak experience is always experienced as good and desirable; . . . at the higher levels of human maturation many dichotomies, polarities and conflicts are fused, transcended or resolved; . . . the person at the peak is godlike [in a number of ways, including] the complete, loving, uncondemning, compassionate and perhaps amused acceptance of the world; . . . is it not meaningful also that the mystic experience has been described in almost identical words by people in every religion, every era, and in every culture? No wonder Aldous Huxley has called it "The Perennial Philosophy." The great creators . . . have described their creative moments in almost identical terms, even though they were variously poets, chemists, sculptors, philosophers, and mathematicians.

In *Brain/Mind Bulletin,* Marilyn Ferguson points out that our normal state of awareness is dominated by low-amplitude, high-frequency brain-wave activity. We are more attentive to the outer world than to inner experience. Altered states, such as relaxation and meditation or deep prayer, are characterized by an increase in slower brain waves of lower frequency but higher amplitude. The electroencephalogram essentially measures a variation in resonance among large groups of neurons. Much the same thing seems to be deliberately induced by the Soviet light-sound relaxer envisaged for the cosmonauts.

Maslow called this state of consciousness B-Cognition—Being Cognition. It has been reported in relatively rare instances through the centuries in every culture. It seems to occur more frequently to highly acute, self-actualized persons during experiences of high perceptual, psychic, or physical stress. It can cause a total shift of paradigm or world view, with compelling Gestalt speed. It has been reported for ages by writers, artists, mystics, mountain climbers, and patients near death.

This fits well with Prigogine's view of the brain as a dissipative structure. Almost everyone has experienced some form of writer's block, for instance, and the explosion of material that follows the breaking or transformation of the block. Almost everyone can remember threshold accomplishments. The old saying goes that once you have learned to ride a bicycle you will never forget; but do you remember what a breakthrough that accomplishment was? After falling repeatedly, you suddenly "knew" how to ride.

Through the ages, mystics have affirmed the value of the great experience that may come only two or three times in a lifetime, if at all, and brings a permanent overall transformation in the psyche. The single mystical experience of Paul on the road to Damascus, for example, changed his life drastically. Such an experience produces a fluctuation of psychic energy which forces the psychophysical structure to complexify into a new state of organization, to resonate into a new pattern. Ferguson pointed out that

It makes sense that the states of consciousness that enhance [brain-wave] fluctuations produce more insight—more significant change—than our everyday consciousness. . . . The Prigogine theory also suggests that learning occurs more efficiently when the brain's fluctuations are augmented [rather than suppressed]. Transpersonal educators have praised the benefits of using music, imagery, meditation, rhythmic breathing and relaxation techniques, all of which tend to increase brainwave amplitude.

These same techniques have been used by prophets, priests, and yogis through the ages, of course, but the first scientific study of altered states of consciousness was conducted by psychiatrist R. M. Bucke in the early 1900s. In his *Cosmic Consciousness* he proposed that while there may have been unique historical exceptions, such as Jesus, Buddha, Mohammed, and Moses, these states of perception were rare until recently and are a new evolutionary development, not a pathology, as is often feared when new and unfamiliar physical experiences and behaviors are encountered. He pointed to evidence of a statistical increase in such experiences in recent centuries. In this regard, Maslow indicated that almost everyone now seems capable of a peak experience at least once in his or her life.

The importance of all this for jurisprudence comes in the rejection by every commentator we have discussed—Bucke, Maslow, Bluth, Ferguson, and Rosen—of any pathological conclusions about psychological or neurological change, both in general and as related to astronauts. From them we can see that the greatest potential for error and disruption of a mission resides not in the peak experience but in a rejection of it or in the refusal of other crew members to discuss it—a break in the flow of conversation.

It is suggested that if the conversation of the group is disrupted the social world begins to totter, to lose its subjective plausibility. This is why total sensory deprivation, as in the isolation tanks used with the early female astronaut candidates, can induce either peak experiences or hallucinations. In a strange sort of way, these early isolation tests were designed to screen out anyone who could not use biofeedback to retain left-brain dominance during the eight hours of floating. According to psychologist Peter Berger,

The subjective reality of the world hangs on the thin thread of conversation. The reason why most of us are unaware of this precariousness most of the time is grounded in the continuity of our conversation with significant others.

This is the basis of the coercive techniques of consciousness control and brainwashing. The meaning of events is not easily decided in isolation. Evidence shows that a child raised in comparative isolation will be neurologically stunted. There is a need for confirmation and feedback from others. Therefore, a tendency to any form of control or suppression of information should be resisted. In criminal law and terrorism we are familiar with the hostage syndrome. We organize our reality by creating human metaphors in the company of others. Understanding is not a solitary act. It is eminently social. The greatest danger is an ostracizing attitude on the part of others. According to Bluth,

Communication [of the experience or perception] may take a different pattern. With a radical paradigm shift the person may be seen by others as having a confused state of identity and distorted thinking processes. If there are any difficulties to be associated with altered states of consciousness that may occur in space, these may be the most probable. The innovator, the person who sees new things, is in a precarious situation for two reasons: First, the old metaphors and symbols are not adequate to the experience, and secondly, no one else had the experience, so it is hard for them to understand. . . . [They] may think he is disoriented or crazy. Paranoia can be described as a game that no one else is playing. . . . An altered state of consciousness may generate a language no one else is speaking or wants to speak. . . . [Yet] in many areas of science and social science it is no longer assumed that the real world designs our understandings of it. Rather, it is thought that [reality] is in our way of seeing, thinking and understanding.

Both Bluth and Rosen indicate that screening out applicants who would be susceptible to peak experiences in space would be impossible, unnecessary, and possibly damaging. Selection criteria that do not favor flexibility and tolerance of the unusual might well precipitate the very kind of breakdown in cultural accommodation and flow of conversation that could cause social disintegration, injury, or death.

The suggestion is that the experiencer treat the event as a personal one, which does not need to be validated, and that the community treat it as a valid experience to be shared and thoroughly aired, but nothing more. The approach is similar to that of religious freedom. Thou shalt not inhibit thy neighbor from transforming and experiencing his or her own consciousness. This is similar to the conclusion of Ferguson:

The common wisdom about transcendent moments is that they can never be properly communicated, only experienced. The Tao that can be described is not the Tao. . . . You cannot describe red to someone who has never seen it. Red is elemental and irreducible.

Perhaps this is why Maslow said that the peak experience is seen as a self-validating, self-justifying moment which carries its own intrinsic value with it and even to attempt to justify it takes away from its dignity and worth. Perhaps this is also why Bluth says that the simple fact of conversation about such an event might be sufficient in itself to deal with it. "Mystery itself," she said, "bestowed on an event, can act as a stabilizing definition because it places the event in a category that need not be fathomed to be dealt with."

The suggestion is, therefore, that it is possible and desirable to devise preflight training for astronauts that would be directed toward the development of an atmosphere that could mediate the experience of an altered state of consciousness. Bluth states that

Rather than try to keep out people who might be inclined to have an intuitive, unexpected, altered state of consciousness, the focus would be upon identification and training which would help the astronaut maximize the event. . . . Preflight training contingencies for keeping up the flow of conversation can be taught. In this way, opportunities for vital human and scientific advancement, as well as personal growth, can be optimized.

Once again we see the importance of diversity, androgyny, and full self-actualization. Once again we see that definitions of actualization may be qualitatively and quantitatively different in space. And once again we see that the gradual emergence of spacekind requires unique reformulations of both our grand internal models and our jurisprudential imperatives. No matter what field of knowledge we have examined, we have seen again and again that we must accommodate the idiosyncratic and constantly evolving natures and bioecological dictates of both earthkind and spacekind if we have any hope of self-fulfillment and survival of the species.

Charles Lindbergh spoke of this type of metaphysical-transcendental view of the human future in his foreward to astronaut Michael Collins's *Carrying the Fire.* Lindbergh recounted an altered state of his own, experienced during his historic transatlantic flight. In his own book, *The Spirit of St. Louis,* Lindbergh described seeing through the fuselage of the plane, which was windowless, "as though my skull was one great eye." In the Collins book he said,

My awareness seemed to be abandoning my body to expand on stellar scales. There were moments when I seemed to be disconnected from the world, my plane, my mind and my heartbeat completely unessential to my new existence. Experiences of that flight . . . have caused me to value all human accomplishments by their effect on the intangible quality we name awareness. . . . Is it remotely possible that we are approaching a stage in evolution when we can discover how to separate ourselves from Earthly life, to abandon our physical frameworks in order to extend both inwardly and outwardly through limitless dimensions of awareness? In future universal explorations, may we have no need for vehicles or matter? Is this the adventure opening to man beyond travel through solar system space?

VI   Astrolaw and Space Law

19 Astrolaw and the Spacekind Declaration

> Astrolaw contemplates the practice of law
> *in* outer space. . . . The direct subjects of
> Space Law are sovereign nations; the direct
> subjects of Astrolaw are natural and legal
> persons in space. . . . Astrolaw focuses not
> upon space as a legal regime, but upon
> space as a place.
>
> *J. Henry Glazer, J.S.D.*
> *White's Inn, Astrolaw Societies, San Francisco*
> *Assistant Professor, Hastings College of Law*

> How will physiological and psychological
> changes in humans living in space . . .
> affect their needs and perceptions and, in
> turn, their own ideas as to what the "rules"
> should be? . . . This field of study has come
> to be called Biojuridics and forms much of
> the foundation of Astrolaw.
>
> *George P. Sloup, J.D.*
> *International Colloquium*
> *on the Law of Outer Space (1984)*

New scientific data and technological applications from seemingly unrelated disciplines have yet to be tapped as resources for the space jurist. The most conspicuous space activities in need of such an interdisciplinary approach are those that involve human habitation. It is particularly important that jurists, policymakers, and the entire general public understand the bioeco-logical foundations of human behavior — which includes thinking — in the synthetic life-support environment of a space habitat if we are to have legal regimes that are responsive to the physiological and cultural realities of living in outer space.

There has been considerable discussion through the years concerning the intent of the people of the United States of America to transplant their "civilization of freedom" into outer space. President Kennedy spoke of a flag of freedom rather than a flag of conquest and of our intent to bar weapons of mass destruction in favor of instruments of understanding. In many ways the communications satellites, and even the moon and Skylab missions, were just that—instruments of understanding.

Yet if we are to have freedom, we must make full and intelligent use of all the technologies, the new extensions of humanity, that are the mediators of the tremendous growth in collective and individual knowledge which is being required of us. The Space Age clearly presents unprecedented challenges to self-government, liberty, and the sovereignty of the individual. Social science is faced with the fact that institutions are more bureaucratic and pervasive, more global in nature, particularly in space communities, where the institution is the ecology.

As we acquire more technological surrogates, as we become more bionic—biotechnologically integrated for survival—our individual autonomy and personality frequently seem to be at greater risk. Being turned into a number, folded, spindled, and mutilated, is a contemporary cliché. This was certainly the apocalyptic view of George Orwell in *1984.*

Meanwhile, the international legal system, which is needed to help fashion a global approach to the rights of space communities and space inhabitants, still denies legal standing to individuals and nongovernmental organizations. Individual human beings are not the *subjects* of international law. They are, at best, beneficiaries of international law—*objects* of international law.

Theoretically, the international legal system exists to aid the status of individuals through their representation by states. A nation-state–centered system of international law, however, that has not yet extended sovereignty below the level of the nation-states is a feeble defense of individual rights, particularly when such rights are not widely recognized in the domestic law of most nation-states. Diplomatic conventions and passports are still the symbols of this state-centered system of representation.

Law is a system of social interaction, whether agreed upon or decreed. It applies, in its various incarnations, to nations, states, organizations, and individuals. In its most socially scientific and ideal sense, law is the creative, just, and efficient institutionalization of ideas, with particular emphasis on the promotion or protection of individual life, liberty, equality, privacy, communication, property—a nonexclusive list within the context of human community.

Therefore, law need not emanate from state officials, nor merely be predicated upon the preservation of the state, since ideally the state should be predicated upon the promotion and preservation of the sovereign person—the citizen—as the spiritual, conscious, and functional basis of the community. In one sense or another, almost every system on Earth, no matter how tyrannical, pays rhetorical or theoretical homage to the functional and protective nature of this supposed social contract.

Yet we all know that preaching is often far from practice and that each nation-state can be counted upon to seek its own survival over any individual right and its own aggrandizement, absent limits. As a socio-organism, each nation-state has a natural evolutionary tendency to complexify and grow. Among our founding fathers, the naturalists understood the tendency of institutions to consolidate and abuse power. This was part of the reason for their emphasis on federalism, republicanism, division of powers, civilian control of the military, and guaranteed individual rights exercised under an independent and supreme constitution and court. Similar thinking may have caused President Eisenhower to fear what he called subgovernments, such as the military-industrial complex.

In his introduction to the twentieth-century edition of *The Federalist Papers,* Clinton Rossiter observed that

The Federalist *is a contribution to political theory only by accident—by the happy accident, one might say, that neither of its chief authors [Hamilton and Madison] could ever make a point in the most Earth-bound debate without pausing, if only for a moment, to put the point in a larger and more abstract perspective. Yet this, after all, is the familiar way in which some of the greatest contributions to political theory come into being. . . . No one can read these pages without being reminded powerfully of both the light and dark sides of human nature—of man's capacity for reason and justice that makes free government possible, of his capacity for passion and injustice that makes it necessary.*

Despite the widely attested brilliance and perspicacity of Hamilton and Madison, however, and despite their rich classical educations, these men were not tending to the larger, more abstract, less earthbound points of view simply because of their personal attributes. They were called to examine the foundations, the cusps, and the interconnections of human society by the very nature of the social and jurisprudential circumstances then existing. It was their task to explain the foundations of a radical, complex, and transformative juridical paradigm to the peoples of New York, the United States, and the world.

These early statesmen were coaxed by the nature of the frontier—not just by its supposed natural emptiness and wild freedom, but also by the necessity to redefine the basis of new communities and social orders on the frontier in ways that would be consonant with the peculiar bioecological requirements of the new environment and, in each successive redefinition, in ways perhaps more in keeping with natural law. Such a recourse to philosophy and interdisciplinary heterodoxy was described by Thomas Kuhn in *The Structure of Scientific Revolutions* as characteristic of extraordinary research: the process of redefinition at the cusps of a body of knowledge within which the interrelations and frameworks are being transformed.

There is a desperate current need for the same sort of broad and deep heterodoxy as that of Madison and Hamilton, in order to protect the ecology of the Earth, to prevent nuclear holocaust, to establish extraterrestrial communities, and to preserve and protect the fundamental rights and freedoms of both earthkind and spacekind. This is a human imperative. Most people should need only brief reflection to see that such an imperative is particularly important for confined, synthetic, planned space communities.

Spacekind may prove to be a central factor in the achievement of this human imperative. Space offers the indispensable new frontier—not the final frontier, but the endless, ever-renewing, ever-expanding, ever-complexifying frontier—an endless laboratory environment. The new communities of space offer the same impetus, the same challenges and opportunities, the same enticements that were offered by the New World during the Age of Enlightenment for men such as Madison, Hamilton, Jefferson, Locke, Rousseau, Kant, and Hegel—only this time it is offered in never-ending continuity.

Still, even with the continuity of the frontier, the new communities of the American West did not alter the juridical constitution of the United States to a great extent. The greatest alteration came about after the Civil War and was the result of things left undone at the original constitutional convention in Philadelphia. Here is yet another of the reasons for our stress on the quality and character of beginnings. The laws of conservation, inertia or least effort, entropy, and evolution predict that stability and slow change will predominate. Acceleration comes only with transformative amounts of energy or acute stress.

The achievement of our human imperative—and of the global and interplanetary constitutions necessary for its realization—will be one of the most monumentally delicate, difficult long-term projects ever undertaken by a human civilization. A poor beginning will seriously threaten its achievement.

Such an achievement, of course, may not come about in our lifetime, perhaps not even for centuries hence. We must be wary and at times tactically self-serving. We shall, of necessity, continue to concentrate on many short-term, realistic goals. Yet the pursuit of such a long-term objective, an attempt to mold reality in this way, may be indispensable—not only to the ultimate achievement of our human imperative, but also to survival of both earthkind and spacekind in the intervening period of continuing instability, destructive change, and confrontation.

Still, it is a rare moment in human history. Few generations have been afforded such an opportunity. Comparisons with the ages of Columbus, Galileo, Aristotle, and even Hammurabi are many. Ideas preserved or generated and institutions invented during such times of fundamental change have far greater, longer-lasting influence than those of other, more static periods. The initial stages of any development determine the vectors. Directions, of course, can be changed or reversed, but the laws of energy tell us that much more energy is needed to reverse a pattern, or to change it to any extent, than is needed simply to flow along with it.

Our task in this time is to begin the definition of founding principles for the self-determination and self-governance of the first semiautonomous and permanent space communities. Beyond that, it is necessary to order Earth law and space law in such ways that the inevitable demand of the interdependent space communities for complete autonomy—the Spacekind Declaration of Independence—can be accommodated peacefully, with a minimum expenditure of wasteful, disruptive energy needed to reverse already established patterns.

A good way to begin is to understand the legal status that has been established for the present astronauts and cosmonauts while they are in space. Their status was somewhat ambiguous in the early space years. Obviously they were profoundly cooperative with and firmly under the control of their home organizations. So, to say that their legal status was ambiguous is mere semantics. Yet dialectics and semantics are at the very foundation of communication today—the communication of an intelligent and compellingly social species. They are the very structure of our law. Indeed, natural law is an aesthetic concept or phenomenon described as having resonance, balance, justice.

We have already looked at many of the early criteria for the selection of astronauts and their pecking order and at the various categories of astronaut. We saw the intimate military-civilian interrelations, and we see them again in the fact that the Uniform Code of Military Justice was one of the first earthly codes to be clearly applicable to the activities of people in space. The reason for this is that the code applies to all U.S. military personnel, "wherever situated." Since most of the early astronauts were U.S. military personnel, the problem of jurisdiction and control was greatly simplified. It is hardly surprising that the Soviets also had no problem with command and control in their hierarchical military space program.

In any event, the 1967 United Nations Outer Space Treaty left no doubt concerning the jurisdiction of the state over its space travelers. In Article VIII it said "a State Party to the Treaty on whose registry an object launched into outer space is carried shall retain jurisdiction and control over such object, and over any personnel thereof, while in outer space or on a celestial body."

This clause, however, did not clarify the matter of jurisdiction beyond all confusion. The emphasis on the launching state still leaves ambiguity concerning jurisdiction in Skylabs, modular space stations, and structures assembled in space. The rule makes little sense in a multinational habitat, regardless of who launched or constructed the modules. A safe assumption on Earth, of course, is that the arm of the law will usually be long enough to protect the vital interests of the state sponsor, and indeed, that is just what Article VIII provides for the types of temporary space activity that were foreseen at the time the Outer Space Treaty was negotiated. The municipal or domestic law of states is clearly extended to objects launched from Earth.

Astrolaw will therefore not be entirely space-indigenous law for quite some time—perhaps for a generation or two. In the interim it is a patchwork of international, intergovernmental, and municipal extensions of law that is normative and largely indigenous to Earth. It consists of contractual agreements between European Spacelab owners or payload specialists or passengers on the one hand and NASA and its pilot and mission-specialist astronauts on the other. These people have special work contracts and life insurance agreements, negotiated with the help of their governments and employers.

Astrolaw also consists initially of intergovernmental agreements such as those between the Soviet Union and other members of their Eastern bloc Intercosmos space program or that between the Soviet Union and the United States during the Apollo/Soyuz Test Project concerning conduct and procedures during space missions. It includes numerous administrative procedures and arrangements within and among several countries.

Under authority vested in its charter and internationally legitimized by the Outer Space Treaty, NASA developed a set of jurisdictional astroregulations relating to conduct in outer space during the late 1970s. They give mission commanders the authority of captains on the high seas. All participants in a flight, both crew and passengers, are considered to be under his control. Under these regulations, there can be no doubt that the president of the United States has authority, both through NASA legislation and the Military Code, over the conduct of any American space mission.

NASA has used these regulations to tighten its control over the values and principles of members of space habitats and to show that space is just another place, a place where people will always be subject to the same social principles of the state of which they are citizens. This is certainly one point on which the United States and the Soviet Union seem to agree.

In 1982, the Congress of the United States extended the territorial and maritime jurisdiction of the United States, including the criminal code, to outer space. This, too, was permitted under the Outer Space Treaty. Indeed, some would say it was compelled by the treaty, which stated in ARTICLE VI that a state must both authorize and continually supervise all private activities in space. The Outer Space Treaty was not self-executing, which means that it did not establish independent municipal standards that could be enforced by a court, yet in the case of the criminal code extension, Congress felt that something was needed to cover the passengers and visitors who would go into space. Congress anticipated well, for in 1984, two new categories of spacefarer were outlined: the civilian observor-participant and the space-station specialist.

Federal legislation provides for special maritime and territorial criminal jurisdiction for the United States, and it is applicable to

Any vehicle used or designed for flight or navigation in space and on the registry of the United States pursuant to the . . . [Outer Space Treaty and the Registration Convention], while that vehicle is in flight, which is from the moment when all external doors are closed on Earth following embarkation until the moment when one such door is opened on Earth for disembarkation or in the case of forced landing, until the competent authorities take over responsibility for the vehicle and for persons and property aboard.

Still, the Congress had not yet anticipated the biocultural diversity of spacekind, for its new claim of jurisdiction included not only American crew members and participants but also those of any other country who are in "any vehicle used or designated for flight or navigation in space and on the registry of the United States." The assertion of this jurisdiction has the effect of applying all the criminal laws of the United States to personnel of space shuttles and, ultimately, space stations, whether or not those laws can be applied rationally to individuals who may perceive values, make judgments, and adopt patterns of behavior in response to an alien and synthetic environment that is significantly different from the Earth environment which molds the criminal code of the United States.

A good example is something known as survival homicide, which is not sanctioned by United States criminal law. Survival homicide involves the so-called lifeboat cases. In these cases a member of a group has been sacrificed to save the others, perhaps because of a lack of food or water or because the boat was overloaded and would sink unless someone was thrown overboard. Such actions are not fully justified under our law, although the Apollo 13 astronauts openly discussed the possibility that one of them might have to be sacrificed if the air supply dwindled further during their well-known emergency. Such an extreme act should not be casually accepted as being necessary in a space environment, of course, but neither can it be ruled out by Earth-sitters as justifiable homicide in those instances in which spacekind might consider it acceptable or imperative.

Preliminary plans for the first permanent NASA space station called for a crew of six, two station specialists and four mission specialists. The astronauts would work in twelve-hour shifts and three-person teams—two mission specialists and one station specialist on each shift. Initially there might be as many as five modules in the station, with separate 150-cubic-foot sleeping quarters, with independent lighting, storage, dressers, and an audio-video terminal for entertainment and to serve as a bulletin board. Large windows are foreseen as important features, with a module for recreation and meetings. A clinic module would have complete facilities for physical examinations and biological monitoring, equipment for minor surgery, and provisions for handling deceased crew members.

The arrival of payload specialists in the station will probably mean additional modules and larger total populations within a very few years. Meanwhile, Russia, Japan, and some Western European countries will have space-station modules, space planes, or shuttles before the turn of the century. Missions will become longer and more complex. Astronauts will tend the new space telescope, for example, and will capture and refuel satellites. And, of course, there will eventually be a station in high orbit, a station on the moon, voyages beyond our planetary system, and private space habitats and vehicles for tourism, space manufacturing, asteroid mining, and interorbital transportation among habitats and different manufacturing or service facilities.

The actual composition of long-term extraterrestrial life, communication, and commerce is, of course, not entirely foreseeable, but whatever it is will be pivotal to the evolving shape of international space laws, just as the composition of each habitat will be pivotal to the nature of each separate domestic or internal astrolegal order. The broad categories or types of law present on the planet today are

1. Public domestic or municipal
2. Private domestic or municipal
3. Public international
4. Private international

Public domestic law embraces all the familiar kinds of law, such as the U.S. Constitution and the statutes of Congress and the state legislatures. In space it would embrace general areas of municipal regulation, such as criminal law, health, safety, and environmental law, and other areas of community policy.

Private domestic law includes such areas of the law as personal contracts, organizational contracts, property rights, and corporate structure. Although private in nature, such orderly rights and obligations require a public context for realization and enforcement. In space the context will initially be provided by extensions of earthborn municipal law and corporate community structures. But as we have seen, some internationally recognized means of self-determination, especially in this area, is going to be necessary early in the proceedings. The Congressional Space Caucus in the United States House of Representatives has also asked for suggestions as to ways in which the private common law of the American states can be made available to space communities, since there is no federal common law.

Public international law involves the United Nations System and other bilateral or multilateral treaties. Examples of public international organizations created by treaty and creating their own bodies of law could include the European Space Agency, the Organization of American States, and the International Telecommunications Union. It is often this public international system that attracts the most controversy. It is this realm that is most likely to be transformed by autonomous space communities, which will be taking their places among the community of nations and, perhaps, loudly insisting on the same type of limits to the sovereignty of Earth states that Earth states might possibly place on space city-states in exchange for recognition of their autonomy as communities.

In this public international realm the Outer Space Treaty of 1967 went beyond its limiting prescriptions of ARTICLES VI and VIII, which make states responsible for the activities of their citizens in space and extend the jurisdiction of states over spacecraft launched from their territory. ARTICLE V provides that "States . . . shall regard astronauts as Envoys of Mankind in outer space." Yet despite the fact that this statement is found in a public international document, and despite the fact that the Universal Declaration of Human Rights and other such documents are also in the public international sphere, there is still almost no individual standing, recognition, or access to international diplomatic or juridical mechanisms that are competent to secure observance of such rights.

Private international law may therefore ultimately embrace more than its traditional areas of multinational corporate contracts, the choice of which national law to apply to transnational activities, agreements between states to afford each other's citizens protection equal to that afforded ones own citizens, and all other transnational, private contracting, communication, and association, such as international trade. What is new is a slow, seemingly inexorable growth in the strength of the idea and practice of transnational civil rights and the legal machinery necessary to cultivate and protect such rights.

These rights would be private rights, but public mechanisms would be needed to secure them. The rights are already available to citizens of certain American and European states through regional, multinational agreements, such as the ones that created the European Court of Human Rights and the Inter-American Commission on Human Rights. All states of the planet Earth may voluntarily agree to bind themselves to similar adjudication procedures under the International Covenants of Civil and Political, and Cultural, Social, and Economic Rights of the International Bill of Rights, which includes the Universal Declaration of Human Rights.

Perhaps some will consider this a heretical treatment of the international private realm, which is a quasi realm at best, with its dependence on the good will or suffrage of the local sovereign. Many lawyers will say that this realm is nothing but the accommodation of conflicts in opposing national legal systems that have simultaneous jurisdiction over a transnational activity. Yet it is still a real realm of human activity, behavior, and action. This can be seen in the operation of transnational corporations such as ARAMCO and Pan American Airlines. It can be seen in the confusion over the liability of Union Carbide for the tragic 1984 accident in Bhopal, India. It can be seen in the access of foreign businesses to American courts and in the compliance of domestic European courts with the decisions of the European Court of Justice, a transnational court that mediates disputes between members of the European Community.

In the final analysis, it is transnational private international law, which really operates among and within all four legal realms, that seems to offer the most promising prospects for the international recognition of individual sovereignty. Philip C. Jessup, late United States Justice of the International Court of Justice at the Hague, described *trans*national, as opposed to *inter*national, law as all law, both public and private, which regulates actions that transcend national frontiers.

The concept of a transnational realm, of a truly private international realm, says that something is happening on the planet, within the species, that is tending toward universal human rights. The way this new tendency is dealt with in the new transnational habitats of outer space will also have a lot to do with directions and outcomes here on Earth. There is much at stake in our initial human occupation and settlement of space—no less than profound influences on the future lives and societies of both spacekind and earthkind.

20 Frontier Justice

[The judge] must first extract from the precedents the underlying principle, the *ratio
decidendi;* he must then determine the path
or direction along which the principle is to
work and develop, if it is not to wither and
die.

Benjamin N. Cardozo
The Nature of the Judicial Process

Space . . . is simply juridically unorthodox,
catapulting both the unwary lawmaker and
jurist headlong into an Alice in Wonderland
setting where a 'trip through the looking
glass' not only dislodges physical perceptions of 'up' and 'down,' but to some
extent, juridical perceptions of 'right' and
'wrong.'

J. Henry Glazer, J.S.D.
White's Inn, Astrolaw Societies, San Francisco
Assistant Profesor, Hastings Collge of Law

Who is spacekind? How do we tell? To what breadth and depth must the
quantifiable changes in psychology, biorhythms, biochemistry, and other
physiological measures go before spacekind is recognized, at least in the
law? We have already seen something of the intricacies and ambiguities of
the changes brought about in a space environment. During long-term missions several astronauts even experienced shifts in physical operating
assumptions that persisted for a short time after their return to the surface
of the Earth. Several, for example, are known to have let go of a glass in
midair after returning to Earth, sending the glass crashing to the floor. They
had forgotten the unforgettable—their lifelong familiarity with gravity.

Is it necessary to change standards of negligence for astronauts in transition between one set of norms and another? What constitutes due care in such inside-out situations? Will normative standards be substantially different in each of the three regimes—Earth, transition, space? Can spacekind truly be protected by a jury of *peers* if such a jury is composed substantially of earthkind, personally unfamiliar with the norms of spacekind? Who is the "ordinary reasonable man" in space?

The last concept, of the typical, average, ordinary, and reasonable person, is the product of the Anglo-American, case-centered system of common law, although in many of the civil codes and legislative statutes there are similar benchmarks for objective comparison of behavior. The idea is to produce an image against which to evaluate the appropriateness of someone's conduct—not, we should hasten to add, its moral acceptability, but rather its appropriateness to public duty and the obligations of free citizenship. What would the ordinary reasonable person have done under like or similar circumstances? This is the question asked daily of juries.

Implicit in this question is the flexibility, relativity, and objectivity of outlook required of an organic system of law, responsive, living, and changing, rather than static or rigid. The common law is the substance of the private municipal law in Anglo-American jurisprudence. It is the law of persons and property, contracts and torts. In short, it is the law of domestic community relations. Since it operates on precedent it naturally follows custom and the laws of least effort and evolution. Since it also seeks equity it operates under the laws of human nature that are discernible by reason, thus allowing for redefinition and acceleration when warranted by the pace of the free community.

The common law developed in England during the two hundred years following the Norman Conquest of A.D. 1066. Yet its roots were even deeper in history. The genesis of common law can actually be traced to the remotest fringes of the Roman Empire, to a region in Germany now known as the state of Schleswig-Holstein. Here on the shores of the North Sea lived a collection of primitive tribes, the Angles, Saxons, and Jutes, who practiced a form of self-government that anthropologists think may have been characteristic of many hunting-and-gathering peoples. When these tribes emigrated from their homelands to the inviting meads of Roman Britain, their ancient traditions of folk assembly and local government went with them.

Common law was, and often still is, considered discovered law. The judge does not just create the law or simply adjust it to particular situations. He also, in a sense, finds the underlying law, the just and ethical solution, which is derived in the light of each particular set of facts or each individual situation. This has led some attorneys of the civil law tradition to assert that the common law is "the law nobody knows," because it is not neatly and precisely spelled out in anticipatory statute books or administrative edicts. It is laid in a mosaic, case by case, through years of published court decisions. Common law is still largely the latent, undiscovered law, awaiting the discovery of further elements of the ideal state of justice.

Perhaps this is why many who have been schooled in the deductive and empirical traditions of civil law think it necessary to spell out, early on, a comprehensive law of outer space in order to preserve public order, prevent militarization, and ensure equitable sharing of the available resources. These are all laudable goals, of course, but anticipatory codes often tend to be rigid, unresponsive, and quickly outdated. This seems particularly likely in a rapidly changing environment. While there may be a need for codes to guarantee the observance of human rights and to lay ground rules in case of international conflict, there will be a particular need for organic, indigenous systems for use in the governance of people in space—by people in space.

There will be a need for self-determination in space, for the right of indigenous inhabitants to develop their own approaches to justice and right reason on the basis of their own unique circumstances. Thus, we should be extremely careful in our initial legal constructions not to preempt the ultimate rights of spacekind. We must not impose our view of what has not yet happened on a group of people who do not yet exist, at least in the eyes of the law.

For the public mentality inside organizations to be primarily concerned with jurisdiction, power, and survival is understandable. This can even be seen in the development of the U.S. Constitution, which was first drafted without its famous Bill of Rights. We are thus summoned again to vigilance in the defense of liberty, since the juridical liberty of the new age must ultimately come from the people themselves. It is not likely to be foisted upon them by philanthropic socio-organisms and nation-states.

In many ways, the inductive method of the common law might prove to be ideal for the domestic jurisdiction of space, just as it did for the young colonies in the New World. It was a pragmatic system aimed at settling real problems, not at expounding abstract theories. The colonial scene was one of novelty and ferment. The old laws frequently did not work. Yet the common law accommodated the new environment.

The organic nature of the common law is undoubtedly responsible for its longevity and success. Indeed, a remarkable faith in the rule of law has generally characterized common-law cultures. The American revolutionaries even felt compelled to justify their insurrection against royal authority legally, thereby producing that remarkable document, the Declaration of Independence.

Although many twentieth-century adherents of the libertarian sentiments espoused in the declaration abhor the idea of a state-centered system of international law and long for a universal, binding code of human rights, the stubborn adherence of our current sovereigns to their regalia of state sovereignty and to its extension into space may nevertheless ensure the transplanting of organic theories of community and cosmopolis, such as common law, into the receptive new environment of space. As we saw earlier, the Congressional Space Caucus is now looking for ways to do just that through U.S. authorization and continuing supervision of its space enterprise. They have asked the question, What sort of device, rule, or jurisdiction can be devised to extend common law jurisdiction into the space environment?

Despite the compelling survival issues of international politics and the desperate need to avert the irreversible militarization of space, it is at least heartening that the right questions are being asked even before the new communities have been formed. These questions are at present being asked primarily by the peoples of the free world, but they are being joined in principle by the people of Poland, South Africa, Ethiopia, and Afghanistan, and perhaps soon they will be joined by the free and independent peoples of space.

What questions are being asked? The questions are those of an idealistic or constitutional nature, those of the metaphysical-transcendental realm of values, needs, and expectations. What are the rights of an intelligent being? What are the duties of the citizen, the social organization, and the state one to the other? What are the limits to coercion? Are there independent mechanisms to assure equal protection and due process? How can an individual assert his sovereignty and free citizenship within his own social organization, as well as those of other communities and cultures? How can we protect our individual personalities and sensitivities in the face of our collective concerns and the unavoidable, collective onslaught of technology?

One way is to foster clearly and organically constituted legal systems, capable of transformative adjustments within a normative and naturalistic juridical framework. This was what the American founding fathers thought they had to do, and, even in the absence of a binding regime of international human rights, it is what we must do today to foster both American and independent transnational space communities for productive service to both spacekind and earthkind. Indeed, there are many who feel that only aggressive pursuit of the lessons of the common law offers any hope for the construction of indigenous space law and free communities in space.

J. Henry Glazer puts his hopes much more squarely in the potential of domestic American law than upon the vagaries of international law, saying,

The elaboration of astrolaw has little to do with treaties, but proceeds instead, upon a reasoned application, or rejection, in space of substantive or procedural municipal law principles. . . . This perception of space as a place in contradistinction to space as an international legal regime is not mere sophistry. Juridical consequences flowing from the distinction, as, for example, in the area of human rights and fundamental freedoms, can be quite profound. . . . Some of the most oppressive and murderous governments on the planet are invariably the first to assume with alacrity all of these solemn treaty commitments and discard them with equal alacrity when found to be inconvenient or annoying. In space as a place, on the other hand, a healthy variety of dissimilar public and private entities operating in space, under U.S. municipal law . . . are bound to advance the cause of human rights and fundamental freedoms far more forcefully and effectively than signatures affixed to multilateral treaties by congeries of dictators, absolute monarchs, theocratic heads of state who still fight jihads in the 20th Century, and gun-toting presidents for life. As between present astronauts and cosmonauts on public payrolls, and future profit-oriented captains of privately-owned space tugs, it is the space tug captains who would be far less likely to brook interference from anyone in the full exercise of rights, freedoms, and prerogatives in space.

One who holds similar views is Congressman Newt Gingrich, former chairman of the Congressional Space Caucus. In 1981 Gingrich, a former college professor, wrote a bill based upon the Northwest Ordinance of 1787, which established the basis of the formation of states in the virgin territories northwest of the Ohio River. The 1787 ordinance became the model for all subsequent admission of states to the union. Gingrich's bill, however, was distinguished by the fact that it applied to communities in free space. Communities of 5,000 would be eligible to apply for self-governing territorial status and would be eligible for statehood at a threshold of 20,000. It is not specified whether the new sovereignties would be equals of the terrestrial states.

Even though the parallels between space habitats and the Northwest territories are tenuous, Gingrich's bill was the first congressional attempt of any kind to call attention to the need of space communities for self-government. It is laudable to propose any serious mechanism for the exercise of self-government in space. Gingrich even admitted that he really did not expect such a bill to pass the Congress for at least twenty or thirty years, despite fifteen sponsors in the House, but he saw some value in raising and addressing the issue sooner in order to spark years of productive consideration.

Yet even the Gingrich bill did not manifest a broad comprehension of the plethora of subtleties destined to be involved in Earth-space relations. The thresholds of 5,000 for territorial status and 20,000 for statehood, for instance, are not fully justified. Although Gerard O'Neill's space-station designs and envisaged moon colonies could accommodate such numbers, it appears likely that habitats for the foreseeable future will have smaller populations than these.

The Outer Space Treaty, moreover, prohibits national claims of sovereignty over locations on the moon or other celestial bodies by use or occupation. Yet it seems inevitable that there will be human settlements on the moon and that it will become necessary for there to be recognition of their independent, self-governing status by nations and international organizations. Thus we see that the questions presented are not all simple and straightforward, and by no means have all been answered.

Serious attention by a broad cross section of concerned citizens is necessary for a responsible juridical result. Open systems and open approaches seem to be called for, particularly when we consider that a new form of neocivil, municipal public law called administrative law has grown to such proportions in the United States as to be euphemistically called a fourth branch of government. NASA itself is a distinguished member of the fourth branch, and administrative regulations predominate in the governance of NASA's activities in outer space at this time. As early as 1980 the federal government alone was promulgating more than a million *new* regulations a year.

As the potential application to space of statutes such as the Occupational Safety and Health Act have shown, without some simple governing principles or mediating devices it will take constant, prodigious efforts to identify the looking-glass perspectives and effects of the domestic "protection" being extended to space by earthborn municipal regulations. One such proposed governing principle can be found in Glazer's call for a requirement for community impact statements, both social and environmental, on all future legislation and regulation that may affect outer space activities. Private space lawyers have already begun, ad hoc, the types of analysis that will be necessary for these statements. One early discovery of space lawyers brought about the passage of a bill to stop the classification of industrial imports from U.S. space facilities as foreign imports.

Such a concern for the unique circumstances, norms, and traditions of a community has been called a concern for the constitution of the community. The constitution of the community represents the way in which any given social unit, given a choice, will actually prefer to solve its own problems and adjudicate its own directions. Yet, as we shall see, this amorphous type of constitution must also be anchored and stabilized by statutory constitutions of laws and philosophical constitutions of ideals in order to be fully protected and fully realized. Otherwise, there could be little justice on the new frontier.

21 Space Law

> I found with the voyagers in Browning's
> Paracelsus that the real heaven was always
> beyond. As the years have gone by, and as I
> have reflected more and more upon the
> nature of the judicial process, I have
> become reconciled to the uncertainty,
> because I have grown to see it as inevita-
> ble. I have grown to see that the process in
> its highest reaches is not just discovery, but
> creation; and that the doubts and misgiv-
> ings, the hopes and fears, are part of the
> travail of mind, the pangs of death and the
> pangs of birth, in which principles that have
> served their day expire, and new principles
> are born.
>
> *Benjamin N. Cardozo*
> The Nature of the Judicial Process

Only during the past ten years or so has the regime of space law become professionally acceptable as a legitimate body of law. Yet, as we have already seen, space law has its genesis in such documents as international conventions on telecommunications, aviation, and outer space activities. As we saw earlier its genesis was also in organizations such as NASA and the Defense Advanced Research Projects Agency (DARPA).

So in one sense, space law is already a middle-aged discipline. Often referred to as "international law and space activities," space law actually embraces all aspects of transnational space activities, public and private, domestic and international. As such, it embraces astrolaw, which is actually one aspect of space law.

Both astrolaw and the spacekind declaration are pedagogical devices of social science, designed to alert space law theorists, practitioners, and sub-jects alike to the fact that the changes in space are not just changes in place, they are also changes in kind. This in-kind shift is multidimensional and multidisciplinary. Although it is true that there are, so far, no permanent, on-site practitioners of astrolaw—or whatever it may ultimately be called—to enunciate declarations of independence, it is helpful to borrow these devices from the artist, dramatist, politician, and historian in order to engender consideration of the future that is rushing upon us at a faster rate year after year—a future that, in space, is totally of our own making.

Space law has been evolving primarily because of the complex legal ramifications of various types of communication, remote sensing, navigation, weather, and intelligence-gathering satellites, as well as the numerous manned space missions. Even in these circumstances, however, space law is practiced primarily by the traditional communications law firms or aviation law firms, by government agencies, or otherwise by consultant professors or even weekend-warrior lawyers who are often not conversant with the entire field, or lack the necessary working knowledge of the natural sciences, but who enjoy speculating in a jurisprudentially virgin area. And of course it is an area about which the public generally has very little knowledge.

As noted in the introduction, space law can be broken down into two broad subtopics. First, there is an evolving body of domestic and international law relating to the essential, mundane aspects of a space law practice. It ranges in scope and variety from obtaining frequency assignments for commercial communications satellites to product liability in the manufacture of equipment for satellites and launch vehicles. It consists of all the private and public domestic and international law necessary to start and maintain any of the usual types of business and related activities, such as communications law, transportation law, contract law, tax law, securities law, antitrust law, banking law, administrative law, insurance law, and so on ad infinitum.

The second subtopic of space law involves what might be considered the more exotic aspect of the evolving discipline, its underlying philosophy, grand internal model, paradigm, or metaphysics. This jurisprudential and jurimetric perspective is concerned with the relations that exist between earthkind and spacekind and among spacekind themselves. This is the subject we have been developing ever since our flirtation with the big bang. It concerns human rights in space and is a large part of astrolaw.

We have concentrated on these exotic, interdisciplinary aspects because even the nuts and bolts embodied in the first, more workaday subtopic of space law, are really understood or created on the basis of reason, values, needs, perspectives, prejudices, and knowledge, the province of the second subtopic. Again, it must be stressed that the law is a tool. It is software, not hardware, but it is a tool nevertheless. It can only be judged by the conformity of its means and ends with some commonly perceived or understood intellectual construct.

With respect to existing international and domestic law, it is almost impossible to determine the nature of anticipated political and legal structures in space societies merely by looking at the provisions of legislative acts and treaties. One must also know the underlying spirit and intent of the legislators and negotiators. What conceptual good was to be served? What social ends were to be achieved? In this light, it is possible to look at the treaties relating to space activities and isolate some of the provisions that imply jurisdictional intent or control over human judgment and behavior in space. The extension of state sovereignty over launched vehicles has already been mentioned.

Many people are surprised to learn that space law is older than the Space Age, itself, or that there is an active international space law and policy process which is well understood throughout the world by participants in outer space activities. What many people deride as esoteric or exotic, or as pseudolegal or pseudointellectual, is nevertheless well understood as practical reality in the Soviet Union and to a growing extent in Europe and the third world. The competition for the constitution of space civilization is already under way. We ignore it at our own peril and abandon it only in contravention of our national ideals.

As early as 5 October 1959, a Moscow Space Policy Symposium was held under the direction of G. P. Zhukov, Executive Secretary of the Space Law Commission of the U.S.S.R. Academy of Sciences. There is no counterpart in the United States Academy of Sciences, or in any part of the U.S. government. Space has traditionally been only one element of, say, national defense, or communications, or diplomacy, and even the NASA lawyers have concentrated primarily on the nuts-and-bolts aspects from an institutional point of view.

Comprehensive, interdisciplinary consideration either of space policy or space law is rare in the United States. Even as recently as the mid 1980s, only a dozen or so American law schools saw the need to add courses in space law to their curricula, although it has been in the curriculum of the Moscow University Law School since the early 1960s.

In a 1962 article entitled "Soviet Attitude toward International Space Law," Robert Crane, director of the Space Research Institute of the World Rule of Law Center at Duke University, revealed that the Soviets saw peaceful coexistence as the juridical prescription for an economic, political, and ideological war. Having decided that modern nuclear war must be avoided, they had accepted the limited value of international law but only as the venue of an ideological cold war. Crane quotes Soviet sources as saying,

"The problem now is whether and to what extent one can create and rely on an entirely new Communist international law . . . to begin to replace in its entirety traditional international law developed to serve capitalist interests . . . to wage an ideological war of law."

Crane continued by saying that the Soviets' strongest emphasis was on their belief that the chief problem of space law was the determination of Communist principles to govern the legality of certain types of space activity. During the late 1950s their main concerns were the use of space for military activities and a formula for delimitation of territorial, sovereign air space from outer space. Recall that Francis Gary Powers's U-2 spy plane was shot down from an altitude of nearly twenty miles, yet Sputnik and later satellites were allowed to pass as low as eighty-five miles above the surface of the Earth without protest.

International law is much grounded in custom and usage, and the unprotested passage of Sputnik over subjacent territory of sovereign nations began a legally recognized custom. This custom was later embodied in the 1967 Outer Space Treaty, to the effect that above a certain, undetermined point, national sovereignty ceases and international space begins, thereby establishing this important first principle of international space law, freedom of exploration and use.

After Sputnik, of course, the real explosion of space law began. Militarization issues got mixed up with disarmament issues, and questions were raised as to whether outer space should be treated like the high seas, or Antarctica, and even whether there should be a set of anticipatory principles from which to deal with possible contact with intelligent extraterrestrials—called *metalaw* by the first American space lawyer, Andrew Haley, who was also instrumental in persuading the nongovernmental International Astronautical Federation (IAF) to found the International Institute of Space Law.

At about the same time—the late 1950s—the United Nations General Assembly created the Committee on the Peaceful Uses of Outer Space (COPUOS), dividing it into a legal subcommittee and a scientific and technical subcommittee. Also, the International Telecommunications Union (ITU), a specialized agency of the UN, and its World Administrative Radio Conference (WARC) began dealing with satellite communications issues. As we have already seen in some detail, in 1958 the United States passed a sweeping space act and set up NASA. The United States also licensed a corporation for space commerce, the Communications Satellite Corporation of America (COMSAT), by passing the Communications Satellite Act of 1962.

In early space law negotiations in the United Nations, it was the Soviet contention that private activities should be banned from space. COMSAT and the Western Union Telstar satellite were President Kennedy's answer. Thus, the Soviets would only be able, realistically, to get a clause in the 1967 treaty calling for authorization and continuing supervision by governments over the private space activities of their citizens. No ban of private commerce would be possible.

The first significant breakthrough in international space law at the United Nations occurred in 1967. The General Assembly ratified the Treaty on Principles Governing the Activities of States in the Exploration and Use of Outer Space, including the Moon and Other Celestial Bodies, popularly called the Outer Space Treaty or the Space Charter. Often characterized as the Magna Charta for space, it is the basic treaty governing conduct in near and deep space. Its noble-sounding, all-inclusive title does full justice to its high aims. As we shall see, however, selfish, less than transcendent motives prompted its approval by at least some of the signatories.

The Outer Space Treaty was spurred in part by the United States National Aeronautics and Space Act of 1958, which espoused a peaceful and beneficial aim to carry out the civilian space program of the United States "for the benefit of all mankind." Naturally, the Outer Space Treaty is primarily a conceptual framework. Since it is called upon to be prospective and anticipatory, and since it mediates among such disparate and competitive systemic paradigms as those of the Unites States and the Soviet Union, it is expressed merely in the form of principles. Some of them are the following:

—Outer space and celestial bodies are the province of mankind and shall be used only for peaceful purposes and for the benefit of all mankind.

—There can be no claims of sovereignty or territory by nations over locations in space, other than over objects launched from Earth, by occupation or use or any other means.

—Nuclear weapons, weapons of mass destruction, military bases, installations, fortifications, maneuvers, and the testing of weapons are banned from space.

—Astronauts and Cosmonauts are to be considered envoys of mankind, they must be given assistance and protection in the event of accident, and there must be no interference with their missions.

—Private interests are recognized as having freedom of action in space, so long as a government or group of governments authorize and supervise their activities. Nongovernmental organizations are recognized as beneficiaries of state authorization.

—States and international organizations shall have certain liabilities for damage caused on Earth by their space activities and for accidents otherwise arising from space exploration. They are under a concomitant duty to authorize and supervise the activities of their citizens in space, including economic activities.

—Efforts will be made to avoid contaminating celestial bodies or harming the environment of Earth as the result of the introduction of extraterrestrial matter. (Nearly everyone remembers the quarantine of the Apollo astronauts. Also, the Viking Landers for Mars and all the early American space platforms and vehicles were sterilized.)

—Space research is to be carried out under international law, the Charter of the United Nations—which calls for the recognition and promotion of fundamental human rights—the Statute of the International Court of Justice, and in the interest of furthering international cooperation, understanding, and peace. Space is to be used exclusively for peaceful purposes.

—The signatory states must consult with each other when there is reason to believe that any harmful interference with others is possible. They must arrange for visual observation by member states, on a reciprocal and equal basis, to encourage international cooperation in space research. (The Apollo/Soyuz flight was formally proposed with this aim in mind.)

There is both promise and risk in the noble language of the Outer Space Treaty. There is the promise of free space, unencumbered with partisan haggling, free of life-threatening weapons. There is the risk of duplicity and uncertainty in the broad, sometimes ambiguous, largely unenforceable, and always idealistic text.

Derived primarily from the ideas of Eisenhower and Kennedy, many of the progressive provisions of the Space Treaty were resisted by the Soviets until the superiority of the space capability of the United States became evident during the mid 1960s. Still, the wording of the treaty survived a process of consensus in COPUOS, alerting us to the reality that both competing philosophies saw potential for the protection or promotion of their divergent views and interests in the principles of the treaty. Otherwise, neither the United States nor the Soviet Union would have subscribed to the treaty at all.

Despite the nobility of its peaceful words, the Outer Space Treaty arose from considerations every bit as practical and parochial as those underlying the early law of the sea, which, in the words of Dutch jurist Hugo Grotius in 1609, gave all nations the "absolute right of innocent passage," a sentiment not too different from Paul Fauchille's desire, three hundred years later, for a freedom of the air. In the days of Grotius, intensely competitive exploration and colonial trade raised fears among the great seafaring nations that individual assertions of exclusive rights on the high seas would disrupt their highly lucrative ventures. Yet, as every American school child knows, there was certainly no universal freedom of the seas as late as the War of 1812, which was precipitated by British interference with American shipping. Nor was there any freedom of the air in the wars of the twentieth century.

In fact, ever since the Outer Space Treaty was opened for signature, lawyers, politicians, and statesmen have consistently tried to interpret and reinterpret the document so as to give their home countries some military or commercial advantage. This was never truer than in the decade of the 1980s, when star wars and commercial exploitation of space frequently made headlines in newspapers and television documentaries. Nations and businesses postured and competed for advantage.

The Soviets even insisted that satellite killers are not "weapons of mass destruction" and are therefore not banned from space. The United States asserted that such satellites are in violation of the "exclusively peaceful purposes" provision of the Outer Space Treaty and that, in any event, their use against a satellite under the registry and sovereignty of another launching state would be an act of war. Yet the United States was simultaneously producing its own satellite killer.

Perhaps an even more telling characterization of the diminishing sanctity of the Outer Space Treaty, and also a reflection of the way numerous Earth cultures and civilizations may see the potential threat of an evolving spacekind culture, is the Declaration of Bogotá, signed on 3 December 1976 by Brazil, Colombia, Ecuador, Indonesia, Kenya, Uganda, and Zaire. This declaration asserted that the geostationary orbit—approximately 22,000 miles out, where a satellite will move synchronously with the twenty-four-hour rotations of the Earth, thereby remaining constantly over one fixed point on the surface—is a scarce natural resource and is "part of the territory over which the Equatorial states exercise their national sovereignty."

Never mind that this declaration was in strict violation of custom, common sense, and the Outer Space Treaty, because it was not in violation of a colonial transplant in the third world cultures that were insisting upon it. That transplant was the doctrine of absolute state sovereignty—the divine right of states. These giddy new states and world actors didn't seem to mind that they were applying the worst aspects of the colonial hegemony they had once opposed.

Perhaps this was because the traditional, reliable rubric of national sovereignty was still strong in the old colonialist and new imperialist powers, both capitalist and communist. It was a rubric that the two greatest juridical adherents to the doctrine of absolute state sovereignty, the United States and the Soviet Union, would almost certainly have to respect in public or else admit to gross hypocrisy, as we shall see.

Without either diminishing or belittling the fervent and aggressive hopes of distressed emerging states for freedom, cultural integrity, and self-determination, the degree to which the state-centered system of international law is fertile ground for both the new international law of peaceful coexistence and also the old capitalist forms of oligarchy is frightening. The new oligarchical potentates use state sovereignty and the threat of communism to obstruct an international communications regime of human rights and the free flow of information, while Kaarle Nordenstreng, a Western communications scholar from Finland, can nonchalantly proclaim in *The Mass Media Declaration of UNESCO:* "Contemporary international law has been called international law of peaceful coexistence. Basic principles of international law . . . have established four minimum obligations of peaceful coexistence for every state."

What are the four minimum obligations? Would it be strange to find them reflected in a March 1962 speech of Planton D. Morozov, Soviet Representative to COPUOS? He said, "In our view the activities of states should be conducted in keeping with the recognized principles of peaceful coexistence, sovereignty, equality, and non-interference in domestic affairs."

These principles are not new, of course, and are not objectionable in themselves. Indeed, it is also good to be sensitive to the fact that the Soviets, however they are motivated, are tacticians and dialecticians. They recognize structure and usually operate openly within it, even if they are covertly in contempt of it for one reason or another. It is true, for instance, that one of the Leninist dialectics is the foment of every sort of subversion and instability to end "the state of war and domination" of the working classes in the capitalist states and to incorporate them into "the state of peace" represented by proletarian communist bureaucracy.

Still, it is also true that only ideology can truly triumph in the information age, for it is also the nuclear age, and the avoidance of nuclear war is necessary for the survival of communist theory, which needs a world and a human race within which to operate. This is an open recognition and firm internal component of the concept of peaceful coexistence. This is the crux of the Soviet-American détente, or cold war—the two are really one and the same.

Robert Crane pointed out that peaceful coexistence had evolved by the early 1960s "into the most radical innovation in Soviet international legal theory since the Russian Revolution in 1917." In the Communist and Workers Party Manifesto, in 1960, it was declared the new ideology of world revolution. Professor Vladimir Korovin, of the Moscow University Law School and the Scientific Research Commission on Space Law, stated that an even more important requirement of the law of peaceful coexistence was that it function to serve the higher principle of proletarian internationalism—that is, coordinated world revolution.

Let no one think, however, that we are sanguine about the occasional Russian or communist paranoia in the United States. Kaarle Nordenstreng is not a communist and would probably claim a Western bias. Labels in themselves are not important, but processes are. All concepts, like the underlying processes which produce them, are multidimensional and omnifaceted. Little by little we may forget what they portend, thus compounding the already nearly impossible task of harmonizing humanity enough to avert nuclear holocaust. The shape of the world, the shape of the law, and the shape of liberty are always at stake, alike and anew for each generation, whether on Earth or in space.

In his speech to the people of Kracow on 22 June 1983, Pope John Paul II expressed it this way: "Freedom is the gift of God to Man. The right of every nation to be free is in the moral order. Freedom is not a relief; it is the toil of greatness."

John F. Kennedy observed that few generations are called upon to defend freedom in its hour of both maximum opportunity and maximum danger. Our care and sensitivity, our cross-cultural, interdisciplinary awareness, and our passion to survive, cooperate, and reach agreement must characterize us in this time. The patterns of acceleration are telling us something.

In *The Fate of the Earth,* Jonathan Schell maintained that the solution is not anything so simple as disarmament. Arms can be hidden or rebuilt in times of tension. The genie is out of the bottle. What threatens humanity is information, the knowledge of atomic physics, and its application to weapons, which portends the permanent ability of human beings to apply the very power of the universe in petty human squabbles. Schell points out that only the annihilation of the greater part of humanity would be likely to wipe out that knowledge. What we have to do is to learn to live with the knowledge.

This generation may well determine whether the species survives and moves to populate the stars, or whether it destroys itself and goes nowhere; and if humanity does survive to populate the stars, it is our generation that will have established the initial vectors and constituted the legal context from which government in outer space will be born. How will we rate as founding fathers and mothers?

VII Space Law and Government

22 The Space Treaties and International Politics

[The Outer Space Treaty] cannot be considered as a final answer to the problem of the exploration and use of outer space, even less when the international community is questioning all the terms of international law which were elaborated when the developing countries could not count on adequate scientific advice and were thus not able to observe and evaluate the omissions, contradictions and consequences of the proposals which were prepared with great ability by the industrialized powers for their own benefit.

Declaration of Bogotá
(1976)

The Declaration of Bogotá is only one of a number of indications that many countries simply do not intend to be held back by the high-sounding principles, not only of the Outer Space Treaty, but of any international law, if it no longer serves their sovereign interests. Here we find the third world taking the Soviet notion of the moral invalidity of "capitalist international law" and turning it into the moral invalidity of "industrialized international law," thus transforming the East-West dialogue into a North-South dialogue. Unfortunately, though, the virtues of the third world's complaints are easily matched by the vices of their solutions, which much too often are sheer territorial mimicry of the industrial countries.

As a role model there is, on the one hand, the Soviet Union and its "sacred territory" over which civilian airliners must take great care. On the other hand there is the United States and its Connally Amendment to the instrument of ratification of the Statute of the International Court of Justice. Pursuant to ARTICLE 36 (2) of that statute, the United States, in accepting the general jurisdiction of the court, declined to submit "disputes with regard to matters essentially within the domestic jurisdiction of the United States of America *as determined by the United States of America"* (emphasis added).

Of course, the Soviets do not even recognize the *general* jurisdiction of the court; but this should not obscure the fact that the latter American provision was clearly in violation of the statute, which specifically provided that in the event "of a dispute as to whether the Court has jurisdiction, the matter shall be settled by the decision of the Court." No other country on Earth has so sweeping a nullification doctrine in matters of international adjudication as *either* the United States *or* the Soviet Union. In no instance did any other state reserve to itself the right of decision on jurisdiction.

Of course, this does not erase the fact that the United States has been a world leader for international law and international institutions since the Declaration of Independence, which was as much an international document as a domestic one. This type of commitment to international law was expressed even in the earliest days of the American republic. Its first foreign war was against the Barbary States of North Africa over piracy on the high seas. The United States also stood for freedom of the seas in the War of 1812. In the Monroe Doctrine it stood for the nonintervention of Old World states into the affairs of the Americas.

Through Woodrow Wilson's Fourteen Points, the United States became the first country to call for the establishment of a League of Nations for the maintenance of peace, and Franklin D. Roosevelt's Four Freedoms—freedom of speech and expression, freedom of worship, freedom from want, and freedom from fear—became the foundation of the postwar International Bill of Human Rights and its two covenants, one on civil and political rights and one on social, cultural, and economic rights.

Yet the deliberately decentralized constitutional government of the United States still has been of two minds as it has contemplated the doctrines of might makes right and divide and conquer that have prevailed in the world until now. Many citizens have felt safer with a fortress America. So the United States did not join the League of Nations, dissented from the Statute of the International Court of Justice, and failed to ratify even the Genocide Convention for more than twenty-five years.

In view of all this, it is no wonder that the concept of absolute state sovereignty and national integrity has been seized upon in the third world as a solution to its international problems. One of the principal present-day complaints of the third world is the existence of a one-way flow of information, in which their cultures are either ignored or portrayed negatively and superficially throughout the largely Western-dominated economic structure and information systems. Some third world countries claim that an ideological imperialism and a cultural imperialism are destroying their cultural integrity and national sovereignty.

This claim is well worth considering, not only because it is being forcefully purveyed in the realm of space communications law, but also because it is a description of precisely the state of affairs that we have warned should be avoided in dealing with spacekind. It also reveals the type of absolute sovereignty being practiced by both the United States and the Soviet Union in their respective space programs. The result of this superpower practice has been to foster the same sort of political and philosophical approach in the arena of third world space policy and thus, potentially, into the practice of international space law.

This is not to say that the countries of the third world have stated no legitimate complaints. Indeed, communications law takes us back beyond the birth of space law to uncover social and political trends that not only are mainstream issues in space law today but also confirm some of the aforementioned complaints from the third world. But no matter how valid the reasons for the complaints, it is still necessary to face squarely the limiting nature of the solutions that have been suggested. In *The Fate of the Earth*, Jonathan Schell does precisely that in suggesting that our current global form of national sovereignty is the single greatest threat to the survival of the species:

National sovereignty lies at the very core of the political issues that the peril of extinction forces upon us. Sovereignty is the "reality" that the "realists" counsel us to accept as inevitable, referring to any alternative as unrealistic or utopian. . . . We are told that realism compels us to preserve the system of sovereignty. But that political realism is not biological realism; it is biological nihilism—and for that reason is, of course, political nihilism, too. . . . Is self-extermination a law of our nature?

We wonder at the answer to the last question as we ponder one of the worst examples of the North-South one-way flow, which is the apparent one-way flow of Soviet legal theory to the third world, and the ramifications of that transfer in the light of the importance to the Soviet system of tightly controlled media—everything from transportation to telecommunications. This is in stark contrast to the importance of open channels of communication in our social system. This importance was well expressed by Lon Fuller, former professor of jurisprudence at Harvard Law School, when he said "If I were asked . . . to discern one central indisputable principle of what may be called substantive natural law . . . I would find it in the injunction: Open up, maintain, and preserve the integrity of the channels of communication."

In opposition to this view the Soviets have a beautiful paradox within their law, which is being aided and abetted, usually unwittingly, by many international theorists of the third world. Soviet doctrine asserts, on the one hand, that the laws of interpretation of treaties arise from global custom and that international law must therefore represent the wills of the socialist countries in order to be binding, while, on the other hand, an absolute meeting of the minds—required for the validity of contract—is impossible between socialism and capitalism. Such a view slams the door on truly open channels of communication between the two systems.

This new version of John C. Calhoun's old nullification doctrine is alive and well in the age of totally sovereign world states. The cries for cultural integrity and national sovereignty are heard around the globe. Such a state of affairs led George F. Kennan, former United States ambassador to the Soviet Union, to say that "covenants without the sword are but words." But former Supreme Court Justice William O. Douglas complained that Kennan's statement was "steeped in the past . . . symbolic of the political bankruptcy of my generation." In *Towards a Global Federalism,* Douglas described the current system of absolute state sovereignty as the rule of force rather than the rule of law.

There is much justification for Douglas's statement. Hugo Grotius, for example, a Dutch theologian and statesman who has been called by some the founder of international law, achieved that recognition from his *Concerning the Law of War and Peace* (1625), which dealt principally with war and the rules of war. He is important in that he is one of several transitional thinkers between the timeless jurisprudential schools of natural law and the rise of schools of positive law in the seventeenth, eighteenth, and nineteenth centuries.

As a schooled natural jurist, Grotius taught that the fundamental principles of international law were eternal, unchanging, and independent of the will of states. Natural law was based on the divine order, the nature of man, and the harmony of nature. Yet Grotius did not limit himself to natural law, but felt that there were also international rules that were established by states and dependent upon their will.

The views of Grotius on international law were therefore in accord with the leading principle of positivist legal thought, which is the decisive importance of the actual practice of states, rather than reliance upon abstract principles of ethics and the laws of nature. It has been pointed out that the simultaneous rise of empirical science with that of nationalist ideology and the birth of new nation-states from the seventeenth to the twentieth centuries created favorable conditions for the advancement of this positivist legal doctrine.

Not surprisingly, greater emphasis also began to be placed on the omnipotence of national sovereignty. This emphasis went to obscene extremes in both world wars—particularly with Hitler's idea of the Fatherland—and is verging on the same extremes, and worse, as we peer over the abyss of nuclear holocaust. To this day, the concept of sovereignty means that a state has exclusive jurisdiction within its territory and that a state is usually bound only by those norms to which it has given its consent. This is why Justice Douglas is not inaccurate in calling the contemporary system of international law the rule of force; it is also why Kaarle Nordenstreng is not really in error in calling it the "international law of peaceful coexistence."

As Nordenstreng rightly observes, international law is different from domestic law, in which there are organs of legislation, execution, and jurisdiction and an effective system of sanctions. Douglas agrees in his suggestion for a more serious, honest approach to all international agreements, an honest attempt to develop the necessary human consensus for the rule of law to replace the rule of force:

Nations, like the men who compose them, are inherently predatory. Conflicts can never be eliminated. That is why talk of peace is usually fraudulent talk. The only talk that is constructive is how to design procedures to handle conflicts between nations. . . . The atomic age has greatly limited man's ability to cope with them in the conventional way. That is why the search for the Rule of Law is the most pressing problem of this century. . . . The Rule of Law [domestic] has survived [in the West] because it is the chosen way of life. . . . Particular decisions, particular judicial regimes have been disliked. . . . But it has . . . survived, because of a consensus of our people to live under a Rule of Law.

The rule of law discussed by Douglas, however, is not the rule of law of "proletarian internationalism"—Soviet communism—which is applicable only within "peaceful socialist territories" that are no longer racked by "class warfare." The Soviet law is "revolutionary," designed to "perfect" the state and the society through the use of "scientific" dictatorship. Soviet law, therefore, is essentially rhetorical. The Soviets say that the ideological purity of the law can only be realized once the bourgeois states of nature have been socialized and incorporated into the "state of peace." But as

Robert Crane warned in his "Soviet Attitude toward International Space Law,"

The rhetorical quality of Soviet international law . . . does not detract from its significance any more than the rhetorical quality of Lenin's statements a half-century ago detracted from the significance of his "scientific theories" of history. . . . To regard peaceful co-existence, or any other product of communist ideology, as a political or as a purely strategic position would be to misunderstand it completely. According to the doctrine of historical materialism [Leninism] law is part of the ideological superstructure, *the passive reflection of reality in the minds of men. At the same time, communist doctrine recognizes the positive function of the superstructure to control the development of reality. . . . Communist law [is] an integral part of the social and political consciousness of mankind . . . by creating thereby a new reality in the minds of men . . . [and] not only in the political order but in what the communists term the spiritual order of mankind* (emphasis added).

Just as one shudders to think of what Lenin and his successors have seen as the proper function of the ideological superstructure or the nature of the new spiritual order, one can simultaneously admire the clarity and brilliance of the consequent legal definition, which, in the subtlety of its formulation, is quite superior to many traditional Western definitions of law. In a sense this description of an ideological superstructure is even naturalistic. It is certainly philosophical in its view of the nation-state as a socio-organism and in its hue toward Machiavelli's end that justifies all means.

This ideological superstructure is incompatible with the Western one that stresses greater liberty in order to do justice to the full potential of each individual human being. The libertarian view holds that the state exists to serve people, not vice versa. So the search for the rule of law has been prolonged and the space treaties have been born into a limbo of quasi status.

This is why international treaties are somewhat quasi law. Indeed, if the state of the international military, economic, political, and legal competition remains largely unchanged for the next twenty-five to fifty years, the purveyors of astrolaw may well be right in saying that ground-based domestic law will prove more important than international law in establishing the foundations of social structures created in space.

We are likely to see a continuous political pressure for the application of limited mercantile and social laws that have been established unilaterally by various launching states and organizations. The principles or characteristics of social order in a space society may be influenced, if not actually dictated, by whatever consortium underwrites a manned space venture. This organizational model is very similar to those of the company towns in nineteenth-century Europe and North America and twentieth-century Alaska and Antarctica.

This is not to say that the Outer Space Treaty has been, or will be, useless, for the Space Treaty is more than quasi law. It is a quasi constitution, not only a culmination but also an initiation. It was intended to be an ideological charter for the Space Age. Readings of the debates, resolutions, and ratifying documents surrounding the Outer Space Treaty confirm its quasi-constitutional function. It was to create a set of fundamental principles that should be adhered to in all subsequent agreements and treaties, whether international or bilateral. Indeed, as we shall see shortly, four subsequent treaties, the first three of which were specifically anticipated in the original Outer Space Treaty of 1967, all refer back to the original.

The various space treaties are all a little unusual, in that they represent attempts to deal with a realm that is as yet largely unknown. Among both the strengths and weaknesses of the law in general, and of common law in particular, is the fact that the law is essentially reactionary. It tends to be a product of whatever social interaction, or technology, or philosophy has arisen.

In this regard, space treaties need the broad, metaphysical perspective of philosophy. They need a perspective as broad as the view from any window of a spacecraft. Given our anthropocentric, earthbound attitudes, the early space treaties especially needed to be merely quasi-constitutional, in order not to preclude the ultimate rights and responsibilities of spacekind. It is also appropriate that the first treaties were idealistic, to act as mirrors for the hopes and aspirations of humanity, just as Renaissance jurisprudence did for the settlers in the New World.

Never before in history have countries set out on such an enterprise or exploration saying that it was "for the benefit of all mankind." Such words are unique to the law of the late twentieth century. The Outer Space Treaty is therefore a good place from which to begin examining the prospects for international space law, and it provides a framework for a number of limited accords between individual countries and intergovernmental organizations, as well as for several subsequent treaties.

These include the Agreement on the Rescue of Astronauts, the Return of Astronauts, and the Return of Objects Launched into Outer Space—the Rescue and Return Treaty; the Convention on International Liability for Damage Caused by Space Objects—the Liability Convention, which was successfully invoked by Canada against the Soviet Union after the 1979 crash of the nuclear-powered Cosmos 954 satellite; the Convention on the Registration of Objects Launched into Outer Space—the Registration Convention; and the Agreement Governing the Activities of States on the Moon and Other Celestial Bodies—the Moon Treaty.

The type of interrelation that exists among these treaties is unusual in international law, except in the case of the United Nations Charter and the Statute of the International Court of Justice, both of which are incorporated by reference into the Outer Space Treaty and many other treaties. Finally, still on the agenda of COPUOS and provoking widely divergent disagreement are draft conventions on direct broadcast by satellites, remote sensing of Earth by satellite, the delimitation of territorial air space from outer space, and an agreement eliminating all weapons from space.

Some international lawyers think that the subsequent treaties have at least deviated somewhat, if not strayed, from the principles in the Outer Space Treaty. And, as we shall see in the Moon Treaty, there are indeed some decidedly new twists to the language here and there. Yet in the main, and especially in the first three subsequent treaties—Rescue, Liability, Registration—it appears that the language is consistent with the goals of the Outer Space Treaty itself. Problems of interpretation and coordination have been created, to be sure, but the real challenges come with the Moon Treaty and the other questions yet to be determined.

A quick review of the three treaties that were anticipated in the 1967 Outer Space Treaty itself shows that, for instance, the 1968 Rescue and Return Treaty requires:

—Prompt notification of the United Nations by a state when any of its astronauts are in trouble.

—All possible efforts by states to assist endangered astronauts.

—Prompt return of any spacecraft personnel who have suffered an accident in another state.

—Notification of the UN and the launching authority or state concerning any space object known to have landed in a nonlaunching state or on the high seas.

—Reporting and elimination of any hazardous or deleterious space object discovered by a state.

—Assumption of the expenses of fulfilling these obligations by whatever state launched the source of damage.

Like the Outer Space Treaty, this agreement appears to be a humanitarian document. Still, just underneath, one can sense fears that astronauts and space objects possessing valuable economic and military secrets could be lost, with no formal recourse for retrieving them. The 1971 Liability Convention is an even more practical accord, which deals with the potential of space objects to inflict damage upon the ground and upon each other. It purports to establish an absolute liability on the part of the launching state for damage inflicted on the ground in a foreign state, while setting a comparative negligence standard for accidents in space. Its greatest weakness is that, like almost every other international instrument, it has no binding force. It calls for consultations followed by a nonbinding, voluntary mediation procedure.

The Liability Convention, however, is a document that is having significant effects. NASA is requiring indemnification from its passengers and payloads on the shuttle for the absolute liability that the government bears. Such indemnification may come to be a common feature of joint ventures between the public and private sectors. Space activities may even become in the common law a component of ultrahazardous torts.

One of the means of determining the launching state or responsible agent in such circumstances is through registration of the space object. The Registration Convention, ratified by the U.S. Senate in 1976, makes mandatory the registration and reporting of launchings into space. Under this convention, data to be reported to the Secretary General of the United Nations include the name of the launching state or states, identifying data, the location and date of launching, orbital data, and the general function of the object.

As we have seen, the Outer Space Treaty itself sets forth an international consensus of solid principles for the orderly movement into and occupation of space upon which all these other treaties have been built. It represents juridically humankind's most radical theoretical approach to the habitation of a new ecosystem.

The Outer Space Treaty takes an ecumenical view. It was forced to be prospective, to anticipate certain events and human capabilities; so even though it is not binding, it has great potential influence. Such a treaty has enormous potential for good as an idealistic exercise, an enunciation of the ideological superstructure. Any sort of reasonably coherent statement that has been signed by nearly a hundred countries around the planet, including the superpowers, in an effort to express a consensus, is important.

When society officially espouses ideas, with the intent to express an ideal or a consensus, the consequences can be enormous. Future generations may very well look back at these space treaties in much the way we look at the codes of Hammurabi and Justinian, or at the Magna Charta, or at some of the early enactments in history, which, though only idealistic exercises at the time and not always directly enforceable, have continued to influence many elements of human law.

Whether or not this will prove to be so in the case of the space treaties, of course, is still somewhat in our own hands—ours, the Soviet Union's and the world's. We of the late twentieth and early twenty-first centuries are the initial custodians and interpreters of these fundamental documents. It is vitally important that citizens of the free world understand and think about this. In our own country, whatever the dichotomy between theory and practice, it is still the assumption expressed in the Constitution that sovereignty resides with the people. If this is going to continue to be so, either on Earth or in space, the people need to be aware of the realities and of what is at stake. Jefferson saw America as the great social experiment, as the last best hope of humanity. This is a vision we must not lose.

23 The Moon Treaty and *Res Communis*

> The great dispute on the applicability of
> international law to outer space came to a
> head at the Second Annual Meeting of the
> Soviet Association of International Law in
> February, 1959. . . . Soviet space law
> jurists exchanged recriminations on their
> respective support or lack of support of the
> sea law principle of *res communis* [often
> equated with freedom of the seas] as an apt
> analogy to determine the status of outer
> space.
>
> *Robert D. Crane*
> The American Journal
> of International Law

> When we . . . evaluate the statements of
> bourgeois jurists on the question, the
> sources of . . . *res communis* . . . are rooted
> in the teaching of Roman jurists on the law
> of property. They saw the bases for owner-
> ship . . . in the thing (*res*) itself, and
> deduced these bases from the character of
> the thing, and not from the relationships
> among people in the process of social pro-
> duction . . . [in order] to justify the rule of
> the exploiting classes.
>
> *S. V. Molodtsov*
> *Soviet Law Professor, (1959)*

Res communis means common heritage, or that which is owned by no one
and for the use of all. In international law *res communis* has been interpreted as the common heritage of mankind and has been primarily associ-

ated with freedom of the seas. Yet its inclusion, in the late 1970s, in negotiations on the law of the sea and the Moon Treaty created a furor in the
United States. It was said that this common-ownership provision was
socialist-inspired and inimical to free enterprise. This reaction should have
been at least a little surprising to those Soviet jurists who saw *res communis* as rooted in the teachings of bourgeois Roman jurists on the law of
property.

The 1979 Moon Treaty is prominent for its use of the term *res communis.* The Moon Treaty is the most recent treaty concerning the use of
outer space to make its way completely through the complex negotiating
machinations of the United Nations. Its specific purpose is to exceed and
elaborate upon the Outer Space Treaty as it touches on the political, economic, and legal issues that will arise from the industrial or commercial uses
of space. It is especially controversial in several significant respects:

—It bans all weapons from celestial bodies but is silent concerning
weapons in Earth orbit.

—It clearly prohibits private ownership of extraterrestrial real estate or
of resources "in place."

—It calls for the eventual establishment of an outer space regime, the
authority of which would be binding and the purpose of which would be to
oversee and regulate the "orderly development and exploitation" of extraterrestrial resources.

Passage of the Moon Treaty through the UN General Assembly for signature and ratification by member nations at first went almost unnoticed in
the American press. Later, however, the roar of the engines of the space
shuttle Columbia on its maiden flight and the growing public realization of
the enormous industrial resources of space reawakened political and academic interest in the treaty.

Debate over the treaty has caused a great deal of confusion, philosophical consternation, and political resentment. President Reagan even with-
drew the Moon Treaty from consideration by the United States Senate,
which has prompted a reciprocal failure of the Soviet Union and certain
other states to subscribe.

Part of the reason for these last-minute problems with the Moon Treaty
is its ambiguity and the ad hoc nature of its composition. There were also
lost opportunities for widespread involvement of the academic community,
the business community, and others in exploring the possibilities available to
the United States to redress the defects of the treaty. The American business, legal, political, and educational communities only belatedly became
aware of the cloistered task of the American delegation, which toiled in virtual anonymity amid public indifference. Meanwhile, as a result of the insu-

larity of the American delegation, fruitful consideration of motivations and objectives of the Soviets and the third world did not come about.

Another of the many difficulties with the Moon Treaty was that the character of the international arena and the negotiating process had changed radically from that which existed twelve years earlier, at the time of the UN passage of the Outer Space Treaty. In addition, the Moon Treaty was approached by the United States as an inexpensive and appropriate opportunity to advance other national goals indirectly.

To elucidate the latter difficulty first, the Carter administration had a laudable desire to advance international institutions and the global rule of law. These have been proud goals of many American presidents, such as Wilson, Roosevelt, Truman, Eisenhower, Kennedy, Nixon, and Ford. Indeed, this desire was expressed in many intelligent and courageous ways by President Carter, but in this instance, he seems to have been unaware of the vitality, the complexities, and the ramifications of the international issues that concern space.

The Carter administration also had a fervent desire to achieve a Law of the Sea Treaty that would increase coastal security zones and clearly establish the neutrality and accessibility of straits, even for warships. With deep-seabed mining and other aquatic commerce far from fully refined, the common-heritage-of-mankind concept was an inexpensive trade, or so it seemed. After all, wasn't res communis also traditionally synonymous with, or at least an integral part of, freedom of the high seas? Did it not traditionally refer, in civil law, to something available for use, in whole or in part, by everyone—such things as air, water, and sunshine?

During the preceding twenty years, however, the composition of the UN General Assembly and its committees, including COPUOS, the Committee on Peaceful Uses of Outer Space, had been altered radically. The membership of the UN had approximately doubled by the late 1970s, with more than ninety new members since the 1950s. Dozens of new, tiny, and destitute countries, each of which barely had the population of a large city or county in other, industrial parts of the world, had joined the club of nations.

Only five countries, Brazil, Nigeria, Mexico, China, and India, hold the great majority of all the people of the third world. Nevertheless, the new majority of countries echoed the Bogotá Declaration and claimed that existing international law was formed before they joined and without their consent—although they formally consented to the UN Charter upon joining—and that international law represents the "imperialist," or "industrialist," or "bourgeois" interests of a minority from an earlier era.

Meanwhile, each of the new sovereignties, often arbitrarily delimited by colonial powers and often lacking adequate educational, communicational, and other modern facilities, has the same voting power as China, India, or Nigeria, for example. As a consequence, there has been a concerted effort, especially among the smaller, nonaligned countries of the third world, to consolidate their individually weak influences in world affairs through the use of the one nation–one vote principle of the General Assembly and of some of the specialized UN agencies, such as the United Nations Educational, Scientific, and Cultural Organization (UNESCO).

The members of the so-called Group of 77 have acted collectively to strengthen their bargaining positions with the industrial countries. They are jealous of their new institutional sovereignty, and many of their new elites are jealous of their power. Understandably they resent the already existing racist and colonial regimes. They fear continued commercial, military, or ideological exploitation. The Group of 77 has called for a new international information order, which would restrict the transborder flow of information, and a new international economic order, which would vest the title to *res communis* in an "authority on behalf of mankind as a whole, [meanwhile] . . . not subject to alienation."

Unfortunately, the concepts behind these new orders are not friendly either to free economic enterprise or to the free flow of information. Arms debates in the United States during the late 1970s, for example, contained continual references to the Finlandization of Europe as a result of this or that policy failure. Finland has been the source of several North-South ideological one-way flows of information. It shares a very long border with the Soviet Union and has known the victimization of the Nazis. These realities, which undoubtedly helped spawn the metaphor of Finlandization, were exemplified in the action of President Kekkonen of Finland in May 1973, when he delivered a speech that became a founding text in the movement toward a new international information order.

Echoing Molodtsov's comment about the property bias of Roman or Western law, Kekkonen told his audience that even the Universal Declaration of Human Rights was a reflection of Western bias and was essentially an expression of the laissez-faire ideas of Adam Smith and John Stuart Mill and their assertions of individual freedoms. "But the freedom of the strong led to success and the weak went under in spite of this so-called liberty," said Kekkonen.

Yet had Kekkonen spent less time polemicizing and more time studying Western jurisprudence he would have discovered that laissez faire and Adam Smith had little to do with the naturalist theory of human rights embodied in the Universal Declaration. Mill and other more often emulated Western political theorists such as Locke and Rousseau, moreover, were strong legal naturalists who were merely attempting to define the most resonant state of community by theorizing about empirical data. Despite Kekkonen's sentiments, and those of Molodtsov, to the effect that Western jurisprudence finds property rights in the thing itself, a study of the real fore-fathers of the human rights movement in global thought does not reveal that any such aspect of property was retained, even as far back as the seven-teenth century.

On the contrary, in chapter 5 of the *Second Treatise on Civil Government,* Locke maintained that the goods of Earth are by nature common to all men—*res communes*—because all men need them for their self-preservation. He maintained further, in contradistinction to Molodtsov's reading of the Roman jurists, that the title to private property flows from one's own labor. He argued that whenever human beings mix their labor with things, they have put into those things a portion of their own personal talent and effort; hence those things belong to the laborer, at least as against any other being capable of possession or custody. Locke said,

Every man has a property in his own person; this nobody has any right to but himself. The labour of his body and the work of his hands, we may say, are properly his. Whatsoever then he removes out of the state that nature hath provided, and left in it, he hath mixed his labor with, and joined to it something that is his own, and thereby makes it his property.

Thus we see, contrary to Kekkonen's and Molodtsov's assertions, that Locke—and other Western thinkers throughout many generations—have indeed been concerned with natural justice and with the "relationships among people in the process of social production." We have only to witness the social welfare system and the legal regimes of antitrust, labor, and con-sumer law in the United States and to recall Carleton Coon's definition of industry as the conversion of energy into social structure in order to see that socialism has no monopoly on scientific theories of social organization. Indeed, Locke himself gave the general name of property to the totality of the lives, liberties, and estates of citizens.

Locke did not hesitate to see his free citizen in the ever-present paradox of social responsibilities and limitations. He spoke of "liberty to follow my own will in all things, where the rule prescribes not; and not to be subject to the inconsistent, uncertain, unknown, arbitrary will of another man." He simply insisted that the individual sources of the relationships not be subju-gated, subverted, or relegated by the relationships themselves. He was con-cerned with the legitimate source and scope of "the rule." He protested against Hobbes's *Leviathan,* which was perhaps the original description of the socio-organism as an entity, but an entity with an insatiable urge for conformity, power, and control, an entity made necessary by the only possible alternative, namely, Hobbes's savage state of nature, which was ruled by the law of the jungle, something later called Social Darwinism.

We can thus see the lack of wisdom in the reformation being called for by those who condemn the concepts of individual liberty and personal sovereignty in modern international law. The Soviets, after long opposing the insistence, primarily of the United States, on the principle of *res communis* in outer space, did a little more research into the breadth of Western legal thinking and into the value of third world voting power for the eventual establishment of an international law of peaceful coexistence. Their tactics in the Moon Treaty negotiations, both during and after completion, were to convince the small nations of the benefit to be derived from redefining the traditional meaning of *res communis.*

As pointed out by Robert Crane as early as 1962, "[Soviet jurists] who support the application of *res communis* to outer space do not necessarily oppose a shift to the new socialist international law. On the contrary, they may consider that . . . the Soviet Union should support *res communis* as a principle which has already acquired a socialist content." As stated anonymously by an experienced Washington, D.C., attorney involved in helping identify the interests of the private sector in the resources of the ocean and outer space, perhaps the underlying sense of fundamental justice demands "that those who receive the raw materials and natural resources which fuel and feed industrialized economies must be required to pay a significant share of their economic wealth in exchange for access to those resources. The so-called North-South dialogue is a direct outgrowth of that declaration."

Third world enthusiasm for this new movement caused the spread of this new ideology to every available forum in the United Nations. These concepts have now been deployed in the UN Conference on Science and Technology and the outer space negotiations and are even under discussion with respect to the use of the natural resources of Antarctica. It should not be suggested, however, that the Soviets have craftily manipulated the third world. Such a view gives insufficient credit to the integrity and intelligence of the people in the third world. The Soviets have rather influenced and benefited from underlying trends that already existed. The change in Soviet thinking on *res communis* can really be traced to opportunities presented by Western objectives in the law of the sea negotiations, by third world objectives in negotiations for new information and economic orders, and in phrases contained in the Outer Space Treaty concerning space as the "province of mankind" and "for the benefit of mankind."

Since the exploitation of space property was not a priority during the evolution of the Outer Space Treaty of 1967, it was given little consideration. The emphasis of the United States was on the "benefit of mankind" and "freedom of exploration and use" principles, which were really intended to embody a *res communis* principle as in the freedom of the seas, this time a transnational, equal access principle for outer space. These principles were not seen as controversial in the West during that period. Rather they were seen as laudable, largely because they were thought of in the abstract, much in the way *res communis* had been thought of in the law of the sea. Space would simply be a place where there would be no national boundaries. Everyone would be free to go there. As a result of activity there the knowledge — and thus the economic base — of the whole Earth would be enhanced.

Nevertheless, it began to be suggested, at first quietly among diplomats and third world jurists, that perhaps the interpretations of these phrases should be changed, in order to vest, in mankind generally, the property rights in the resources of outer space. This would be accomplished by using the UN or some other world body as the title holder. The circumstances that aided the move in this direction were paradoxical. First, the United States had again, almost reflexively, suggested a *res communis* principle for the resources of outer space, and second, *res communis,* already a principle of sea law, was about to be reinterpreted and embraced in the ultimate act of opportunism by many communist and third world states as meaning common property in its literal sense, a principle pressed vigorously and somewhat successfully in the negotiations on the seabeds.

Yet except for the acceptance of a sort of quasi title to seabed resources in a global institution — the so-called Enterprise, or international seabed authority — the new socialist interpretation of the concept of *res communis* for space is quite weak. In fact, before withdrawing objections to the American version of *res communis* in the Moon Treaty negotiations, the Soviets attempted to insert into the treaty a clear statement that there should not be private ownership or property rights of any kind in resources on the moon or any other celestial body.

In many ways this was simply a replay of the demands they had placed on President Kennedy before the establishment of COMSAT. It was a revisionist effort, when seen in the light of the prohibition in the Outer Space Treaty of Earth-based national sovereignty over the moon or other celestial bodies, which were to be, from the point of view of inhabitants of Earth, a no-man's land — *res communis* — in the sense originally described by Locke. The Soviets were, again, attempting to extend this no-public-sovereignty provision into a no-private-property provision.

This time they succeeded in part and might have succeeded fully, at least in the negotiation phase, had pressures from the American public not awakened the U.S. delegation to the peril of potential reinterpretations of these terms and definitions that had previously been considered fully acceptable. The U.S. negotiators thus quickly quelled consensus on any concept of *res communis* different from the one traditional to the law of the sea. In the law of the sea, *res communis* as applied to, say, the fish, has traditionally followed the formula spelled out by Locke. The fish are *res communes* in their natural state, but become private property once they have been caught.

The Soviets were thus ultimately forced not to oppose this position, simply because they, too, have the advantage of being able to exploit movable resources once they are "entitled" to them as a property interest through their own industriousness. In order to strengthen further the American contention that ownership of extracted materials as personal property would be allowed in space, whether by public or private sources, the American delegation not only squelched the Soviet attempt at an outright ban on such ownership, but also requested that the words "in place" be inserted in the consensus ban on ownership of fixed resources. No country objected publicly to the belated Lockean interpretation of the Americans during the final statements of consensus in COPUOS. Yet because of the American desire to prevent Soviet claims of territorial sovereignty on the moon, a firm ban on ownership of real property in space had been established.

Since the formulation of the Moon Treaty, moreover, the fear has persisted that the increasingly strident insistence of the third world on a title theory of *res communis* may threaten even the negotiating history on personal property. The mandate in the Moon Treaty for an outer space regime, possibly similar to the seabed regime, and the possibility that some American president might again feel the need to relegate space negotiations to strategic territorial concerns pose a threat both to the extension of free enterprise into space and to the free existence of spacekind communities. This, along with the ambiguous wording of the treaty, seems to be at the crux of the American opposition to the Moon Treaty. The primary objection is that the kind of regime or space government called for is not made at all clear within the four corners of the document itself.

Again, it should be remembered that the considerations just mentioned not only impinge on earthbound economic policy but also help to determine the types of community that spacekind will eventually form and the rights and obligations vis à vis earthkind and each other that they will eventually have. The Moon Treaty itself may well reflect the anthropocentric attitude with which spacekind may be regarded by earthkind. The treaty is nondis-criminatory in declaring the whole solar system, including all "celestial bodies" and all "natural resources in place," to be the "common heritage of mankind." Conceivable interpretations of these phrases might even include certain fabricated bodies, such as large space stations made of extraterres-trial resources, as the common heritage of mankind.

All this helps set the tone for insensitivity to the evolving unique natures of spacekind. The Moon Treaty provides that no sovereign nation can, by act or assertion, appropriate a celestial body or its resources. Fur-ther, neither the surface nor the subsurface of any celestial body, or any part of it, can become the property of a state, corporation, or private person. Although this concession may once have been understandable in the light of the American desire to prevent Soviet assertions of sovereignty in space, it could eventually prevent space societies from evolving as they must evolve, according to the dictates of space habitation and not those of Earth habita-tion or of political and economic imperatives that may arise out of imperial-ism and colonialism of whatever economic stripe.

To a large extent, the original sociopolitical vectors will be established by the terrestrial founders. Free enterprise will almost certainly give rise to free communities, which will prefer organic, responsive legal systems. Ironi-cally, from this perspective, if the United States should ever ratify the Moon Treaty, at least without several strong reservations, it could well serve as a public announcement that the United States does not support free commu-nities in space, or, by logical extension, on Earth.

Even more ironically, the passage of the Moon Treaty might facilitate arrangements whereby NASA and the Department of Defense would become the leading U.S. entrepreneurs in the industrialization, exploitation, and commercialization of space, since such a treaty, negotiated by absolute sovereigns, is friendlier to government agencies than to private ones. NASA is certainly in the business of space, with its shuttle operations, and it should be evident, by any interpretation, that NASA is free to do whatever the Soviet Union is free to do, perhaps even with a competitive advantage over its own private sector through developing interpretations of *res com-munis*.

To the extent that the Moon Treaty is an attempt to prohibit free enter-prise or abridge the freedom of citizens, it becomes a body of tyrannical wishful thinking that fails to reflect thoughtful consideration of the political and economic systems of several space powers in both the Western and Eastern hemispheres. It certainly reflects the absence of any consideration of the basic tenets of natural laws or rights. Such rights must be granted to spacekind, the on-site industrializers of space resources, if we hope to avoid the destructive cycle of imperialism, colonialism, and violent revolution seen in earlier frontier migrations.

Seen in this light, the all-encompassing nature of the prohibition on occupation and use may prove to be a little like the decree of King George III that established a line of demarcation approximately along the crestline of the Appalachians beyond which English pioneers were forbidden to settle. The exploits of Daniel Boone and others are testimony to the ineffectiveness of such decrees.

In the evolution of space law, too many nations and people have blissfully accepted idealistic wording at face value. We recognize the value and indelibility of ideas, but the wishful desire for an environment of cooperation for peaceful purposes in near and deep space may have distracted some of the decisionmakers from consideration of the true military, economic, political, and ideological motivations of the primary negotiators of space law. The failure of the United States, until recently, to face the reality of an emerging Soviet military space doctrine, for instance, and the failure to recognize, accept, and deal openly with the postcolonial attitude of sovereignty and equality espoused by many of the developing countries has brought the industrial countries of the West to a critical determination: Is there any place for private free enterprise in space?

If we are to consider the likelihood of economic freedom and the application of the principles of private enterprise in the industrialization of space, then we must also consider how these principles and characteristics will influence the type of sociopolitical order that will evolve in space communities. And for practicing lawyers and jurists, that consideration must involve unique and creative legal approaches that will encourage the private sector to invest risk capital in space ventures.

With the rise of the commercial European Arianne rocket and President Reagan's commitment to facilitate the private development of space, private investment in space ventures has finally begun to happen. New principles are evolving in the insurance industry that are designed to spread the risk of inordinately large financial losses across the entire spectrum of domestic and international resources of government and industry. Imagine the attitude of investors or underwriters confronted with the prospect of the seizure of their assets by spacekind in the quest for independent socioeconomic and political status.

Still, there are as many theories about the way to institutionalize and stabilize the exploration and exploitation of space through international legal institutions as there are creative jurists, crafty practitioners, statesmen, economists, and prudent or careless investors. Despite the vast array of formal international and domestic law that is likely to serve, at best, as wishful statements of intent, the real law of near and deep space will probably turn upon hard business, political, and military decisions made by individual countries and economic-political-military alliances or organizations. These will largely help to determine how far into the future we must go before we are able to look back upon the highest and most naturalistic aspirations of the space treaties as faits accompli, much in the same we now look at such documents as the Magna Charta. It is in this paradoxical cosmic context that the work of the first space lawyers is taking shape.

24 Self-Government in Space

> The exploration and use of near and deep
> space, including all celestial bodies accessi-
> ble by humankind, shall be carried out for
> the benefit and in the interest not only of
> Earth inhabitants, who shall be called
> earthkind, but also of inhabitants of near
> and deep space, who shall be called space-
> kind. Such areas of habitation shall be con-
> sidered the province of spacekind in the
> first instance, and of earthkind in the sec-
> ond. There shall be free access by both
> earthkind and spacekind to all areas of
> space and celestial bodies, consistent with
> the best interest of the mental and physical
> welfare of spacekind and their existing hab-
> itats, regardless of their political or Earth-
> sovereign origins.
>
> *A Convention for Spacekind*
> *ARTICLE 1*

To facilitate an understanding of the influence of international law on early space settlement, perhaps a brief look at an earthly parallel might be helpful. By the late 1980s all the continent of Antarctica had been mapped and permanent settlement had begun. A 1961 treaty forestalled all claims of sovereignty by any country over portions of Antarctica until 1991, but as the eighties wore on, two of the most serious early claimants, Argentina and Chile, actually began establishing civilian settlements, much in the way that settlements had been established on the East coast of North America from the 1580s to the mid 1600s.

These first settlements had at least some civilian characteristics, including the presence of wives and children. In the austral summer of 1985, three Chilean women were expecting the births of the first native Antarcticans. Yet these Antarcticans were due to be born on an island claimed not only by Chile, but also by Britain and Argentina, the participants in the war over the Falkland, or Malvinas, Islands. Also, the children were due to be born into a young society in which some colonists already spoke openly of the way the isolation and military discipline encouraged depression and discord. While these first Antarctican children are likely to be granted the citizenship of their parents and their sponsor government, many legal and social issues have yet to be resolved.

One such issue was exemplified in 1984, when a wives' rebellion at a Chilean settlement forced the base commander to relax standards for volunteer work at the school, the post office, and the library. As a result of the dispute, there was a break in the flow of conversation. Families avoided each other, and both efficiency and the quality of life suffered. Still, plans for the Chilean village called for twenty families, a supermarket, a gymnasium, and a forty-room tourist lodge to accommodate visitors.

In addition to these new "colonies," even countries without claims have established permanent stations in Antarctica, including the United States and the Soviet Union. In view of that fact an international conference was held in January 1985 at a temporary base in the Transantarctic Mountains in order to give the political and diplomatic representatives of the fifteen countries with interests in Antarctica a chance to meet with each other in the native setting, a setting expected to convey something of the true nature of the environment. The representatives and observers would be able to visit the various communities in Antarctica and talk to the inhabitants about their needs, their outlook, and their problems. The American contingent was coordinated by the Polar Research Board of the National Science Foundation.

Only three quarters of a century after Norwegian explorer Roald Amundsen first reached the South Pole by dogsled in 1911, the Antarctic was being settled and was bracing for a coming era of mining and tourism. We would do well to remember this parallel as we consider space settlement. Is our only thought for the development of homes and industry in space to be that of extending the administrative jurisdiction of NASA and domestic criminal laws of the kind examined earlier? Our own early forebears did better.

During the 1580s, for example, after England's first attempt to establish a permanent outpost in the New World on Roanoke Island had failed, Sir Walter Raleigh pressed upon Queen Elizabeth I the rationale that the outpost had failed because it was purely a military outpost, isolated in a distant world from the comfort and amicability of kith and kin. Raleigh convinced Elizabeth that the best chance for permanent settlement was to organize the next attempt with a civil government and to include men, women, and children in what was intended to become a permanent and flourishing community.

Although the first "Cittie of Ralegh in Virginia" was lost from unknown causes during the Anglo-Spanish wars, it became the prototype of subsequent English settlements, both at Jamestown and even in the dissident Plymouth colony. It is a moving experience to stand in the only remaining original structure at Jamestown and read a monument to the transplanting of the common law and liberties of citizens to the New World.

It is also instructive to read the Mayflower Compact and to understand that the Pilgrims who composed it were exiles of a sort, establishing a permanent, essentially private community in the New World. Their compact, enacted before their craft had been abandoned, also directly addressed the organic needs of unique communities for self-definition: "We whose names are underwritten . . . do by these presents solemnly and mutually in the presence of God, and of one another, covenant and combine ourselves together into a civil body politick, for our better ordering and preservation."

Forty-one men stood on the deck of the tiny wooden ship on 21 November 1620 for the purpose of affixing their signatures to the small document that would constitute them as a self-governing community. Perhaps it will be November 2020, before a private community first attempts to establish itself permanently in extraterrestrial space, but the first outposts have already been established. NASA's space station, originally planned to coincide with the 500th anniversary of Columbus's first voyage to the New World in 1492, is a second-generation outpost. Advance planners are already dusting off the old plans for the third-generation moon bases and Mars missions for the turn of the century.

Is it too soon to begin thinking about the way these first, necessarily Earth-dependent outposts and communities will set the stage for spacekind communities? Even Queen Elizabeth I started considering self-government for semiautonomous settlements as early as the first generation of New World outposts. In each field of study we have looked at—cosmology, quantum physics, the evolution and dynamics of systems, biology, psychology, sociology, history, politics, and legal philosophy—we have seen the natural tendency of both physical nature and human nature to be free, exhibiting random choice, self-direction, and diversity.

The early Antarctic stations also found that a civil regime for ordinary daily life was a social necessity. The more hierarchical military or militia regimes were reserved for the most critical survival decisions. How, then, does one go about formulating or permitting the natural evolution of a realistic scheme for free, autonomous, self-governing space communities in the complex, dangerous, and parochial arena of international law and politics, the first real legal environment of space? There are two basic approaches, both of which we have already examined superficially.

One is the determination of a nation or group of nations to develop, from the outset, semiautonomous models of internal governance for space stations as extensions of their Earth-based municipal authorization and jurisdiction. This degree of autonomy for a space community would be more likely to encourage the participation of a broad range of dissimilar public and private actors than would merely government-controlled stations. The other approach is to develop international principles, conventions, or mechanisms of recognition through which communities could attain a kind of autonomy that would be recognized internationally.

The first approach—the extension of municipal jurisdiction—can be taken immediately, a prospect of particular importance when you consider that the United States is still one of the predominant actors in space. Principles of municipal law that should be considered for space should include requirements for social and environmental impact statements on domestic regulation and legislation that may potentially affect space communities. Some form of common law or local government must be established, and eventually some mechanism must be considered for support and recognition of the autonomy of a space community once a certain threshold of longevity and population has been attained.

Legal modeling for space communities should include the right of the space inhabitant to be judged by standards applicable to space habitation as applied by administrative fact finders, judges, or juries composed of space inhabitants. Even though applicable laws, regulations, and precedents might continue to be predominantly earthborn for many years to come, this guarantee of no final judgment harsher than a space community could countenance should go a long way toward smoothing the transition to fully autonomous spacekind communities.

This is by no means an unprecedented approach, as it reflects one of the foundations of federal-state relations in the United States. The aim is to give the benefit of the doubt to the individual, the sovereign citizen. Even though the federal constitution is supreme and thus superior to the laws of the states, the citizen is entitled to that decision, from whatever level, which affords him or her the greatest liberty and the government the least power.

Attention to the image of the autonomous city-state in space is growing, both among space jurists and among industrialists and the general public. At least semiautonomy would be a given in an environment of dissimilar public and private communities in space, since such dissimilarity could not exist under a highly centralized system of controls external to the communities. This was precisely the point of Glazer's comment, reported earlier, that private space tug captains would be more insistent upon their liberties than would government representatives.

American lawyers Patricia Sterns and Leslie Tennan also elaborated upon the reason for greater freedom in a diverse and decentralized legal regime in their paper entitled "International Recognition of 'The Art of Living in Space': the Emergence of Settlement Competence," delivered at the Twenty-Second International Colloquium on the Law of Outer Space. They suggest that the terrestrial founder or sponsor of a space community is not in a position to administer the day-to-day operation of the settlement realistically. Whatever decisionmaking system is established, moreover, it will have a significantly greater effect on the settlement community than on the terrestrial sponsor.

Although the interests of the space settlement and the Earth sponsor may often overlap, it is very important to the objectives of any terrestrial founder that those issues deemed vital by the indigenous space community be resolved to the satisfaction of that community. No other solution is compatible with the productivity of the community. This is the same conclusion reached by Bluth and Kramer in the NASA Human Productivity Program.

Perhaps this is one of the reasons that not only Sterns and Tennan, but a number of other space jurists as well, have spoken favorably of the idea of the city-state in space. Ancient Greek philosophers maintained that the city-state was superior to other forms of political association because of the heightened commonality and the practicality of participatory decisionmaking in local communities. The Greek city-states ultimately fell, of course, to such destructive factors as internecine warfare and the military technologies of richer, more powerful nation-states. Perhaps, though, the time for idealistic community experiments has returned with the advent of unique space habitats and societies.

Urban historians remind us that before the industrial era cities seldom had more than 50,000 inhabitants. Rome managed a city of twice that size with its efficient, far-flung network of transportation, communication, military bureaucracy, and slave labor, but it, too, fell back to fewer than 50,000 people after the imperial era. In the new megatrend from centralization to decentralization, we see a growing preference for smaller cities of 50,000 to 100,000 inhabitants — that is, communities well able to handle interruptions in energy supplies, maintain civic pride, and promote peace and justice.

In an article written before the final negotiation of the Moon Treaty, "Domicile and Industry in Space," J. Henry Glazer mentioned the growing concern for space communities:

In view of the mounting evidence that steps toward space settlement are feasible within the present state of the art, it is hardly premature for the United Nations conferees to consider the inclusion of certain escape clauses in the draft Treaty Relating to the Moon. These clauses should not merely protect the rights of future space settlers but rather enhance those rights and assign to them an order of priority which would take precedence in futuro over those for mankind domiciled in states on Earth. In article 1 of his proposed convention for spacekind, Robinson has furnished the model for such a text, which should become a staple for all future multilateral conventions elaborating regulatory regimes applicable to outer space and celestial bodies. . . . It seems rather bizarre that the future of space settlement has not been permitted to intrude upon the deliberations concerning the [Moon Treaty]. The vice of the proposed treaty is that if it is negotiated within the existing framework of debate, then the enlarged rights of states on Earth could pre-empt entirely the future rights, needs, and priorities of space settlement with respect to vital and indispensable extraterrestrial resources.

Yet this did not seem to be of serious concern to Soviet space jurists. In 1978, the same year Glazer set down these thoughts, Soviet space lawyer and InterCosmos Chairman Vladlin S. Vereshchetin asserted at the Twenty-First International Colloquium on the Law of Outer Space,

Article 8 of the Space Treaty [states] . . . "A State, Party to the Treaty, on whose registry an object launched into outer space is carried, shall retain jurisdiction and control over such object, and over any personnel thereof, while in outer space or on a celestial body. . . ." In our opinion, by jurisdiction in international space law we should mean the rights and authority to exercise not only judicial power [most often associated with jurisdiction], but also legislative and executive power in regard to personnel and objects in outer space, including celestial bodies. In the Space Treaty, the term jurisdiction *stands next to the term* control, *and they both are often used in international space law to denote one and the same meaning. . . . We accept a certain juridical significance of this [envoys of mankind] provision in the Treaty, but in our opinion, it does not provide any reason to recognize mankind or astronauts as the subjects of international law. Nor does it lead to depriving astronauts of their civic origin nor to granting them any supernational status.*

Vereshchetin, however, did not rule out all hope for new community rights and cosmic citizenship; he also said, regarding both the near and distant future,

Though present-day international space law is a ramified system of legal rules and institutions, it does not yet contain provisions specially dealing

with the preparation and carrying out of international space flights. . . . This problem will be more acute in the event of building in the future of permanent international space colonies where the questions of exercising legislative, judicial and executive power will require their special regulation. . . . Only in the future, when flights to other planets become a reality, will astronauts represent mankind, Earthmen as a whole, and then this phrase of the Treaty [Envoys of Mankind] will acquire its literal meaning.

What the juridical advocates of the city-state idea for space are saying is that the idea of envoys of mankind—envoys of humankind—should acquire its literal meaning now, in our own time, in order to assure a smooth and orderly transition to a state of affairs recognized as inevitable even by the Soviet representative. It can well be argued that the present system of international space treaties—with the possible exception of the Moon Treaty—is already amenable to independent space jurisdiction.

In the 1967 Outer Space Treaty, for instance, we see phrases that characterize the intent of signatory nations to consider their envoys in space as simply mankind in a different, largely hostile, environment. This was a logical approach for statesmen flushed with the euphoric and speculative promise of things to come in space. On the other hand, many of these seemingly parochial provisions of the treaty might well be interpreted as embracing the potential biocultural differentness of spacekind.

In the preamble to the Outer Space Treaty, for example, we find such wishful statements of intent as "the exploration and use of outer space should be carried on for the benefit of *all* peoples" and that international cooperation will "contribute to the *development of mutual understanding and to the strengthening of friendly relations between states and peoples*" (emphasis added). ARTICLE 1 of the Outer Space Treaty speaks of the exploration and use of outer space as being the "province of all mankind" and states that the exploration and use of space shall be for "the benefit and in the interests of all countries." ARTICLE 2, in asserting that "outer space, including the moon and other celestial bodies, is not subject to national appropriation by claim of sovereignty, by means of use or occupation, or by any other means," gives some sense of the possibility that spacekind might have the right to exert jurisdiction over their own activities.

A case for the independent status of spacekind might be made here, particularly if an acceptable interpretation of "celestial bodies" included those synthetically altered or fabricated bodies called space habitats and if the prohibition against asserting national sovereignty over celestial bodies and space resources was interpreted to apply only to the Earth states that promulgated it. ARTICLE 5 of the treaty indicates an intent of the negotiating and signatory states to consider astronauts as envoys of all people, regardless of fortuitous national origin and despite their undoubted initial function as single-combat warriors:

States Parties to the Treaty shall regard astronauts as envoys of mankind in outer space and shall render to them all possible assistance in the event of accident, distress, or emergency landing on the territory of another State Party or on the high seas. . . . States Parties to the Treaty shall immediately inform the other States Parties to the Treaty or the Secretary-General of the United Nations of any phenomena they discover in outer space, including the moon and other celestial bodies, which could constitute a danger to the life or health of astronauts.

Although ARTICLE 8, cited by Vereshchetin as the source of jurisdiction and control by a launching state over a space object and space personnel, clearly indicates that jurisdiction and control are determinations between states or nations on Earth, it does not preclude the exercise of jurisdiction and control over a space habitat by its indigenous society. Neither is there a prohibition of any of the city-state ideas we shall discuss in more detail later. There is, therefore, no obvious reason that a space habitat, having received international recognition, whether through the diplomatic recognition of key countries or through an international instrument of recognition, could not itself become either a signatory or a beneficiary of the Outer Space Treaty and its successor treaties.

Even the errant Moon Treaty might be salvageable if the United States were to couple any decision to subscribe to the treaty with a request of its allies to apply concerted reservations to their instruments of ratification — reservations that would contain clear affirmations of the principles of free self-determination by space societies. Such a statement of national intent to accept no less than a libertarian transnational legal regime to help our descendants cultivate and evolve their own sensitive and responsive principles of social order in space societies would have enormous philosophical and psychological influence on the ideological accommodations among earthkind and between earthkind and spacekind.

All the issues of jurisdiction over astronauts and spacekind are interrelated with the initial space treaties, the United Nations Charter, and all the formal and customary provisions of international relations that constitute the body or regime of public and private international and transnational law. Although it seems clear that in formulating these treaties and related laws the negotiators and signatory states did not consider astronauts as representing themselves independently, there is room for a reasonable interpretation of these documents and laws as permitting independent jurisdiction of spacekind over their own activities.

It seems equally clear that the development of a self-governing space community need not struggle into existence only in an ad hoc way. It is possible to facilitate, ease, and cultivate a smooth transition to self-determination. It is possible to have a Convention for Spacekind (see the epilogue for the complete proposed text) that would establish substantive provisions and international procedures for the issuance of articles of recognition to space communities, articles that would recognize and accept or accommodate the unique requirements of space communities for social order and survival. It is possible to interpret *res communis humanitatis*—the common heritage of humanity—as including diversity, freedom, equality, and universality.

This is not to say that it will come easily. It will be a difficult political task in the international environment and a difficult educational task in the domestic environment. Sterns and Tennan point out that, in a very practical sense, it may be unrealistic to expect the terrestrial founder-investor to want to lose total control. They suggest, therefore, that the early international mechanism be constructed so as to allow a form of semiautonomy for purposes of municipal jurisdiction or home rule. In the system they propose, there would be legal recognition of three fundamental subjects or realms, the norms, rules, and regulations of which would, presumably, overlap somewhat. They are

1. The terrestrial founder of a space settlement,

2. The political city-state in space, and

3. The supreme judicial authority of the community, which they characterized as home rule and which is also often characterized as the police power. This might resemble some of the models of astrolaw discussed earlier.

The existence of the second and third components would be achieved by the International Agreement of Recognition and Capacity (IARC) proposed by Sterns and Tennan, which could exist as a function or instrument of a specialized agency of the UN or, presumably, as an article or instrument of some other agency or convention, such as the Convention for Spacekind.

The Convention for Spacekind envisages a new, interdisciplinary, specialized UN agency, the International Organization for Sentient Space Activities (IOSSA). IOSSA would not only provide a structural framework in which the IARC could be negotiated in a fair and equitable way—at arm's length—but would also establish an international academy composed of expert representatives from all relevant disciplines of the arts and sciences. This academy would review constantly all aspects of interaction between earthkind and spacekind and would serve as the sole expert advisory body to the International Court of Justice, and to any successor space court or court of international human rights, on matters concerning space communities.

Sterns and Tennan suggest that the IARC should recognize the autonomy of a settlement as beginning when the first citizens of the space habitat establish permanent residence in the habitat. Statehood usually denotes a legal regime with a permanent population, a territory that it occupies, a form of government, indigenous or otherwise, and international capacity and recognition. Once the first three requirements have been satisfied, the recognition of the space community should be authorized and guaranteed pursuant to the IARC. Dual citizenship would be recognized to accommodate those persons who might desire to retain a genuine link with a terrestrial state.

Yet how realistic is the prospect that any of this will come about? How can we really expect the international system to accept international city-states in space as part of a set of civilized, solar system communities? Perhaps one answer is that, at least on Earth, such city-states have already been tried. Many of the essential elements of the IARC idea are already present in terrestrial treaty contexts.

The free city of Danzig, established by the Treaty of Versailles after World War I, and the Free Territory of Trieste, established after World War II under the terms of the 1947 Allied Peace Treaty with Italy, both furnish examples of less than fully sovereign communities considered sui generis in international law. As was pointed out by Glazer in "Domicile and Industry," even these old city-states seem to be almost tailor-made as models for space settlement. The inhabitants of the free city of Danzig enjoyed a great deal of freedom and internal autonomy. Their rights and obligations were governed by a melding of treaty law and municipal law.

With this early experiment in international city-states in mind, the convention for Spacekind, the IARC, or whatever other specific form might be adopted, might contain models similar to those set forth in ARTICLES 100–108 of the Treaty of Versailles. ARTICLES 103 provided for the drawing up of a constitution by representatives of the free city in agreement with the High Commissioner of the League of Nations. The city constitution that emerged not only stressed the nonmilitary constraints imposed upon the free city, but enthroned personal liberty and freedom as well. In fact, between 1925 and 1935 the affairs of the city were examined by the World Court on six occasions, and, in the last opinion rendered, the court held that certain penal laws issued at the behest of the Nazi authorities violated the fundamental rights of the inhabitants of Danzig under its constitution as a free city.

Unfortunately, four years after the invalidation of these unsound penal laws, Nazi Germany annexed Danzig and ended this promising experiment. Yet the precedent stands, not only as a monument to the potential dangers that unlimited state sovereignty may pose to space communities, but also as a rehearsal for the type of arrangement that will be needed to effectuate the early self-determination of spacekind.

Indeed, more recent experiments are already being examined, such as the fully sovereign city-state of Singapore and the Maltese proposal for an international sea-space service to engage in cross-cultural training for the kinds of population mixture that may be attracted to the early space polities. Perhaps this time the experiments will be allowed to come to fruition. We can only hope and work toward the achievement of that goal.

VIII

Metalaw

25   Metalaw: Self-Evident Truths

Humanity must rise above the Earth, to the
top of the atmosphere and beyond, for only
then will we fully understand the world in
which we live.

Socrates, 500 B.C.

Here social man a second birth shall find,
And a new range of reason lift his mind,
Feed his strong intellect with pure light,
A nobler sense of duty and of right,
The sense of liberty.

Joel Barlow
The Columbiad

The spirit of liberty is the spirit that seeks to
understand other men and women.

Judge Learned Hand

We began our look at the next human migration, at our emerging space pioneers, our envoys of mankind, with a look at the basic nature of our
makeup. We watched the evolution of our star-stuff envoys from the primordial big bang, through the primitive communities of early *Homo sapiens,*
to the organizational and episodic histories of our first and current explorers.
Then we examined their new neurologics and biojuridics.

In so doing, we have seen increasing hierarchies of community, from
the original community of subatomic particles, to the eventual, ever-
evolving and complexifying communities of atoms, molecules, celestial
bodies, organisms, and human beings, and finally to socio-organisms great
and small, including the UN, the Soviet Union, the United States, NASA,
and postulated free city-states in space.

Our focus has been primarily on the kinds of people who are going into
space as progenitors of longtime and permanent inhabitants and the reasons they are going there. We have been especially concerned with the val-

ues they take with them and their special physiological, psychological, and communal needs. In focusing on this aspect of human evolution in space, we have really been focusing on the irreducible foundations of space community and space jurisprudence. We have been trying to catch at least a glimmer of what the natural constitution of the community in space may be.

In his influential monograph *Liberty in the Balance,* H. Frank Way, Jr., indicated that there are really three types of constitution, based roughly on Aristotle's three constitutional ideals, that must be taken into account in the day-to-day establishment and maintenance of liberty in any human community—the constitution of the community, the constitution of laws, and the constitution of ideals. Way's description of the constitution of the community is roughly analagous to what we have briefly described as the survival realm of human activity. It might also be roughly equated with the school of legal positivism, the belief that the law—or a community belief or norm—is best understood or described as a body of community structures, practices, and prejudices—an empirical, behavioral, and ethological approach.

As Mr. Justice Holmes said, it is what the courts actually *do* in real life situations that counts. What they do shifts from time to time, of course, depending on new facts, changes in social values, and the like. The Anglo-American system of common law, based on case-by-case decisions, is a particularly good example of an approach designed to reflect the evolving nature of the values and needs of a society.

Almost everyone is familiar, for instance, with the fact that the United States Supreme Court reinterprets the U.S. Constitution of laws significantly from time to time. In the famous nineteenth-century Dred Scott decision, for example, the Court held that slavery was constitutional, while in the 1954 case *Brown* vs. *Board of Education of Topeka,* the pendulum had swung so far to the opposite view that even "separate but equal" schooling among free citizens of different races was considered inherently unequal and therefore unconstitutional. In this regard, Way pointed out that

Liberty is not essentially a legal matter. Liberty is an integral part of the politics of citizenship and the forum for its preservation is not just in a court of law . . . ; the attitude of society and of its organized political forces, rather than its legal machinery, is the controlling force in the character of free institutions. . . . [Still] it is interesting to note that it is frequently observed that our courts are the last and basic protectors of civil liberties. All that can be meant by this is that the courts do attempt to reconcile ideals, the law, and community practices.

Yet even this type of reconciliation is not the exclusive province of the courts. The necessary synthesis among these interdependent constitutions and their inextricable interrelations is equally the province of the jurist, the philosopher, the social scientist, the natural scientist—indeed, of all citizens. It is for this reason that we have been at some pains to describe the constitution of the community in space in a context larger than simply that of community practices and prejudices. It is why we have tried to examine it at every level of existence—from the communities of atoms that are a part of us to the communities of people of which we are a part.

In doing this we have been laying the groundwork for a fourth category of constitution, a metalaw or metaconstitution, which would embrace and interrelate the other three in a coherent, resonant, and understandable way. This was the original task of philosophy and of its various practitioners, such as Aristotle, Plato, and Socrates. They were not only attempting to understand and merge theory, practice, and emergent, observable reality but also to discover the underlying concepts and nonmaterial realities upon which the cosmos was based—a metaphysics.

As we indicated at the outset, *metaphysics* has often been considered a synonym for the mystical or supernatural in the scientific, empirical nineteenth and twentieth centuries, but in the original Greek philosophies, metaphysics was nothing of the sort. A metaphysics was simply the principle, the underlying concept or idea upon which emergent reality relied and was based. It is not surprising, therefore, that the early Greeks were the first group known to develop thoroughly the conception of a natural law, which was derived from a sort of metalaw—the undiscovered, universal basis for existence—the grand metaphysics.

The conception of natural law as developed by Plato, the Stoics, and other classical idealists, was really more an ethical than a legal conception. It bore little resemblance to most positive man-made law. It was not, moreover, a true metalaw—a universal, nonanthropocentric conception of intelligence and being. It was instead a human moral design or blueprint. It was essentially a constitution of ideals upon which the constitutions of laws and of the community would be based to the extent that could be realized.

Of course, there was a desire to discover the underlying laws of intelligence in the cosmos, metalaw, and the laws of human nature, natural law, but because of a lack of knowledge of the cosmos, the Greek pioneers were limited. Except for their grand metaphysical approaches to unrealized knowledge, their conceptions of natural law were derivative, secondary, even relative ones such as justice. They were limited to the realm of the legal positivist, empirical and theoretical observations of human individuals and communities and the way ideals are embodied in laws and community practices.

Still, the Greek idealists were seeking to discover the common ethical heritage of all humanity, a natural code of morality that individuals and communities could turn to in spite of their cultural differences. Indeed, we are still seeking the same thing in the late twentieth century. We search for some universally recognized, ecologically based ethical concepts. As Frank Way put it, "The problem for liberty is how to achieve a harmony of our ideals, our laws, and our daily lives." This task has been made much more difficult by the inherent relativity of natural law and the diversity of human culture, not to mention the security instincts and parochialism of nationalism and absolute state sovereignty.

Through the years there have been several schools of natural law, with confusing differences in approach and emphasis, even within a single school. This confusion undoubtedly contributed to the rise of positivism in the empirical and mechanistic nineteenth century.

The classical or idealist tradition of natural law includes not only the early Greeks, but also Roman philosophers and jurists such as Cicero, Seneca, and Marcus Aurelius. The Christian or theological approach to natural law was first manifested in the works of St. Paul and St. Augustine and continued through the Middle Ages and the Renaissance with St. Thomas Aquinas and the early progenitors of international law, Francisco de Vitoria, Francisco Suárez, and Hugo Grotius. This tradition borrowed from the late Romans, who were the first to take a predominantly legal approach to natural law. They were also the first to formulate the idea of *jus gentium*—the law of peoples and nations.

As early as the 1600s, a constitution of ideals was already seen by most of the West as underlying the ideal constitutions of laws and community. Through the years the Magna Charta had been strengthened in England by the evolution of the Parliament and the common law. Science and technology were beginning to flourish, and the continental philosophers of the Enlightenment began to apply the new sciences to the old Greek and Christian ideals of natural laws.

The Enlightenment school of natural law has been called the rationalist, mechanistic, or individualist school. Actually, this new rationalism and individualism, very much influenced by Newtonian science, were mechanistic and empirical in approach. As stated by Francis Eterovich in *Approaches to Natural Law,*

To the philosophers of the seventeenth and eighteenth centuries, the law of nature—an expression they preferred to natural law—was either the primi-

tive instinct of self-preservation (Thomas Hobbes) or logical reason (John Locke) or liberty unspoiled by civilization (Jean Jacques Rousseau) or human reason concerned exclusively with the preservation of one's own being (Montesquieu). A state of nature is affirmed in this tradition as the basis for a genuine understanding of human nature and its laws of development.

The state of nature was the pretribal era of individual families and kinship groups alone against the elements—John Pfiffer's egalitarian hunter-gatherers. Rousseau portrayed these early people as living in an idyllic state, emphasizing human reason and creating the archetype of the noble savage. Hobbes, like Darwin after him, saw primitive humanity as the uncivilized, ignoble savage. He equated the state of nature with a state of war, the law of the jungle. Many others portrayed the state of nature as some sort of combination of these. Yet nearly all of them relied on the same organ of association, the social contract, as the measure that terminated the state of nature and began the human community, city-state, and nation-state as we still know them today.

The real innovation among this group, however, was the idea that the state is based upon the individual, who has inalienable rights that the state exists to protect, and that the social contract must be a reciprocal arrangement, freely entered into by the members of society. In addition, a juridical metalaw began to develop. It was a framework, a paradigm upon which all the three constitutions would be based. It was an attempt to accommodate pluralistic cultures, beliefs, and practices that might be vital to an intelligent or sentient community, a commitment to the three transcendental principles of Jefferson—life, liberty, and the pursuit of happiness—as the culturally neutral, ecologically based elements underlying the constitution of the community, the constitution of laws, and the constitution of ideals.

Jefferson realized that a community, in all its aspects and all its constitutions, must accommodate uniqueness, diversity, and individuality. To the extent that natural law was still seen as divinely inspired, and therefore extraterrestrial or incorporeal, Jefferson and the other founding fathers interpreted natural law from a metalegal point of view—a point of view that is ecumenical rather than parochial and that attempts to be culturally, even religiously neutral. They made no real attempt to enunciate an intricate code of natural law. Rather, they offered a simple model of what now might be called metalaw—a framework to embrace, and by which to judge, all the constitutions of intelligent beings.

Jefferson called these metalaws self-evident truths and cautiously refused to identify more than three general needs of any conceivable conscious entity. When he spoke of the inalienable rights of humanity, those that we term *metalegal,* he simply said, *"among* these, are life, liberty, and the pursuit of happiness." He clearly realized that a mere constitution of laws is not enough, that survival, liberty, and freedom are always in the balance, anew in each generation—throughout the irreversible processes of nature.

Jefferson knew that ideals and community practices, as well as the constitution of laws, would have to embrace these metalegal concepts and that his personal commitment to this end would be forever necessary. In 1800 he wrote to Benjamin Rush, "I have sworn upon the altar of God eternal hostility against every form of tyranny over the mind of man." In 1816 he wrote to Pierre du Pont de Nemours, "I believe with you that morality, compassion, generosity are innate elements of the human spirit." As recalled by Frank Way,

Much of Jefferson's program is dated, but as Lincoln observed, his principles remain "the definition and axioms of a free society." A personal dedication to liberty, a belief in the essential goodness and moral capacity of man—these were the principles of Jefferson and they remain the principles of all free societies.

As we approach the constitutions of community in space we would do well to remember the lessons of our past frontiers, historical, scientific, and philosophical. One of the most poignant lessons was highlighted by John Stuart Mill in his essay, *On Liberty* (1848). That lesson was the extent to which an original vision of the American Revolution had somewhat been lost in practice. That vision was the concept of individual sovereignty— every person a state, a being. The founding fathers enshrined this constitutional ideal into the new constitution of laws for the republic.

The very first words of the Constitution are, WE THE PEOPLE. They are tall words, proud words, written larger than the rest. New York attorney Joanne Irene Gabrynowicz indicated to the authors her belief that the success of the founders may have derived from their adherence to four essential, metalegal principles that were designed to enshrine and ensure the supremacy of personal sovereignty. Gabrynowicz describes them as four essential "factors of self-organization." Along with our elaborations upon them, they are,

—*conscious exercise of choice*—guaranteed personal sovereignty through constitutional, due process of law; and a symbiosis of equal, sovereign entities;

—*awareness of a natural order*—and the necessity to discern a system in accordance with its dictates;

—*spiritual motivation*—an intuitive belief in cosmic consciousness and potential human transcendence;

—*acknowledgment of a relation between a part and the whole*—a metalegal paradigm of the entireties, according to which each individual is seen as one juridically equal, intelligent entity among a community of others.

As an example of their awareness of a natural order, the founders based the structure and underlying assumptions of the new constitution on their knowledge of natural structural forms, such as the triangle and the pyramid, and on natural processes, such as crop rotation and diversification—exemplified in the staggered terms of congressmen. Every builder knows, for instance, that the strongest structure is a triangle. According to Buckminster Fuller, "What we . . . call structure in our universe is a complex of energy events interacting to produce a stable pattern. The triangle is the only inter-self-stabilizing set of events. Triangle is structure, structure is triangle."

In a triangle each point is attached, checked, or opposed by two other points. The result is dynamic equilibrium—a coherent system. It appears that a similar analogy may have been uppermost in the minds of many of the American founders, who devised a dynamic system of checks and balances, both vertically and horizontally, in which each center of collective power or sovereignty is checked or opposed by two other such centers.

The point is that the founders did not simply base their system on moral, ethical, or even political theories. They did not leave the protection of natural law to the shifting consensus of the community. Their vertical division, for instance, was between individual, state, and federal authority. Their horizontal division was between executive, legislative, and judicial. There seems to have been a definite intention to divide and conquer concentrations of social power and natural institutional tendencies.

The structure embodied in the United States Constitution is a pyramid—a three-dimensional triangle. The pyramidal model not only allowed each point of aggregate power to be offset by two other points, but it also allowed the identification of internal segments of the pyramid with the natural, metalegal factors identified earlier by Gabrynowicz. The pyramidion, the capstone of a pyramid, for example, is an idealized model of the entire pyramid itself. It is seen as the great eye on the Great Seal of the United States. In ancient times, precious metal would be used to coat the capstones of the great pyramids so that they would gleam in the sunlight. The constitutional capstone is the Preamble, and, by subsequent popular demand, the Bill of Rights.

There is little doubt that the framers had the form of a pyramid in mind when fashioning the Constitution. It was a favorite conceptual metaphor of James Wilson and James Madison, the most advanced legal theorists at the Constitutional Convention. Thomas Jefferson himself kept a scale model of the Great Pyramid of Egypt in a place of honor on a mantle in the entrance hall at Monticello.

The democratic principle is the base or center of the founders' conceptual pyramid. Division of powers and the republican or representative principles constitute the bounds or sloping sides. Inside the pyramid, the workings of government proceed according to principles of dynamic systems theory, in which directionality and orientation are always beckoned and transfixed by the principles in the pyramidion. A good example is ARTICLE I, SECTION 10, called the Contract Clause, which forbids states from interfering with the freedom of contract, a freedom that gives individuals the right to make private laws which are enforceable in the courts of common law.

The U.S. Constitution was revolutionary precisely because it embodied concrete, positive steps to protect and promote fundamental, natural ideals. It was an attempt to make natural law more than simply a code of ethics. It advanced the juridical evolution of natural law. In this respect it is not only a code of positive laws unique to our culture and circumstances, but also a naturalistic system and statement of ideals.

This is why Jefferson considered America to be the world's last best hope. He felt that the frontier, the intermix of cultures, and the free, organic framework of government, would combine to create a true *novus ordo seclorum*. There is no doubt that many of the leaders among our American forebears saw America's destiny in just this way. Above the cosmic eye on the Great Seal is the additional statement, *Annuit Coeptis,* said to have been suggested by Benjamin Franklin. Perhaps inspired by Virgil's *Aeneid,* it means, roughly translated, "heaven approves."

Still, as we have seen, the socio-organic leviathan is nevertheless alive and well, and unless we are very careful it can be stronger in space than anywhere else. Yet we really haven't been thinking about it or preparing for it.

Walking among members of the most activist American space groups of the 1980s, one would often hear discussions about the capacity of exorbitantly wealthy musical or religious groups to construct a space habitat at L-5, a gravity-neutral zone between Earth and its moon. Of course, there is nothing inherently wrong with the idea. Why shouldn't free groups with the means to do so move out and establish self-supporting communities? Our support for this type of activity is explicit in our references to past exploration and in our examination of the exploratory nature of life itself. Our point is simply that the establishment of these communities can either be peaceful, beneficial, and promising for all concerned, both earthkind and space-kind, or the communities can be catastrophic fiascos—experiments in power politics and imperialistic bionics.

The choice is ours. The early vectors are ours to determine. How can we go about securing settlement rights, city-state status, and spacekind conventions for our new settlers? What are the legal mechanisms that would have to be used, existing features of international law that are friendly, protective, and naturalistic? We have already begun to look at these questions, but we need to broaden our look at the international legal system, which will be the metalegal forum for the interaction of both space and Earth communities.

What can we discover about the type of metalaw necessary for interaction with spacekind, eventually perhaps even with interstellar extraterrestrials? How can this metalaw be discovered by earthkind, sufficient to enable them to embrace the global constitutions that will be necessary, not only to guarantee the rights of spacekind, but also to guarantee the survival of earthkind?

26 Metalaw and International Law

Natural theory of international law . . .
[received] its most searching examination
at precisely the time when man was last
faced with a major expansion in the effective size of his universe and with the resulting need to devise new systems of law. . . .
We are on a similar threshold today. . . .
Unfortunately . . . such treatment as positivist jurists accord the foundation upon
which international law is based—that is,
regarding it as based on a mere system of
mutable, man-made laws—is completely
antithetical to the idea of law itself. Certainly, to disregard the law of nature and
place wholly in its stead man's positive law
is not a sound way for the world community to build its rules of conduct in opening
the new frontier of space. It means accepting the structure and throwing out the foundation.

Andrew G. Haley
Space Law and Government

In today's world the international system includes virtually everything organizational in character that influences, but operates beyond, a local or
regional community. Even some local activities have international over-
tones. This is equally true in both public and private organizations, from
governments to corporations and associations.

Take, for example, the growing number of domestic businesses that use
communications satellites. Even local television stations now have mobile
satellite ground stations for coverage of remote events. More and more disparate businesses have daily operations that depend on mass communica-

tions and that indicate the growing interdependency in organizational and legal life.

This trend toward interdependency is also indicative of the rise of the kind of cosmopolis or universal city envisaged by the Greeks, or of the global village described by Marshall McLuhan. Thus, the early settlers of the first space communities will not have the opportunity to be solitary individuals like Daniel Boone, or even bands of iconoclastic explorers like the Plymouth Pilgrims. As we have seen in many different ways, spacekind will be born of and by the community, if not for the community. Spacekind will assist earthkind in fabricating their own space communities from the inside out, and, in turn, these totally technologized communities will reform spacekind from the outside in.

As we see and say this, and as we think about it, it is important not to get lost in the complexity, in the cold, hard machinery of the process, and in all of the new biotechnological and philosophical jargon. It is important, because what is at stake is no less precious and fragile than the qualities of intelligence, life, and love.

It might reasonably be assumed, for instance, that the development of efficient shuttle and space-station crew members will be consistent with American jurisprudence. Yet this is the type of assumption that cannot be mindlessly or carelessly embraced in an environment dictated solely by biotechnological objectives designed to serve an almost exclusively Earth-based public consisting mostly of military institutions, entrepreneurial organizations, and government agencies.

We are once again reminded of the iron hand of government and the blunderbuss of bureaucracy, which are the antithesis of sensitivity, liberty, and justice. Almost every American lawyer is aware of instances, even in the organic *novus ordo,* where the objective, empirical, mechanistic, didactic, indiscriminate social machinery of government and the courts has bludgeoned its way into situations in which a gentler, more private, and more sensitive approach would be eminently more appropriate.

The blindfold on justice bespeaks a paradox, reflecting not only the image of objectivity, but also one of a blind, groping giant, thundering about in a closet containing priceless and fragile works of art. The founding fathers saw this paradox in their time, a time as far removed from the Space Age as it was from early humanity—the hunter-gatherers of antiquity. How much greater is the threat of the socio-organism to intelligence, life, and love today, especially in a planned, synthetic space culture?

It is not possible for space settlers simply to bang a few planks together and float away toward a mooring on some unknown shore in the Infinite Ocean. There are too many complex interrelations to be considered and too many interested parties. Meanwhile, despite the lessons of the free city-state experiments on Earth, an international system that is weak politically and legally is a perilous scaffold upon which to build the kind of space polity that will be required to protect the most precious, fundamental, metalegal essences of life and intelligence in space.

As we examine the evolutionary characteristics of the existing international framework, we should keep this in mind. Perhaps it has become necessary again to see the present international system in the way many of its founders did, as the mere starting point, the first single step on a journey of a thousand miles to peaceful, organic, international, and, now, interplanetary communities and institutions.

In fact, the international legal system is really metalegal in two important ways. One is found in firm present reality and the other was intended by the founders of international law to approach the balance demanded by the polarities of existence. The firm reality is that much of international law is scarcely positive law at all. It is *metalaw,* in the sense that the realm in which it functions is primarily theoretical, ethical and ideological.

The required balance is also metalegal, in that the hope, anticipation, and study of its essential elements may be the very unifying and motivating force necessary to assure survival of the earthborn sentient genome. What is necessary is even more than a species-normative ideology. A cosmic, interspecies consciousness and an objective understanding of subjectivity are needed.

John Stuart Mill felt that "the practical question is where to place the limit—how to make the fitting adjustment between individual independence and social control." Yet there has been only painful, grudging success in making the fitting adjustment even in the "libertarian" United States, much less in the international arena. We have yet to reach the point of legal development in the international community that Jefferson and his compatriots accomplished at the nation-state level, even though we know, ideally, that the only true legal definition of liberty exists in society, which in turn means that liberties, whether of individuals or nation-states, carry with them responsibilities to society.

This realization is what led William O. Douglas to observe that the international system is based more on the rule of force than on the rule of law. In his remarks we see a human race still so primitive in its evolution that its international communities have not yet emerged from the state of nature described by the Renaissance jurists. Our international relations, moreover, resemble Hobbes's violent state of war more than they resemble the natural states described by Hobbes's contemporaries.

We have thus returned once more to our often-stated paradox—

parochialism, isolation, and entropy versus evolution, ecumenism, and transformation. These are polarities within omnidimensional reality, the oppositions of nature, both animate and inanimate.

There is a need for a fusion of these polarities, for transcendent paradigms and metalaws to supply the intricate neurological and ideological structures, the connective tissues for the next epoch of human social life, an international and interplanetary epoch. Such metalaws are vitally necessary for space communities, which are more than transnational. These communities will be transplanetary, perhaps even transspecies.

We continue our search for these metalaws with an examination of the current matrix of the international system and all its components. In examining the components of the international system, one is immediately struck by the fact that, because of the great degree of interdependency in modern organizational life, it is sometimes difficult to determine where a public component or realm becomes private, or where a domestic one becomes international. This is why it is difficult to base a perception of the international system merely on the fractiousness of the United Nations Security Council or the more famous examples of the ineffectiveness of the International Court of Justice, such as its inability to enforce its order to Iran to release American diplomatic hostages. Such a limited perception of the international system does not even accurately reflect the numerous other activities of the United Nations itself, much less the whole panoply of public and private transnational relationships.

In *Law and Force in the International System,* Soviet jurist G. I. Tunkin pointed out that the international system actually transcends, or operates beyond, the United Nations. He described the international system as a decentralized community, a community which, because of continuing conflicts between socialist and capitalist nations, functions without legislative, executive, and judicial organs. Since the United Nations does not provide these organs in any enforceable or legally positive way, Tunkin suggested that the UN is merely a subsystem within the larger international system. Apparently, Tunkin's emerging international community can find juridical union only in socialism. Tunkin's arguments are ironical, moreover, in view of the fact that Soviet insistence on the absolute sovereignty and "sacred inviolability" of socialist states is largely responsible for the generally quasi-legal, theoretical, and functionally hamstrung nature of existing public international organizations.

Still, even the briefest perusal of the United Nations system, surely the preeminent subsystem in the international sphere, will reveal a breadth and depth of activity and international coordination seldom apparent in the headlines of the mass media. The UN embraces a multiplicity of functions.

Some, such as the UNICEF Committee and the World Bank and the International Monetary Fund, which have been in the forefront of news coverage during periods of economic upheaval, are familiar to most Americans.

Among the many noteworthy organizations of the UN are such specialized agencies as the UN Educational, Scientific, and Cultural Organization (UNESCO), the Universal Postal Union (UPU) for foreign mail, and the International Labor Organization (ILO), which has been the originator of many human rights conventions and initiatives. The World Health Organization (WHO) and the Food and Agriculture Organization (FAO) have done much to coordinate vaccination practices, isolate epidemics, modernize agricultural practices, and facilitate the exchange of information. The International Civil Aviation Organization (ICAO) coordinates international air traffic control and route selections pursuant to the various air conventions mentioned earlier. Indeed, the list is seemingly endless and extends far beyond what can be covered in this chapter. We shall therefore focus our attention primarily on those aspects of the UN system that have to do with activity in outer space.

The most relevant purposes of the UN, as expressed in ARTICLE 1 of its charter, are to

1. Develop friendly relations among nations based on respect for the principle of equal rights and self-determination of peoples; and

2. Achieve international cooperation in solving international problems of an economic, social, cultural, or humanitarian character and in promoting and encouraging respect for human rights and for fundamental freedoms for all, without distinction as to race, sex, language, or religion.

The central organ of the United Nations is the General Assembly, which might be loosely compared to an international parliament. The General Assembly adopts the general budget, assesses members, and has the authority to establish associated committees and subsidiary organizations on questions of specialty. The Committee on the Peaceful Uses of Outer Space (COPUOS) is one such committee. Each member nation has one vote, although each can send as many as five representatives to the assembly. A two-thirds majority is required for votes on particularly important matters such as international conventions.

In constitutional theory, the actions of the assembly do not carry the force of positive law and are considered by the World Court only as subsidiary or tertiary sources of international law. Nevertheless, they carry moral weight as a result of their assumed representation of the consensus of nations. Also, actions of the assembly are often the sources for treaties and other binding — to the extent that anything in the international system is ever binding — positive international law. Assembly actions can also be examined for emergent features of underlying customary international law.

In reality, therefore, the General Assembly is somewhat more influential in the constitution of the international community, even if only politically, than is generally realized.

Still, in the original conception of the United Nations, the Security Council alone was to be given executive authority. To it alone would be given the power to levy sanctions, dispatch peacekeeping forces, enunciate binding international law, and even engage in collective military action. In this sense, it had the potential, theoretically, to be a real world government of sorts.

Originally, a nine-vote majority of the fifteen-member Security Council was to be required, although action could be vetoed by two negative votes from among the five permanent members, the United States, Britain, France, China, and the Soviet Union. The Soviet Union, however, insisted on a one-vote veto, and as most Americans are now painfully aware, the one-vote veto rule has shackled the council ever since, thus accounting for Tunkin's unwillingness to consider it an organ of juridical authority.

The Secretariat provides administration for the United Nations organs and committees and for some of the specialized agencies as well. The Secretary-General must be nominated by the Security Council and elected by the General Assembly. Within the Secretariat are both outer space and human rights divisions, which are very important and quite active in coordination and education in their respective fields.

The International Court of Justice—the World Court—has only permissive jurisdiction, which in the case of the Iranian hostages, for example, was possible only because both parties had previously agreed to an international diplomatic convention. Although the results in such cases may have enormous diplomatic, political, or even moral force, it is obvious that enforceability requires either the consent of the charged party or development in the future of more effective mechanisms of enforcement. Nevertheless, these structures could serve as a framework for future relations among spacekind and between spacekind and earthkind.

The Trusteeship Council was set up to administer the orderly transition of former colonies or other unincorporated communities to an independent, self-governing status. Since the initial work of the Trusteeship Council is essentially complete there has been talk of abolishing it and even of reforming it to perform some other task. Perhaps it will reemerge as the coordinating locus for international agreements of recognition and capacity (IARCs) for space settlements, and for the type of specialized, cultural coordinative and study agency called for in the Convention for Spacekind (see the epilogue).

Last among the principle organs of the UN is the Economic and Social

Council (ECOSOC). ECOSOC addresses the myriad problems of the world by coordinating the work of the specialized agencies, each of which is constructed independently on the basis of a separate, multilateral treaty. Each works in its own specialized field and cooperates with the UN pursuant to an agreement that defines the relationship.

In this respect, the UN did not seek, as did the League of Nations, to bring all international activities rigidly into one system. Although most of the specialized agencies are organized similarly, each is an independent, international legal entity, with its own legislative body and secretariat. Specialized agencies are destined to be ever more important, especially in the field of astronautics, and especially if an entity such as the International Organization for Sentient Space Activities (IOSSA) is created to grant IARCs and monitor the interdisciplinary complexities of space communities, with priority given to the protection of spacekind.

Beyond the organs, committees, and intergovernmental specialized agencies of the UN lie the various private nongovernmental organizations (NGOs). These range from domestic interest groups to the transnational corporations and the great international unions or federations of professional associations, some of which were instrumental in the formation both of the UN itself and also of the early space treaties. The NGOs work at the public international level. Indeed, almost any nongovernmental organization may affiliate itself with the UN system in one of several designations, as several American prospace citizens' and professional groups have done.

The International Astronautical Federation (IAF) is a good example of an NGO which has affiliated itself successfully and prominently with several specialized agencies, notably UNESCO and the International Telecommunications Union (ITU). The IAF began as an ad hoc international congress of professional astronautical societies, such as Hermann Oberth's German Society for Space Research, the British Interplanetary Society, and the American Rocket Society, now the American Institute of Aeronautics and Astronautics (AIAA). The IAF has held International Astronautical Congresses annually since 1950; they have included countries in the Soviet bloc since 1957.

The IAF vigorously and successfully pursued UN affiliation under several visionary natural and social scientists. Andrew Haley, an American pioneer in international space law, became the first social scientist elected president of the IAF and was its first legal counsel. The first suggestion of the "benefit of all mankind" language used in the initial space treaty appeared in 1956 in Haley's article "Basic Concepts of Space Law." Under Haley's guidance, the IAF held, in 1958, the first International Colloquium on the Law of Outer Space. Such colloquia have been annual events ever since and are now held under the auspices of the IAF's subsidiary organization, the International Institute of Space Law.

The IAF has been particularly effective in its advisory relationship with specialized UN agencies such as the ITU and the World Meteorological Organization (WMO). Indeed, the ITU itself is a good example of an element of the UN system which actually seems to have some real, practical, and functioning authority. The primary authority of the ITU is the allocation of radio frequencies and satellite orbital slots. This is seen to be enormously important when one considers the vitality of communications to any community and the tremendous number of communications satellites from many different countries, each requiring access to an integral segment of the electromagnetic spectrum and the geosynchronous orbit.

Few people are able to recognize the importance and influence of international intergovernmental and nongovernmental organizations such as the ITU and the IAF, shrouded as they are in the general perception of the international system as ineffective. Yet the days when even domestic communications policy could be developed without regard to international implications are long gone.

Secure, recognized frequencies, for instance, are necessary especially for the types of private investment that characterize the American communications market. The ITU alone has about seventy-five different committees, study groups, and interim working parties. Many people are surprised to learn that the ITU's predecessor in interest, the International Telegraph Union, antedates the UN by many years. It was established in 1865, was renamed in 1932, and became a specialized agency of the UN in 1949.

Indeed, several of the specialized agencies of today, such as the WMO, the roots of which go back to 1853, when shipowners throughout the world began formally to exchange meteorological observations on the oceans, have venerable origins. The WMO is a clearinghouse for cooperation among the weather services of the member nations. Little imagination is required to perceive the complex and valuable exchange of information now taking place, not only from satellites and ground stations, but also from comparative meteorological studies of other planets in our solar system.

This description of the international system as it relates to space activities does not even include many important intergovernmental and domestic organizations, such as the International Telecommunications Satellite Organization (INTELSAT) or the European Space Agency (ESA). Even NASA, like many other domestic organizations, has an office of international relations, which negotiates launch services for international astronauts and payloads and advises the government on questions of international law related to space. There are far too many similar organizations for us to list them here.

At the Twentieth Colloquium on the Law of Outer Space, Isabella Diederiks-Vershoor, then president of the International Institute of Space Law, even suggested the establishment of a World International Space Agency, patterned after the International Civil Aviation Organization (ICAO), which would not only be empowered to engage in cooperative launch ventures along lines originally envisaged by President Eisenhower, but would also perform coordinating functions for spaceflight roughly equivalent to those performed by the ICAO for civil aviation.

So the international community seems to have the organizational experience and expertise necessary to provide a smooth transition to space habitation. What remains to be seen, however, is whether the international community has either the vision or the will to do so in a way in which the unique circumstances of living in space and the needs of space societies for self-determination are taken into account.

This vision and will of earthkind, and of earthkind and spacekind working together, may prove to be of enormous importance to the development of the type of cosmopolitan world view necessary even to save the species from self-extinction. Although this assertion may seem to represent quite a leap in cause-and-effect reasoning, it is valid in view of the level of destructive technology we have created and its potential for reducing human population to a level from which a recovery of the species cannot be made. Any contribution made to avoidance of that eventuality is positive. Perhaps a good place to begin looking for this type of will and vision is in the ideology and the courage that produced these international systems in the first place and that have continued to enlarge the international definition of fundamental human rights.

27 Natural Law

> In man's ascent . . . from the primordial
> hydrogen atom through a series of associ-
> ated atoms, thence into the molecular,
> thence into megamolecules, thence into
> cellular life, and through an amazing and
> myriad series of steps to the numenon, the
> monad, the "thing in itself," and on to
> become the psychosocial individual known
> as *Homo sapiens,* one finds only "onward-
> ness" and "upwardness" and there is no
> positive evidence to indicate that the evolu-
> tionary process has stopped or that *Homo
> sapiens* (or his successor) may not emerge
> as a creature having such transcendental
> qualities as to render another and even a
> different classification on the ladder of life.
> Indeed, a new order of sapient creatures
> may evolve on Earth having origin in
> entirely different atomic combinations and
> surpass man in all sentient and intellectual
> capabilities.
>
> *Andrew G. Haley*
> Space Law and Government

In Latin, *meta* has been defined as a goal, a bound, a turning point. It is one of the few words available to describe adequately the interstices — the underlying weave of existence. It is one of the few words available with which to describe the structural interconnections of Prigogine's continual and irreversible processes of nature and society.

Unfortunately, in the early development of English common law the term *meta* was used as the name of a boundary landmark, a benchmark with the characteristic of a fixed point. It was still a turning point, of course, but it took on the connotation of stasis or immobility.

Metalaw, as we envisage it, is characterized by the relative, mobile "exstasis" of the Latin definition. Its only fixed characteristic lies in the irreversibility of its initial vector, its direction toward a goal. As we have seen, though subsequent events may tend in a perpendicular or even an opposite direction, the reversal of a movement or the change of a pattern is fraught with unavoidable consequences.

In order to be truly *meta,* therefore, metalaw must be consonant with the fundamental, diverse, constantly evolving nature of universal being. It would therefore be based upon metaphysics — a science of being. In essence, of course, this is what law really is — or, at least, is ideally conceived to be. Unfortunately, law has too often become equated with specific rules and regulations, thereby invoking the cliché about the inability to see the forest for the trees.

In *Legal Research in a Nutshell,* Morris L. Cohen complained of "the lawless science of our law, that codeless myriad of precedent, that wilderness of single instances." Cohen implied that the law is, in fact, cumulative and dynamic, operating within interstitial, somewhat stable, metalegal frameworks. The frameworks are interstitial or metalegal because they represent connections or references to people and communities separated by time and space. Jurisprudence is, essentially, a social intervenor, a mediator between individuals and organizations. Within these interstitial frameworks of the legal process, individual cases both derive from and lead to the legal principles that define the frameworks.

What we are seeing here is the ecological and cumulative nature of juristic sensing, a sort of ecological metalaw that is characterized by societal shifts in response to evolving cultural ecotones. When whole systems are examined and the cumulative nature of experience and consciousness are considered — the approach of philosophy — more and more parts of the basic pattern can be discerned. Juridical planning for space habitation has inevitably been required to adopt precisely this type of approach — this paradigm of the entireties — in order to be able to plan sensitively and soundly for healthy space communities.

In his perceptive article "On Teaching Natural Law," David F. Forte examined the great difficulties confronting the practitioner of the type of natural law that will be needed in the space age. Many of these difficulties are exemplified in the second and third years of legal study by the continuing, nearly exclusive use of the case method in all legal instruction. One of the principal problems has been the lack of so-called practical applications of natural law in the rather mechanical daily workings of the highly departmentalized, case-bound and precedent-bound judicial causes of action. The concentration on actual cases, their outcomes, and the precise enunciation of their rules has often led to neglect of the need to examine the meta, the interstice, and the synthesis between rules and naturalistic theory systematically.

One of the first jurists to examine the possibilities for synthesis between natural law and positive law was Harvard Professor Lon Fuller, who developed a case method for natural law. It was his decision to present natural theory in action, in applied contexts, such as the study of the natural principles applied by the American Constitutional Convention.

As Forte notes, because of the lack of such examples and of scholarly research on the largely nonquantifiable, diffuse underlying reasons for cultural rules and organizational regimes, Fuller was forced to use his famous imaginary cases as a means of illustrating different jurisprudential analyses. His own view of natural law was "woven in amongst other philosophical threads in the fictional opinions" in these concocted cases. Fuller's intention was to go intensively into fewer instances so that he could consider more of the ramifications in each. He aimed to achieve greater analytical depth and a greater appreciation of the ecological nature of the sociological and philosophical foundations of law.

Although sociological jurisprudence was originally perceived as a positivist school of thought, its founder, Roscoe Pound, decried the moral nihilism of positivism. In his article "Social Control through law," he observed that "Absolute ideals of justice have made for free government, and sceptical ideas of justice have gone with autocracy. . . . If the idea is absolute, those who wield the force of politically organised society are not. Sceptical realism puts nothing above the ruler or the ruling body."

Obviously this is not always true, as has been demonstrated in Ayatolla Khomeini's Iran, where a supposed absolute ideal and its attendant juridical enforcements have helped to create havoc and have given autocratic power to one theocrat. The potential for absolutism in systems based on so-called divine law is, of course, what motivated the American founders to include among the natural rights of Americans religious freedom and separation of church and state.

The same fear of autocratic tendencies is what leads many American jurists to forget the ease and familiarity with which the founders also called upon Divine Providence. This fear, therefore, is what has led many jurists away from the study of natural law and toward an exclusive reliance upon positive law in an attempt to achieve cultural neutrality through strict, mechanistic empiricism, the so-called rule of law.

Before we can extend this rule of law into space, however, it is important to understand, as Plato, Thomas Kuhn, and others have demonstrated, that even the empiricists operate on the basis of unstated, fundamental assumptions. Positivist jurisprudents, for example, search for the "correct" rule in cases where no direct precedents exist. The correct rule is to be based on "justice," and "right reason," even though these are recognized as relative terms.

It is ironic that one of the psychological supports for positivism has been the fact that relativity in society often seems frightening to those who seek stability and order. Yet even time and space are relative. Perhaps much of society's future shock is really due to the fact that the social scientists have yet to uncover fully their own special theory of relativity.

In *The Law and Its Compass,* Lord Radcliffe pointed out that there are numerous examples of the application of right reason, community wisdom, and unspoken consensus, the famous common sense of the silent majority. He points to the importance of custom in determining global norms of international law and to the domestic equity jurisdiction and its remedy of quasi contract. Quasi contract gives an equity judge the power to create in public law a contract that did not exist in private law. The judge is empowered to declare that because no remedy is available to an unjustly injured party, either in statutory law or case law, a remedy will be created by the court.

What has too often been forgotten is that the case method itself, like the experimental method in science, was intended to be a metalegal tool, one that opens precedent to change, that allows each case to be considered in the light of current evidence, reason, equity, and justice. This type of searching discrimination is really at the heart of the so-called Socratic nature of the case method, which is ideally founded upon and embraces the philosophical and cultural dimensions of each case. Ideally, the temporal role of each case is examined in the context of the continuing legal process.

The supreme rule that governs cases in almost every naturalistic jurisdiction is the rule of reason, which gives judges the authority and the latitude to administer cases that are not covered by written law, much in the same way that the Roman praetors displaced the narrow, highly technical civil law of the Roman citizens with natural law. The rule of reason is also used in the civil courts of continental Europe in the absence of a definite law governing the transactions in question, whenever, in the opinion of judges, it should be applied. As Lord Radcliffe observed,

We cannot learn law by learning law. . . . It is not strong enough in itself to be a philosophy in itself. It must still stand rooted in that great tradition of humana civilitas. . . . Cut it away from that tradition, no matter for how good a reason, and it will lose what sustains its life. We must never, then, lose touch with the idea of natural law or give up the belief that all positive law bears some relation to it.

Yet the English word *law* has too often been associated with gavels, rules, and stasis. The Latin word for law is *jus*. As with the definition of *meta,* the classical Latin meaning is more fluid. *Jus* was envisaged as the honeycomb or web of cultural definition, a natural order that binds into cohesiveness, yet shifts through time along with the conscious consensus of cultural self-definition. Traditionally, the classical Latin word *jus* meant law considered in the abstract — that is, as distinguished from any specific enactment.

The *jus* is the legacy, the embracing, structural entropy and irreversibility, the public response to the passion and logic of social-cultural existence. This is why the juristic perspective, like the scientific perspective, is only now beginning to reemerge from the foggy empirical and mechanistic bias of the Newtonian paradigms. As Einstein himself noted, "It is characteristic of Newtonian physics that it has to ascribe independent and real existence to space and time as well as to matter." The hallmark of the Newtonian approach, both of its failures and of its successes, is separation.

Of course, it was the still valid aspects of this spirit of structure and separation that gave rise to the greatest political and humanitarian experiment in history — the United States. Yet when the revolutionary and transcendental naturalists began to die out, they were replaced by a wave of mechanistic positivists, concerned primarily with operating the new governmental physics and building a national sovereignty and identity — still the prime concern of Russian communism and of much of the third world.

Since the early nineteenth century, rampant nationalism and positivism have characterized global politics. In the late twentieth century, we are only just beginning to see a practical resurgence of naturalistic thinking, spurred on by Einsteinian paradigms, the new physics, and the astral perspectives revealed to us through space science and exploration.

The juristic exercise is again being seen as the never-ending, idealistic attempt to bring social machinery into harmony with the various laws of physical nature and the indescribable insights of conscious entities — the heartfelt sense and survival necessity of simultaneous human independence, interdependence, and cohesiveness.

A commitment to this type of flexible cohesiveness, to an integrated, interdisciplinary approach, is essential to the continuing health of a free society and the development of free institutions in space or on Earth. Perhaps this is because liberty actually depends on and carries with it a continuing and unstinting commitment to liberty for all other individuals.

As we have seen, it has historically been recognized that there must be certain rights ascribable to humankind, regardless of the particular community sovereign to whom a given individual owes allegiance, whether by birth, conquest, or choice. In American legal history, these rights flow from an inflexible keystone principle, individual human freedom—on land, on the sea, in the air, and now in space. These rights, moreover, if their basis is to be universally accepted, must be ascribed to human beings independent of their individual worth or merit.

This, again, is the doctrine of natural rights and natural law, *jus naturale,* that is, in some sense, traceable back to the Greek and Roman Stoics. In *De republica,* Book 3, Cicero said that natural law is "distinct from the laws of Athens and Rome, a law binding upon all men in such a manner that whosoever is disobedient is fleeing from himself and denying his human nature."

Down through the centuries, these rights have come to be considered so fundamental, perhaps even congenital, that an individual cannot alienate them, cannot relinquish, transfer, or forfeit them. The United States Supreme Court has rendered decisions time and again on the inflexible premise that citizens of the nation, indeed, of all other nations, who have submitted to the jurisdiction of the United States cannot contract away their natural rights and freedoms as enumerated in the United States Constitution. In *The Spanish Origins of International Law,* James B. Scott stated,

The Constitution of the United States is itself a tribute to the law of nature. The Constitution is a supreme law; it is not to be changed by the legislature, as an ordinary statute. It can be amended . . . and in that sense is not immutable; but it can only be amended by an express vote of three-fourths of the States of the American Union. Every written constitution made by its framers superior to a statute of the legislature is a recognition, unconscious perhaps, of the law of nature—that is to say of a law of general effect, beyond the power of the ordinary law-making body to modify.

A positivistic, practical explanation for the supremacy of the Constitution over autocracy can be found in the belief of the American founders that government structures should be balanced and limited and inclined toward the centrality of the sapient being and the golden rule. They knew that rights have clear costs—opportunity costs. Sometimes the guilty go free, for instance, because of constitutional protections.

History suggests that such costs often appear too high when placed in direct competition with other needs, particularly survival needs. This is why the American people, supposedly the fountainhead of their new naturalistic Constitution, demanded the protections of the Bill of Rights before they would assent to the more perfect union the Constitution was purporting to form. They thought it necessary to guarantee that no government official be constitutionally authorized to jettison human rights, whatever the compulsion, exigency, or opportunity.

The violation of these fundamental rights, whether by tyrants, governments, other organizations, or individuals, has been seen as the violation of the very humanity of the victims themselves. Such destruction of the integrity of a person has been characterized as being as serious as the taking of the life of another, since it involves the degradation and demeaning of human life as a whole, evoking profound revulsion.

These inviolable, fundamental human rights are what Andrew Haley had in mind in formulating his Interstellar Golden Rule for space inhabitants, regardless of their national or planetary origins: "Do unto others as *they* would have you do unto them," a basic bioecological dictate for survival where cultures overlap and intermix. It is a dictate that finds roots in the medieval idea that natural law was instilled in the minds of human beings by God and that it was discovered by intellectual reasoning of the type recommended by the Greeks, particularly when applied to study and understanding of the Holy Scriptures.

Haley noted the correspondence of the Interstellar Golden Rule with the anthropocentric golden rule of almost every Earth culture and religion. In 1955 he introduced his concept of metalaw and the Interstellar Golden Rule to an unreceptive diplomatic and scholarly audience. Haley courageously asserted that an "indefinite projection of a system of anthropocentric law beyond the planet Earth would be the most calamitous act man could perform in his dealings with the cosmos." He was convinced that the human occupation of space would provide, not only technological advances and increases in empirical scientific data, but, more important, new potential for peace, cooperation, and "advancements in medicine, science, and philosophy." Yet he warned that

To extend our existing systems of law, with their imperfections and ideological limitations, their inherent conflicts and inconsistencies, under the guise of an "international law" which is to apply to "outer space and celestial bodies," would be to spread our terrestrial conflicts and intolerances wide and far through the universe.

The subject of metalaw was discussed by many of Haley's contemporaries, but always in the context of *Homo sapiens* versus exobiological or extraterrestrial life forms not of the same species or the same planetary origin. Metalaw in space would encompass the inflexible rule that human beings must treat all extraterrestrial life forms, regardless of where they fit into the total spectrum of sentience and sapiency, "as they [the extraterrestrial] would have done unto them."

In an anthropocentric context, the essence of metalaw is described by the great theologists and the scriptures in such words as those of Jesus Christ, "Therefore, all things whatsoever you would that men should do to you, do you even so to them; for this is the law and the prophets;" the prophet Mohammed, "Do good unto others as God has done unto you;" the Babylonian Talmud, "What is hateful to thyself do not unto thy neighbor;" Bidpai, "Men are used as they use others;" and Confucius, "What I do not wish others to do unto me, that also I wish not to do unto them." In the Torah, the Mahabharata, and the Sutra Kritanga and in the writings of Epictetus, Seneca, Ahikar, Abdullah Ansari, Sadi, Gandhi, Martin Luther King, Bishop Desmond Tutu—wherever humanity has set down the essence of law—the same simple concept emerges.

The Ten Commandments, the Koran, and the Torah are actually something of a self-evident, derivative subset of rules based on the golden rule. They are not so much imposed by God on his unwilling people, a misimpression often drawn from the metaphor of Moses the lawgiver, as they are revealed by God to his people as the keys to harmonious and transcendent survival of humanity on the planet Earth. They are the bioecological dictates of *Homo sapiens.* Haley pointed out that "all of the precepts of the great law-givers, even that of the heterodox Hindu religion of Jainism, are, in each case, starkly anthropocentric."

This sense of anthropocentrism in law has continued to prevail in the development of a social order in space, except in the imaginary cases of serious jurists regarding the natural sociolegal relations that must be established if human beings should ever interact with extraterrestrial life forms. Yet these discussions seldom include any perception of the reality of psychophysically altered spacekind children of *Homo sapiens* within the definition of extraterrestrial life forms.

We continue, in positive practice, to extend our traditional earthly legal positivisms into space in a way that clearly prevents the projecting into outer space of free and enlightened groups of human beings who are spiritually inclined to carve out new habitations from new land on new planets and to proceed on their quest under rules of law that require respect for the whole integrity of other sapient beings, including ourselves and our spacefaring sons and daughters.

We are establishing civil and criminal laws for our own space inhabitants on the premises of the tried and true human sanctions of force in shaping and controlling human conduct. These sanctions are less and less sensitive to the collectively unique biological demands of human beings living in space. Truth, the main object of natural law, has too often been subordinated to winning in a highly competitive legal system which was ideally intended to exhibit only a philosophical form of competition.

In his 1984 article, "Astrolaw Jurisprudence in Space as a Place," J. Henry Glazer noted that the perception of professional responsibility of those people involved with the practice of law in space must be one of a "helping profession" rather than an adversarial one, thus resurrecting the full meaning of the classical title of counselor. Glazer pointed out that

If extended into outer space, the adversarial approach to dispute resolution, accommodating primitive systems of courtroom combat moored to the Middle Ages, will greatly exacerbate physical dangers there, and, as a consequence—with the possible exception of capital offenses or high crimes—adversarial systems of jurisprudence should have no place in the inventory of dispute resolving mechanisms developed in and for space through Astrolaw jurisprudence.

May not spacekind require even more sensitive and more highly evolved forms of natural protection for community cohesiveness, harmony, and individual growth and actualization? Much of the practical, affirmative answer to this inquiry, unfortunately, can be seen in the earthly cycles of imperialism, colonialism, integration, rejection, independence, and accommodation.

The imposition of an imperialist culture on societies considered to have primitive cultures has gradually given way, albeit with boundless bloodshed, to recognition of the need of a primitive society to abide by cultural institutions that have evolved in response to the demands of that society's specific ecosystem. Not only, therefore, does the individual have inherent natural rights, simply because it makes sense to give a unique dignity to the individual existence of humankind, but there is also a measurable set of natural rights that inhere in a societal grouping in order to ensure flexibility for survival of that society. If this concept holds true for the technologically primitive societies on Earth, it holds no less true for the highly advanced biotechnological societies in space.

28 Universal Law of Humankind

Law defines a relation not always between fixed points, but often, indeed oftenest, between points of varying position. The acts and situations to be regulated have a motion of their own. There is a change whether we will it or not. . . . One is reminded of the Einstein theory and the relativity of motion. . . . If there were infinite space with only one object in it, motion for that object would have no meaning in our minds. . . . There is need to import some of this conception of relativity into our conception of the development of the law. We render judgment by establishing a relation between moving objects—moving at different speeds and in different directions. If we fix the relation between them upon the assumption that they are stationary, the result will often be to exaggerate the distance. True constancy consists in fitting our statement of the relation to the new position of the objects and the new interval between them.

Benjamin Cardozo

A system of justice, an organic, balanced, independent, synthetic justice, is sociocultural clothing. Without it we are naked to the world, fair play for the unrestrained scientific power now available to the animal impulse, the ancient biochemical reality. Even with justice, or, at least, an advanced articulation of it, how many American citizens still feel free from crime and economic imbalance and the machine mentality of bureaucracies, whether military, commercial, administrative, or judicial? Are not all of us also potential victims of a nuclear holocaust and economic hostages to a global military-industrial complex run rampant?

With this as a background, it is perhaps worthwhile to state that in no way do we envisage spacekind as a master race or a horde of elitists. Such has been one of the greatest misunderstandings of the supposed nature of potential human transcendence. Higher intelligence has too often been seen only in conjunction with higher power and higher organization. Even theology has been susceptible to such Aristotelian and Newtonian paradigms. The separatist paradigms, for example, led to the "conquest of nature" by mankind its "master." The positivist school of theology held that one is judged upon highly legalistic canons of denominational ethics. The outward appearance was of paramount importance. This certainly held true during the puritanical and ceremonial Victorian period.

What has been overlooked is that higher intelligence also requires heightened sensitivity and greater wisdom. It requires that the historical heritage of experiences be realized, cherished, and reflected. With the change of consciousness being produced by Space Age perspectives and scientific knowledge come the responsibilities and realizations inherently necessary for survival at the new level of capability.

Again, as an example, the ability to make use of atomic energy is an intellectual capability. Science and technology are merely the informational, social, and organizational tools of that intellectual capability. There are opportunity costs associated with higher intelligence just as much as with stronger protection of human rights. There are the unavoidable entropy and the cogwheel, printed-circuit mentality of organizations and biotechnological integration. There is a need, therefore, for empathy, balance, even a passion to agree. Perhaps the ultimate dogma of the ultimate new age must be a disdain for dogmas. In *Magister Ludi,* Hermann Hesse expressed a similar idea:

Whatever you become . . . have respect for the "meaning," but do not believe it can be taught. If I were introducing pupils to Homer . . . I would not . . . tell them that the poetry is one of the manifestations of the divine, but would endeavor to make the poetry accessible to them by imparting a precise knowledge of its linguistic and metrical strategies. The task is to study means, cultivate tradition, and preserve the purity of methods, not to deal in incommunicable experiences which are reserved.

This sense of religious privacy is found not only in the American separation of church and state and freedom of religion but also in the doctrines of the founders of various religious faiths. The Prophet Mohammed, for example, spoke of faith in extraordinarily private terms. For this reason, Egyptian President Anwar Sadat, a devout Muslim, complained that the world was drawing the wrong impression of Islam from the experiment in Iran. Sadat insisted that Mohammed had taught the most private, least ecclesiastical, most ecumenical version of the three principal faiths, accepting Jesus and Moses as prophets and pivotal figures.

Jesus exhorted his followers to effect social transformation through the force of aggressive but nonviolent example, an unbending insistence on truth called *satyagraha,* or soul force, by the Mahatma Gandhi. This is exemplified in Handel's *Messiah.* Quoting Isaiah, its words emphasize the active, vital element in what has often been misnamed passive resistance: "He gave his back to the smiters, and his cheeks to them that plucked off the hair: He hid not his face from shame and spitting."

Gandhi disowned the term "passive resistance" because of its suggestion of weakness and inaction. Satyagraha derives its powers from two apparently opposite attributes: fierce autonomy and total compassion, in which one does not simply turn the other cheek but offers it. As Marilyn Ferguson pointed out in *The Aquarian Conspiracy,* satyagraha says, in effect, "I will not coerce you. Neither will I be coerced by you." The dynamic integrity is seen in the individual's willingness to suffer, to go to prison, or even to die.

Gandhi said, "I am Christian and Jew and Muslim and Hindu." Indeed, it was this attitude that led to his death at the hands of a militant, fanatic Hindu. Gandhi's attitude is also characteristic of the Sufi and Baha'i faiths, which, in some sense, consider their members to belong to all other faiths. There is an Einsteinian element in the approaches of these revered religious leaders in history. It is the spirit of satyagraha that reveres both individuality and community.

The name of God itself is often the most enigmatic word or concept in a linguistic tradition. The story of Moses, for example, tells of his vision of a burning bush, which though it burned was not consumed and from which a voice seemed to emanate. The voice identified itself as the God of Moses' fathers, of Abraham and Isaac. Yet when Moses inquired of a name to tell the people, the voice responded, "I Am That I Am . . . say . . . 'I Am' has sent me unto you."

YHVH (pronounced Yah'wey or Ya'howay), and Allah, which are anglicized as either Jehovah or God, were the corresponding Hebrew and Arabic versions of "I Am" or, more accurately, of the verb "to be." The word *YHVH* has generally been understood to mean existence, as if "he that is," "the self-existent," "the one ever coming into manifestation," or "the eternal." Some have portrayed this element as Father-Mother, an androgynous deity, a male-female dyad similar to Shiva-Shakti in the East. In early Judaism it was forbidden to speak the word *YHVH,* a juridical recognition of the ephemeral, unapproachable, all-encompassing nature of Ya'howay, the higher intelligence, the spirit of the universe.

It was a spirit that was well understood by the American transcendentalists of the nineteenth century, Ralph Waldo Emerson, Henry David Thoreau, Walt Whitman, and other members of the Lyceum and Theosophical Societies. Their understanding is exemplified in Walt Whitman's poetic tribute to "Him That was Crucified":

My spirit to yours dear brother,
Do not mind because many sounding your name do not understand
you,
I do not sound your name, but I understand you,
I specify you with joy O my comrade to salute you, and to salute those
who are with you, before and since, and to those to come also
That we all labour together transmitting the same charge and succes-
sion,
We few equals indifferent of lands, indifferent of times,
We enclosers of all continents, all castes, allowers of all theologies . . .
Compassionaters, perceivers, rapport of men,
We walk silent among disputes and assertions, but reject not the dis-
puters nor anything that is asserted,
We hear the bawling and the kin, we are reach'd at by divisions, jealou-
sies, recriminations on every side,
They close peremptorily upon us to surround us, my comrade,
Yet we walk upheld, free, the whole Earth over, journeying up and down
till we make our ineffaceable mark upon time and the diverse eras,
Till we saturate time and eras, that the men and women of races, ages
to come, may prove brethren and lovers as we are.

Long before Einstein, the American transcendentalists believed all observations to be relative. Marilyn Ferguson noted that they sought companions rather than disciples. Despite the still enthroned Newtonian paradigm of their day they believed that mind and matter are continuous, and they saw the universe as organic, open, and evolutionary. The views of the transcendentalists were among those covered by William Irwin Thompson in *At the Edge of History,* in which he said it would "seem that we are at one of those moments when the whole meaning of nature, self, and civilization is overturned in a re-visioning of history as important as any technological innovation."

Many modern historians, philosophers, social scientists, and ordinary citizens have echoed the words of George Leonard in *The Transformation:* "The current period is indeed unique in history and it represents the beginning of the most thoroughgoing change in the quality of human existence since . . . the birth of civilized states some five thousand years ago."

Yet, as David Spangler noted in *Emergence,* there is a shadow side to most new age movements. "Glamour, imbalance, withdrawal from society, and a false sense of righteousness (and separative) superiority were some of its manifestations." These movements often lack a truly participatory element. As Spangler said,

The problem with the prophetic new age vision as often conceptualized in the fifties and sixties was that it shifted this accountability away from individual persons and onto the back of vast, impersonal cosmic forces, whether astrological, extraterrestrial, or divine. It took away an individual's sense of being a cocreator with history, being involved in a process of conscious and participatory evolution. . . . I have already mentioned in passing some of the distortions and imbalances one is likely to find: a desire for power, the tyranny of the group over the individual in the name of community, glamour, an attachment to novelty for its own sake, a withdrawal from the world.

One thing we seem to have learned is that transcendence requires a certain critical distance, a type of involved, disciplined renunciation, which may not be possible until survival needs and all lower-order needs have been met. It was this realization that originally spawned Marxism, socialism, actualization psychology, and Franklin Delano Roosevelt's modern reformulation of the basis of freedom.

Recall that Roosevelt's Four Freedoms included freedom from want. What this is saying to us is that transcendence must come in concrete ways. Autocracy and transcendence are inherently at odds. Injustice and transcendence are inherently at odds. Liberty for all must be a social consensus as well as a constitutional reality. The constitution of ideals must be realized in a truly supreme constitution of laws preserved by a truly independent judiciary and fulfilled by truly democratic and representative forms of self-government and transnational association.

Transcendent intelligence, satyagraha, and sensitivity are now necessary for the survival of the species. It is time to turn again to macro questions, to the basic human constitutional needs and inherent rights. Let those who doubt this consider a world filled with injustice, a breeding ground for resentment, separation, misunderstanding and anger, and a place where the powers of the universe itself are becoming widely available.

It is evident that we have entered a period of acute evolutionary stress in which liberty can be hard to come by or maintain. We shall be called upon to adapt with lightning swiftness, in evolutionary time. And whether we adapt successfully or not may well be predetermined in the next few decades or generations. We must cultivate a new and continuing emphasis on our metrical strategies, the legal, ethical, spiritual, social, and biotechnological frontiers of our cosmic pioneers—our astronauts-cosmonauts-settlers-selves.

We have relegated these pioneers to entertaining but static descriptions such as "the right stuff." We have subjected them to a nation-state, sovereign-centric form of international law in which they are mere beneficiaries without real citizenship or standing. What are the rights of a cosmic citizen, whether earthkind, spacekind, or extraterrestrial? What should they be?

Elites in most of our sovereign subdivisions rule with an iron fist of repression under the guise of one philosophy or another. True political freedom and guaranteed individual freedom are rarities on the planet Earth. It is this state of affairs that rivets our attention and that leads to great concern for the initial human inhabitation of interplanetary space.

We must recognize the inhabitants of space as our extraterrestrial children. They are couriers of Earth's ethics, legalisms, beliefs, and cultures that will eventually be translated into a form that is space-indigenous and ultimately of great influence upon the cultures and cross-cultures of both earthkind and spacekind. It is from them that an undeniable insistence on a more global and absolute form of freedom may first emanate.

Again, however, a primary obstacle to this form of freedom is the doctrine of classical international law that only states are proper subjects of the legal order and possess *locus standi,* or the right to standing before a court of justice or some international policy forum regarding specific issues of law. Until recently, individuals had no legal rights or means to assert any claims they might have against nations or citizens of other nations. Only the claimant's own state could assert his or her claim, and in most states there were no mechanisms by which a citizen could claim this service from his or her government. Those states willing to provide the service did so under the legal fiction of diplomatic protection, by which the claim of an injured national is deemed to be that of the state.

At the end of World War II, however, the nation-states of the world did finally begin, really for the first time in history, to assume some international obligations to their own citizens in forms that are defined as precisely and formally as are most of the legal obligations they had until then owed only to each other under international law, such as respect for the immunity of diplomats.

States bound themselves under the UN Charter and the Statute of the International Court of Justice to respect fundamental freedoms and human rights. The Universal Declaration of Human Rights was one of the first declarations of the new UN General Assembly following its convocation in the late 1940s. Yet the assembly was not satisfied with its own declaration, since it failed to become a part of the charter and was therefore nonbinding.

Thus, it was decided that a binding International Bill of Human Rights should be drafted. Because of the varying emphases within states on various elements of human rights and natural law, it was decided that the Universal Declaration should serve as a nonbinding preamble and that the subsequent, binding bill should be divided into two covenants, the International Covenant on Civil and Political Rights, which stresses traditional Western versions of rights and Roosevelt's freedoms of speech and worship and freedom from fear, and the International Covenant on Economic, Social and Cultural Rights, which stresses the socialist right of "distributive justice," social security, and Roosevelt's third freedom, freedom from want. President Harry Truman expressed the belief that "this bill will be as much a part of international life as our own Bill of Rights is a part of our Constitution."

Unfortunately, the provisions in these covenants that give *locus standi* to individuals in international tribunals and that make the covenants binding on the subscribing states are optional—mere protocols. Neither the United States nor the Soviet Union has subscribed to them. Still, by 1985 nearly thirty nation-states had ratified them. These protocols and other regional agreements, both through formal treaties and informal practice, oblige states not to torture or summarily execute their citizens, to convict them without due process of law, to dissolve their trade unions or discriminate among them on the basis of race or religion, or to do a great number of things that in earlier ages were matters entirely at the discretion of the sovereigns.

Despite the continuance of the almost overwhelming degree of absolute state sovereignty in our positive international law, the age of unbridled sovereignty is really past. One of the beauties of the unrealizable ideal, of the true natural law or metalaw, is that it is inexorable. Survival itself comes to depend upon it.

In the atomic age, or the Space Age, sapient interrelation and interdependence are an undeniable and irreducible reality. This compelling reality of survival, moreover, only mirrors Einstein's "special theory of relativity," which reveals a universal omnipresence in every quantum of energy. His startling theory predicts that, at the speed of light, mass is infinite and time is nonexistent. In a sense, every single quantum is everywhere in the universe at once.

Jesuit theologian Thomas Berry observed that this must also mean, a posteriori, that every atomic particle is present to every other atomic particle in an inseparable unity, "a unity that enables us to say that the volume of each atom is the volume of the universe." As Andrew Haley put it, "the center of the universe resides in each of us as truly as it does in the Milky Way or in the Constellation Andromeda." In *Emergence,* David Spangler writes,

The idea of a planetary culture is less a political vision than one of creating relatedness. . . . Life is interrelated and interdependent. . . . The formative elements of creation are not bits of matter but relationships. . . . Evolution is the emergence of ever more complex patterns and syntheses of relationships . . . empowering and nourishing the biological, ecological, and spiritual relationships that already deeply make us one, while making accountability to those relationships the guiding factor in our cultural, political, and economic lives. It is less an image of government than an image of communication and communion, of bringing the music of the human and natural worlds into harmony.

Spangler suggests that this harmony can be enhanced by a recognition of the interdisciplinary nature of his three prime values — ecology, community, and spirituality — values that are closely related to the other triads of values we have examined, from Jefferson's values of life, liberty, and the pursuit of happiness to Frank Way's constitutions of community, laws, and ideals to our own categories of survival, social, and transcendental values. Interestingly enough, the world's *people* seem to be recognizing this. We have seen this recognition in the universal archetypes, not only of God, but also of process, and even of "ET" — in whatever linguistic form.

This recognition is also embodied in the growing number of guarantees of human rights embraced by formal international documents. For this reason, it may even be that spacekind, if precluded from an internationally recognized status around which to assert its unique requirements for social order derived from natural law and metalaw, may still benefit from the positive international laws that relate to individual rights, such as the 1949 Geneva Convention on the Protection of Prisoners and Civilian Populations.

A subtle shift toward the ultimate subrogation of national sovereignty in favor of peoples and individuals is evident. The Nuremburg Trials, for instance, and the Helsinki Accords, the European Convention on Human Rights, the American Convention on Human Rights, and the Andersonville Trials that followed the American Civil War, all recognized that there are certain acts, such as genocide, the sovereign cannot, or must not, be guilty of.

In both the Andersonville and the Nuremburg trials it was recognized that there are times when a soldier has a natural duty to disobey the legal order of a superior. However ineffectual they now may be, these juridical tribunals constituted a legally recognized ideal much in the mold of the Magna Charta, an ideal of limiting sovereign action in favor of the people.

In this regard, the word *mankind* first slipped into the international language during the negotiations surrounding the formulation of the 1967 Outer Space Treaty. Thus, we have seen the phrases "for the benefit of mankind," "common heritage of mankind," and "envoys of mankind" come into wide usage. We are slowly evolving a doctrine of customary law, if not of treaty law, that mankind—humanity—is a legal beneficiary of the exploration and exploitation of outer space.

Despite the increasing specificity and positive character of space law, the meta upon which the law of space is founded is one of naturalism. Under natural law the welfare of people is considered to be the basis of human society; human beings are considered to be the holders of fundamental, nontransferable rights. The fact that space law has incorporated the United Nations Charter and its call for human rights and fundamental freedoms merely confirms that view. Perhaps the next step is to distinguish spacekind and earthkind as components of humankind, for purposes of asserting certain rights of spacekind as separate from those of earthkind.

In the meantime, however, spacekind will continue to be considered within the context of space law as objects of that body of law and not as subjects. Until space habitats and their societies are considered competent in international law to assert indicia of nation-state or city-state sovereignty, the legal rights, claims, duties, and responsibilities of nascent spacekind must be tended, asserted, and defended by parental earthkind.

Earthkind must develop the abilities necessary to perceive in nonanthropocentric, extraterrestrial ways. Yet this type of perception will require disciplined sensitivity. As Spangler said, "It is less an image of government than an image of communication and communion, of bringing the music of the human and natural worlds into harmony." It has often been said that with freedom comes responsibility. Real human transcendence requires the shouldering of the types of responsibility described by Spangler. Sometimes, as John F. Kennedy said in his inaugural address, "God's work on Earth must truly be our own."

Argentine space lawyer Armando Cocca pointed out that the cycle followed by human beings as subjects of law is as follows: individual, society, state, international community, humanity. If these categories are placed, in order, upon discrete sections of the circumference of a circle, or a Möbius strip, the loop is completed by the joining of the individual with humanity.

Jus humanitatis is the law of and for humanity. It is not traditional international law, which governs international relations among and between states. It is rather the law of the human race as a whole, the fourth dimension of political reality. Space law has been a positive contributor to the identification of that dimension, for the Outer Space Treaty speaks not only of states and nations and the international community, but also of mankind and peoples. Nor is it a dimension unrecognized in other disciplines. Political scientist Raghavan Iyer calls this fourth, transnational dimension of political reality *Parapolitics,* the political counterpart of metalaw and *jus humanitatis universalis,* the universal law of humankind.

29 Relations with Alien Intelligences

> Can a religious person . . . be legitimately
> involved in, even be excited by these dis-
> cussions of the possibility of other intelli-
> gent and free creatures out there? . . . It is
> precisely because I believe theologically
> that there is a being called God, and that he
> is infinite in intelligence, freedom and
> power, that I cannot take it upon myself to
> limit what he might have done. Once he
> created the Big Bang . . . he could have
> envisioned it going in billions of directions
> as it evolved, including billions of life forms
> and billions of kinds of intelligent beings. I
> will go even further. There conceivably can
> be billions of universes created with other
> Big Bangs or different arrangements. Why
> limit Infinite Power or Energy which is a
> name of God?
>
> *Theodore M. Hesburgh*

The American public is quite familiar with the concept of alien life in outer space. Since Orson Welles's shocking radio rendition of H. G. Wells's *War of the Worlds,* broadcast during the 1930s, when there was widespread belief in canals on Mars, Americans have been avid devotees of close encounters, cosmic consciousness, Carl Sagan's search for extraterrestrial intelligence, and Star Trek's Mr. Spock.

The United States Air Force has long since conducted its famous Project Blue Book, an attempt to identify unidentified flying objects (UFOs). With the discovery, in the late twentieth century, of other solar systems and with NASA programs to detect and make contact with extraterrestrial intelligence, almost everyone has an opinion on the likelihood or even the statistical probability that intelligent forms of life exist elsewhere in the universe.

Metalaw is the branch of theoretical law that deals with a generalized natural law relating to all sentient beings, be they on Earth or in other worlds. Metalaw deals with different perspectives and frames of existence, with sapient beings different in kind. This is made plain in Andrew Haley's ironic statement to a somewhat more skeptical, less well informed public of the early 1960s:

It is quite obvious that speculation on metalaw beyond the application of principles of pure justice which flow from man's nature is quite purposeless . . . if two conclusions are posited:

1. the human evolutionary process has been concluded and there is no further prospect of changing the nature of man; and

2. in the universe there exist no other sapient creatures.

Having said this, however, Haley devoted much more attention to the possible existence of extraterrestrial beings than to the possible existence of different human natures. Although he said "we already find that metalaw has a most vital place in any juridical system because man now has the power to change many aspects of the reproduction and functioning of *Homo sapiens,*" he nevertheless balanced his three-page coverage of bio-juridics on Earth and in space with a ten-page consideration of the possibility of extraterrestrial life. In his enthusiasm for his basic premise of metalaw—that is, absolute equity between human beings and sentient or potentially sentient nonhuman beings of extraterrestrial origin—Haley unwittingly largely excluded from metalaw our first contact with extraterrestrial life, Earth's own spacefarers. Haley said,

The natural law of man . . . is anthropocentric in kind, and while such law must govern in space among human beings, it nevertheless is the law of human nature alone. With the concept of absolute equity, we shall be prepared to face the possibility of an indefinite number of frameworks of natural laws.

In one breath, Haley prepared us for principles of social order applicable to our spacekind progeny and descendants and disfranchised those progeny by not recognizing the speed with which biotechnological integration in space would change the value-forming processes and consequent behavior patterns of our astronauts, our emerging *Homo spatialis.* There is a practical need for jurists to recognize the natural rights of social groupings to evolve their own cultural institutions that respond for survival to their own respective ecosystems.

This can be seen in the history of various interactions and peace treaties between alien groups, such as, on the one hand, Native American tribes and nations and, on the other hand, either the governments of the Old World, primarily Spain, or the new United States government. In the case of Spain, the record is particularly shameful. Great civilizations in Mexico and Peru, on the order of the ancient kingdom of Egypt, were pillaged and destroyed, and a virtual genocide was practiced upon their people, whose descendants today still do not enjoy full citizenship, much less full human rights, in most Latin American countries.

This occurred despite the fact that the greatest Spanish jurist of the time, Francisco de Vitoria, disapproved of the practices of the king's American conquistadores and said so openly. In his classical and courageous lecture to his students at the University of Salamanca around 1532, "De Indis et de ivre belli reflectiones," he stated, "The Aborigines undoubtedly had true dominion in both public and private matters, just like the Christians, and . . . neither their princes nor private persons could be despoiled of their property on the ground of their not being true owners."

Vitoria's naturalistic inclination was to recognize that the "Indian nations" were states of the New World to which the rights of Old World states should be attributed. Yet the attempt of the newly formed, naturalistic government of the United States of America to effectuate that recognition in an environment of manifest destiny and a widely held view of the aborigine as a subhuman savage is a testament to the difficulty of achieving, in positive law, the metas of Vitoria's naturalistic inclinations.

The nature of this difficulty can also be seen in the history of the many treaties negotiated between Native American tribes and nations and the U.S. government. Because of the different characteristics of their physical environments and the different evolutionary nature of the cultural institutions that they developed to cope with their survival needs, most of the Native American societies perceived the components of their environments in metaphors and as relations among objects.

In contrast, government representatives, with roots in the industrial history of Europe, were captives of the Aristotelian, Baconian, and Newtonian paradigms and conceptualized and reasoned primarily in a logical, empirical, linear fashion. Although terms and symbolic references understood by both parties were used in the treaties, the conceptualizations of the subject matter were different and the consequent levels of expectation by each party remained different and unrecognized until the failure of each party to meet the expectations of the other, as embodied in the treaty document, led inevitably to disillusionment and hostile confrontation.

As demonstrated by our earlier discussion of the principle of res communis, this remains a serious problem for negotiators of international agreements that incorporate disparate cultures evolving in disparate ecosystems.

This cultural diversity, a product of social parochialism, is largely the reason the developing international law of space has perpetuated the same type of misunderstanding and reflects insufficient attention to the natural rights of human beings occupying space.

Yet, as Haley pointed out, the essence of metalaw has been examined by philosophers, ethicists, and jurists, whether in the form of natural law, cross-cultural sociology, or biojuridics, "without the conscious knowledge of the definitive label metalaw." These examinations are thus available for our use as we face the onslaught of biotechnological, psychological, and sociocultural future shock that is accompanying our move into space.

In a thoughtful and far-seeing address at the Georgia Institute of Technology in 1963, Earl Warren provided a particularly good example of the type of metalegal musings referred to by Haley. Warren noted the gap between the social and physical sciences, saying "The simple fact is that law has not kept abreast of science." Warren emphasized that new powers acquired by human beings through their rapidly expanding knowledge and technology required "new decisions by the courts, new interpretations by theoretical philosophers and ethicists." He continued,

The challenges of our time . . . are so different from those of even our imme-diate ancestors and even of our youth . . . [that] what is conceived to be just when human beings are engaged in one sort of activity may become unjust when they are engaged in another. . . . How much better the world would be if we would develop a kind of Maser for the Rule of Law — if the elemental principles of law and justice could be broken down and reflected and re-reflected, striking sparks from all who want freedom under law, and if the mixture could produce a beam of coherent legal light of immense power capable of revealing the Rule of Law in its full glory to any and every part of the Earth.

Although upon first reflection this may seem a whimsical bit of wishful thinking, it nevertheless characterizes the principles of social order neces-sary for spacekind-earthkind relations. It also characterizes the search of enlightened philosophers, scientists, ethicists, jurists, and natural theorists through the ages for the fundamental principles of natural order.

Perhaps it is not such a whimsical observation after all. Indeed, it could well be that the changed nature of human beings functioning in space will serve as the lens that separates and focuses the spectral components of that elusive universal justice by virtue of earthkind having to study space-kind from every possible perspective in order to ensure survival in an envi-ronment alien to that on the surface of Earth. Perhaps an understanding of the unique requirements of space societies will produce a beam of coherent legal light for those who want freedom in space, simply because they are couriers of their parents' values.

Yet all this presupposes that earthkind is prepared to use its evolving technology to preserve for spacekind the natural right of freedom. We may, on the other hand, actually be inclined to use our technology to suppress changes in social values being wrought by new social ecologies. We have already seen this tendency to some degree in the Soviet space program. Soviet space planners are aware that, even in the Soviet Union, newly evolving technologies are combining with changing social values to encourage and cultivate certain expressions of individual freedom within that country and its political satellites. As noted in the March 1982 issue of *New Age,*

[There are] profound changes happening in the Soviet Union that have generally gone unreported by the American media and unnoticed by professional Soviet watchers. [It is] a cultural awakening . . . not unlike the awakening in America in the 1960s, though it's far more quiet. A growing subculture there is exploring esoteric religions, gestalt and encounter groups, alternative healing methods, UFOs, the search for lost continents, parapsychology. As in the '60s in the United States, the exploration ranges from the sublime to the ridiculous, but what unites it all is a growing conviction among many Soviet citizens and scientists that hidden human reserves must be discovered and developed.

Some Soviet theorists, for example, see the use of computer technology as creating the conditions necessary for a hungerless, well-cared-for, socially classless people who approximate the concept of a perfect collective society. At the same time, as S. Frederick Starr observes, "their American counterparts look to computers to fulfill the promise of the Declaration of Independence and the Bill of Rights." Starr continues, "Let us allow the possibility that both perspectives are to some degree valid." Meanwhile, the big difference between the ideological use of high technology in the two countries is "the policies by which the state seeks to confine the effects of that technology within acceptable bounds."

In the Soviet Union that web of policies is still characterized by Leninist centralized control, perhaps one of the reasons that many Soviet watchers—who are primarily Soviet *government* watchers—have missed some of the popular ferment discussed above. Centralized control of technology was critical to Lenin's tactics for the Bolshevik revolution and was a necessary part of the effort to establish and stabilize a proletarian dictatorship on the basis of Marxist philosophy. Lenin even went so far as to say, "We must be ready to employ trickery, deceit, lawbreaking, withholding and concealing truth. . . . We can and must write in a language which sows among the masses hate, revulsion, scorn and the like toward those who disagree with us."

This alien philosophy of centralized control and management, not the cultivation and preservation of individual freedom, is still the cornerstone of Soviet philosophy. Concurrently, the availability of new technologies such as the automobile, mass communications, and individual apartment units has given Soviet citizens growing mobility, privacy, knowledge of the outside world, and independence from collective decisionmaking and central control. Sovietologist Starr notes, in this regard, that "the number of people in this unfamiliar state has become so great that it is beyond the powers of even the huge Soviet security apparatus to keep track of every individual's actions."

Unfortunately, this is not so for the embryonic but growing space societies of the Soviet Union. Cosmonauts are carefully selected to participate in the official Intercosmos program on the basis of academic and technical skills, psychological and physiological characteristics, and—perhaps most important of all in relation to the Soviets' perceived extraterrestrial imperative—the cosmonaut's commitment to communist ideology and personal attachment to Mother Russia. This personal profile, combined with the technological control over the economics, social order, and survivability of space societies, makes individual freedom, even to the limited extent so far observed among the single-combat warriors of the American astronaut corps, a highly limited prospect for the societies of the present and envisaged permanent space stations of the Soviet Union.

Perhaps the best way to deal with this situation is through the force of example. It is within the power of the United States to make the independence and quality of life in space a highly visible element of superpower competition and to engage in joint programs that expose cosmonauts to our communities and our theories of social science. At the same time, on Earth, it is within the power of the United States to carry out a policy of international satyagraha, a return full circle to John F. Kennedy's "long twilight struggle."

Historian Warren Wagar reported that Kennedy's advisor, Walt Rostow, offered a projection of the struggle in which he indicated that as Soviet Russia enters the era of high mass consumption and mass communication, communism "is likely to wither" and Russia is "likely to fall prey to the familiar affliction of families and nations that have achieved prosperity and want to enjoy it in peace. Like the Buddenbrooks in Thomas Mann's early novel, they no longer care for empire building." Yet, such could not come about without unending Western satyagraha. Rostow warned that "the

Buddenbrooks dynamics will operate in Russia, [only] if given time and a strong Western policy that rules out as unrealistic Soviet policies of expansion."

In *The City of Man,* Wagar indicated that communism has won nearly all its victories by direct political and military action rather than by waiting for economic conditions to topple the bourgeois state. "Lenin substituted for Marxist economic determinism his own messianic political determination." After Lenin the party line became sacrosanct. "Good communists today are taught to suppress all doubts and skepticism. The truth is known." This justifies suppression of "false" knowledge. Leninism may thus prove to be one of the greatest obstacles in the path of world cultural synthesis.

Wagar summarized Charles Moore's *Asia and the Humanities* with the observation that the philosophical attitudes of the traditional Orient and the traditional Occident are in fundamental harmony, even though emphasizing different things, "whereas communism, with its materialism, determinism, totalitarianism, economic obsessions, ethics of class expediency, and rejection of all spiritual or divine power, is basically incompatible with both." Wagar, quoting Karl Jaspers, went on to say,

This may be a harsh and extreme judgment born of Cold War hysteria, but there are times when the most cheerful observer cannot help but agree with it. . . . A world totally planned would be a world totally despiritualized, closed to transcendence, reduced to insecthood. "Either we have confidence in the chances of the free interplay of forces, notwithstanding the frequency with which they give rise to absurdities . . . or we stand before the world planned in its totality by man, with its spiritual and human ruin."

Still, the Soviets aside, natural laws that characterize natural, human, or absolute rights do not constitute a discipline of decided rights whose properties have long been agreed to and laid to rest. In practice, it has proved extremely difficult to apply the doctrine of natural rights. Even in the United States, the individual has no absolute rights or privileges.

Individual rights and individual sovereignty are compromised to varying degrees by what a society requires for survival and by its definitions of justice. As Locke said, a right is limited, "by that reason, and confined to those ends which required it." It can be said, for example, that a person has a right to life, but not necessarily the right to live. An example of this seemingly hollow, and certainly subtle distinction is the convicted murderer who has compromised his right to live, but not his right to life.

The irony in this distinction is similar to that of the long-debated issue of the lawfulness of civil disobedience to a recognized government having de facto or de jure jurisdiction over those who are being disobedient. The answer has always been characterized in one fashion or another as incorporating the thesis of Thoreau's "Civil Disobedience" — that is, civil disobedience is a right if the disobedient individual is willing to accept the legal consequences of his actions.

Many lawyers, however, have urged a new positive defense of "conscientious civil disobedience." Such a defense would still allow the state to arrest disrupters but would also allow defendants who had admitted the infraction, disobeyed openly, disobeyed nonviolently, and disobeyed for stated reasons of conscience to be declared not guilty by virtue of conscientious civil disobedience. Like freedom to contract, this would be a recognition of equity between the state and the individual, a recognition that there are times when the needs of the one outweigh the needs of the many as well as times when the needs of the many outweigh the needs of the one.

Such ideas, once dismissed by jurisprudents and philosophers as the intellectual curiosities of the dead past or of the fictional future, are alive and well in the present. We need only review the genocide policies, even the laws, of some countries to realize that civil disobedience is still a critical tool for safeguarding diversity, individual life, and personal sovereignty. It is primarily the various governmental and legal policies or endorsements of war or of discrimination on the basis of race, sex, religion, and age that have helped to regenerate practical philosophical interest in universal human rights, including those of human progeny existing in space. As noted by Margaret MacDonald,

The claim to natural rights has never been quite defeated. It tends in some form to be renewed in every crisis in human affairs, when the plain citizen tries to make or expects his leaders to make articulate his obscure but firmly held conviction that he is not a mere pawn in any political game, nor the property of any government or ruler, but the living and protesting individual for whose sake all political games are played and all governments instituted.

Perhaps it is time we understood positively the natural reasons that natural rights have never been totally suppressed or destroyed. Could it be that only the complete destruction of sentient life on Earth could ever extinguish those rights? Is not the assertion of those rights, essentially, the aspiring nature of life, of intelligence, of energy in organized interaction?

Although it may soon be easy for any political system to destroy life on the planet, if survival is to be the collective human choice no system of political theory will have the absolute right or absolute sovereignty to kick against the membranes of true natural laws. "Something will explode," said

Teilhard de Chardin in *The Future of Man,* " if we persist in trying to squeeze into our old tumble-down huts the material and spiritual forces that are henceforward on the scale of a world."

This realization is the basis for the survival of natural rights. As long as there are injustice and repression there will be dislocation, aberrant psychology, vengeance, and violence. How many years will it be before any high-school whiz kid can understand how to make atomic devices? How long will it be before terrorist groups and numerous small nations have access to the atomic bomb? Can they make the bombs now? Do they have them now?

The identification of natural laws and metalaws is a necessity for survival. Still, as the Greek and Roman philosophers knew, natural law is an abstract, intellectual ideal, a standard never fully embodied in or characterized by a legal code or set of positive rules. Rather it is fixed by nature to be applied by humanity. It is realized only imperfectly in the positive laws of humanity. How is this limitation to be overcome?

We should not despair. The premise of evolutionary learning by trial and error has led inexorably upward at every level of evolution. It has led, as well, to the recognition in free countries today that all the natural rights of humanity flow from natural law and are the foundations of positive civil rights as they are now understood.

Subtending the foundation of natural rights is the unique capacity of humanity to reason. When we turn our gaze back toward the stars and consider the infinite dissimilar frameworks within universal existence, even more new perspectives are presented, and new questions are raised to be answered on Earth.

When we contemplate contact with other species of greater or lesser intelligence, or the moral issues involved in terraforming, or physically transforming a planet to sustain human life even though there are indigenous microorganisms living on it, or when we consider the possibility of Earth people and space people actually being somewhat different in kind, we are even led to ask whether the capacity to reason is really the distinguishing characteristic of legal personhood or an intelligent species.

Other so-called lower orders of animals show capacities to reason and use both tools and abstract symbols. When do they achieve juridical recognition as sentient persons? In attempts to identify the elusive characteristics of sentience such traits as mental ductility, the ability to transmit culture, the ability to fashion tools, the ability to symbolize, a predisposition to learn from experience, and self-awareness have been suggested.

So far, in Earth law, raw intellect alone has not been enough to qualify one for personhood. Dolphins, whales, and many other animals have a high brain-to-body ratio and demonstrate surprisingly high intelligence in certain situations. They also exhibit loyalty, perhaps even love. Yet the law does not consider them persons. At the same time, the law does consider permanently comatose, insane, and severely retarded people as persons.

In *Should Trees Have Standing? Toward Legal Rights for Natural Objects,* Christopher Stone even suggested that natural objects and the environment in general should be treated as having legal rights, something that has, indirectly, come about. This development has evolved simply because of the need to recognize that our very survival depends upon the intricate chains of life within our biosphere.

In *Persons: A Study of Possible Moral Agents in the Universe,* Roland Pucetti proposed another kind of test for personhood. His suggestion was to find an objective way of identifying creatures capable of moral awareness. Moral persons, he suggested, should be considered legal persons. Is the creature capable of taking a moral attitude or of making moral judgments? Does the creature possess a system of ethics? Pucetti would also allow intelligent machines which—or who—could pass the tests be considered persons and therefore immune from disconnection without the exercise of some form of due process.

Probably the most commonly agreed-upon answer is that only at a certain level of intellectual development do creatures become persons and claim rights. The difficulty with this formulation, of course, is that it can be interpreted to mean that human beings and other creatures not fortunate enough to have achieved the requisite level of intellectual development— usually defined by the formulator of the rule—possess only some form of second-class natural rights and remain subject to the whimsical arguments supporting altruism.

Yet even altruism answers requirements of quantifiable sociobiological dictates—and thus we come to our premise yet another time. The fact remains that human freedom as a natural right can now be identified as the true state of nature. It can be seen as a quantifiable, external, and internal biochemical interaction with the environment that adds to the physical survivability and homeostatic sense of well-being of a specimen—at this time a specimen of the human species.

At some point in the intellectual articulation of natural law into the form of positive laws, it is necessary to express freedom as a biological dictate, not merely a moral or purely intellectual requisite. Teilhard discovered what he considered the biological key to the true nature of this requisite in two basic trends, perhaps even laws, of evolution. The first, complexification, we discussed at the outset. It is the path to higher synthesis, organization, and intelligence. It is characteristic of Prigogine's self-organizing systems. The second, individuation, is the tendency for individual members of a species to grow in importance in relation to the species as a whole as each ascending branch of the tree of life is examined, until, in humankind, the "phenomenon is precipitated" and "personalization" occurs, which is the birth of the self-conscious, self-directed person.

A metalaw of inalienable personal sovereignty is the only one that can be simultaneously relative and fixed, the only one that can be universally applied, regardless of species or origin. Metalaw is personal sovereignty and personal sovereignty is metalaw. This is at the heart of Haley's variation on the traditional golden rule for interaction with interstellar extraterrestrial beings.

The reason the traditional formulation of the golden rule is "starkly anthropocentric" is because to treat other sentient creatures as *we* would desire to be treated might well mean their destruction. Instead, we must find out how *they* wish to be treated and then treat them that way. This is the bare essence of Haley's Great Rule of Metalaw, his prime directive of noninterference in the legitimate affairs and natural evolution of other sovereign entities, whether individual or social. Absolute equity is the only principle of human law we should permit ourselves to project into the universe. The Great Rule preserves this principle by granting individual sovereignty to each member of every sentient race in the cosmos.

Margaret MacDonald believed that a good intellectual articulation of the natural rights of this emergent individual sovereignty might be the simple statement:

In any society and under every form of government men ought to be able to think and express their thoughts freely; to live their lives without arbitrary molestation with their persons and goods. They ought to be treated as equal in value, though not necessarily of equal capacity or merit. They ought to be assured of the exclusive use of at least some material objects other than their own bodies; they ought not to be governed without some form of consent. . . . It is by the observance of some such conditions that human societies are distinguished from ant hills and bee hives.

To this we should add that they should be assured these things through enforceable guarantees of equal protection and due process of the law. This is simply yet another way of stating the ecological foundations of Andrew Haley's metalaw. For if you asked an extraterrestrial being how best to implement the Interstellar Golden Rule of doing unto others as they would have done unto them, he or she or it might respond with certain minor variations on MacDonald's words, along with the one final corequisite of Haley's Great Rule:

It is sufficient at this time to establish the simple proposition that we must forego any thought of enforcing our legal concepts on other intelligent beings in the manner we have on the American Indians, i.e., on the theory that they could not withstand our force. Quite apart from all considerations of altruism, we must bear in mind the hapless possibility that the situation might be reversed, and we may turn out to be the savages who are decimated and enslaved. It follows, therefore, that in the realm of space law the principle of enforcement is malum in se. *In establishing spatial relationships of any kind, no force of any kind may be used* (emphasis added).

In response to objections to the absolute pacifism of this suggestion, Haley did finally retreat somewhat to the position that "reasonable force" could be authorized in dealing with less than benevolent extraterrestrial beings, but just enough force to restrain them from damaging us: exactly that much and no more. In the first book-length treatment of metalaw, *Relations with Alien Intelligences* (1970), Ernst Fasan built upon Haley's Great Rule and Immanuel Kant's Categorical Imperative—act in such a way that the maxim of your will can at the same time always be valid and desirable as a general rule. From these and a few basic assumptions about the character of a sentient creature—alive, four-dimensional, physically detectable, intelligent, and possessing a will to live—Fasan identified eleven fundamental components of metalaw. In descending order of importance, he identified them as follows:

1. *No partner of metalaw may demand an impossibility.*

2. *No rule of metalaw must be complied with when compliance would result in the practical suicide of the obligated race.*

3. *All intelligent races of the universe have in principle equal rights and values.*

4. *Every partner of metalaw has the right of self-determination [personal sovereignty, self-organization].*

5. *Any act which causes harm to another race must be avoided.*

6. *Every race is entitled to its own living space.*

7. *Every race has the right to defend itself against any harmful act performed by another race.*

8. *The principle of preserving one race has priority over the development of another race.*

9. *In case of damage, the damager must restore the integrity of the damaged party.*

10. *Metalegal agreements and treaties must be kept.*

11. *To help the other race by one's own activities is not a legal but a basic ethical principle.*

How can we human beings dare to venture an examination of the very metas of existence? We can venture to do so because we were destined to do so, and because now we *must* do so in order to assure the survival of the human race. We must go beyond conventional dictates of good and evil and exceed established ecclesiastical moral and ethical mandates. We must model a universal legal framework that fosters harmonic interrelations by creating organization within diversity—a framework for diversity.

By identifying any natural right to govern as rising from the people—the aggregate of sovereign individuals—we can regard ourselves and others, earthkind or spacekind, as only one intelligent entity within a cosmic community of intelligent entities. For humanity, despite its millenia of geocentrism, is not entirely anthropocentric. As stated by Robert Freitas in "The Legal Rights of Extraterrestrials," "While some may argue that the essence of humanity is strictly defined by the human genome, the sounder view is that the essence of man is mind—the rationality of a sentient organism."

This has been our premise in this book since page one. The phenomena we know as life and consciousness may very well be the true substance of creation, the primal energy or implicate order from which everything arises. This might be called the social or psychic law of self-organization—the conscious nature of the cosmos. It is the internal reflection of Prigogine's physical law of self-organization. Self-organization comes about through the natural tension and interplay between the tendencies toward complexification and individuation—the structural and convergent features of energy-dissipative structures.

In science, *law* is defined as universal generalizations about classes of phenomena. The law of gravity is a familiar example, as is the newly discovered law of self-organization. Such laws must be truly universal to be considered laws, not merely accidental patterns found among a specific set of facts or expedients for the achievement of transient values. Just as in natural law, science considers that true laws can only be discovered, not created by the scientist. Also, the laws, in and of themselves, do not create anything. They simply summarize things as they are. They are intellectual articulations—biotechnological approximations of the optimum realm of being.

Making these approximations is the grand task, one in which Herman Hesse's warning against the conceit of an exclusive grasp of "the meaning" must be kept in mind. Yet the construction of humanity's grand internal models will go on unceasingly, as long as the species and its future variants survive. The "little creatures" of H. G. Wells's *Shape of Things to Come* will never cease the exploration, an exploration defended by the protagonist in that piece of dramatic art in response to a frantic victim of future shock who asked, "Oh God . . . ! We're such little creatures . . . little animals. . . . Is there ever to be any age of happiness? Is there ever to be any rest?" Wells's hero answered,

Yes, for the individual, too much and too soon, and we call it death. But for man, no rest and no ending. He must go on, conquest beyond conquest. And when he has conquered all the deeps of space and all the mysteries of time, still he will be beginning . . . [for] if we are no more than little animals we must snatch each scrap of happiness and live and suffer and pass to dust . . . mattering no more than any others do or have done. It is this [with a gesture to the ground] or that [with a gesture to the sky]. All the universe or nothing! Which shall it be? . . . Which shall it be?

Conclusion:
New Conventions for Earthkind

> Behold, the nations are as a drop in the
> bucket and are counted as the small dust of
> the balance.
>
> *Isaiah 40:15,17*

> Let us break their bonds asunder and cast
> their yokes from us. . . . You shall break
> them with a rod of iron. You shall dash them
> in pieces like a potter's vessel.
>
> *Psalms 2:3, 9*

> And they shall beat their swords into plow-
> shares, and their spears into pruning hooks:
> nation shall not lift up sword against nation,
> neither shall they learn war any more.
>
> *Isaiah 2:4*

At this early stage of the space migration, space law is still a strange and often bewildering mosaic of both public and private, national and international law, based upon a strange and often bewildering cultural diversity on planet Earth. To the extent that the law governing this basic diversity is to be a true metalaw, it must be a law capable of equitable application to any cultural framework or ecosystem, on Earth or in space. It must embrace all sentient communities as a framework for diversity, a template for survival, and an endless resource for continual conscious transformation.

In this last quarter of the twentieth century politicians, diplomats, scientists, artists, educators, law professionals, and others are continuing to write the history of nature and democracy. Professionals from all areas are moving away from restrictive, narrow conceptions of specialties. They are talking of interdisciplinary approaches and are beginning to discern a natural order.

Yet the discovery and definition of that order are not only the magnificent trends but also the tedious, timeless tasks. As we have seen, differences in experience, perspective, and expectation can seriously complicate the harmonizing of Haley's "infinite framework of natural laws." New conventions for earthkind and spacekind are well and good in theory. We should like to think that consideration of them has even made for interesting and provocative reading. Yet the cold, hard fact is that such recognition and respect among and between earthkind and spacekind will not come easily from an international system that cannot even establish recognition and respect for all of earthkind.

It has often been said that we are at some sort of turning point, and truly the air is pungent with the flavor of apocalyptic stories of nuclear winters, star wars, and Armageddon theologies. Indeed, there is every reason to believe that we must either abandon force as a means of solving international problems—renounce and enforceably outlaw it—or the existence of the world will, at best, continue to hang by a thread. The rescue, survival, and stewardship of our fragile, threadbare tendril of a link between the past and the potential human future are now in our keeping. If we fail in our quest to preserve that link, there may be no human future, either on Earth or in space.

Our embryonic envoys have been essential intelligence agents for greater understanding of this survival vision—a total view. Through our efforts to propagate our envoys into the cosmos, through their own personal preparations and adjustments, and also through our remote biotechnological reception of their new transglobal outlook, our envoys have helped us begin to understand the systematic, dynamic, multidimensional, and continuous nature of the cosmos.

From this point of view we see that there are really no shortcuts to a truly dynamic, organic, and diverse civilization, whether local, regional, global, interplanetary, or interstellar. The skeleton for such civilizations really depends, whether we like it or not, on community consensus, a shared ideological superstructure, which, at the very least, must involve a commitment to survival and to the resolution of disputes by law instead of force—a law that incorporates, understands, appreciates, and protects the fundamental diversity and individuality of sentient creatures and their societies, a true metalaw. In *The City of Man*, Warren Wager discussed the thoughts of Reinhold Niebuhr on the difficulties faced in accomplishing this possibility:

The world community cannot be integrated "purely by artifact and conscious contrivance," by a world constitution, or a world police force, or any

*of the merely mechanical schemes favored by world government zealots.
"If we are patient enough . . . we could cultivate the gradually growing
organic factors of world community and perfect them at opportune
moments by the constitutional contrivances which always express and perfect what the forces of life and togetherness have established."*

Wagar's treatment of Neibuhr's statement suggests that a constitution
of laws is not organic if it does not reflect the underlying constitutions of
ideals and of the community. True as this is, however, perhaps our teetering
on the brink of nuclear Armageddon has changed the necessary order of
development. Nuclear knowledge, the development of a technological,
global nervous system, the reengineering of DNA, and the birthing of spacekind are all requiring that jurisprudence recapture its ancient role as synthe-
sizer.

Jurisprudence, in free societies, is being forced to realize its ideal definition as the art and science of harmonious, symbiotic human interaction. We
are already upon the meta or turning point of the next age. We must choose
between punctuating our accustomed equilibrium with transformative evolution or presiding over the disintegration of humanity.

It is time for jurisprudence to take the lead in discovering and defining
the politically and culturally neutral metalaws of sentient survival in the cosmos. Perhaps this is the opportune moment to recognize again that there
are objective laws of nature, reflected even in biological and conscious
nature, which are the inevitable and inexorable requirements for the symbiosis of individuals, communities, and nations on the planet Earth and also in
space. Such a survival necessity will inevitably overwhelm any industrial,
political, or legal artifact which, for the sake of any interim expediency,
either ignores or flouts the metalaw, the fragile template for the symbiosis
of dissimilar conscious entities, cosmic brothers, sisters, and cousins of one
degree of relation or another.

Symbiosis is defined as the intimate living together of two or more dissimilar organisms in a mutually beneficial relationship. The goal of law and
of organized human community is social symbiosis, which is a natural
requirement for human survival in a postnuclear Space Age.

There is beauty in this portrayal of the possibilities of our juridical inventions. These inventions actualize the potential for conscious choice in natural, living, open, self-organizing social systems. This view beckons us to the
challenge of influencing the social systems and their policies toward vital
metalegal structures and processes, toward natural rights and natural
requirements for human survival. It calls upon us to know who the policy

leaders are and what the policy networks are, in order to force them out of their now deadly parochialism.

Law should be visualized by all sentient cultures as a set of articulated interrelations between individuals and their cultures and between their cultures and their respective ecosystems. These articulations are essentially descriptions of the way a society is coping with what is happening at any given instant. With this view of natural law and metalaw as quantifiable bio-ecological dictates for sentient survival and evolution in the cosmos, it can be seen that, ultimately, not even the seemingly implacable communist systems will be able to survive, unaltered, in the systematic, dynamic and continuous realms of our cosmos without gradually conforming to metalaw.

In order to survive, a system must grow and evolve. It must open itself to change. This is a simple evolutionary requirement. Yet, in the age of the atom, terrestrial military or territorial expansion is no longer a workable means of accommodating this bioecological need for growth and change. This is also true in the fragile, biotechnologically integrated habitats in space.

Growth must therefore be rechanneled into other outlets, other productive, industrious, and transformative forms of the use and dissipation of energy. Such outlets must now be turned inward—to knowledge, for instance, including transglobal, juridical structures, whether legal, scientific, economic, or communicative. Such outlets must also be turned outward—to space—in order to avoid the inevitable charnel of the human species in the explosive, closed systems of a parochial, ethnocentric, earthbound species.

Prigogine's new physical-scientific law of thermodynamic systems, of dissipative structures, requires open systems—systems based on nonanthropocentric, universal ethics of relativistic, indeterminate, individual sovereignty and equality. Given the dissimilarities and uniquenesses of individuals and societies on Earth and elsewhere in the cosmos, such bases will inevitably become requirements of societies that wish to survive racial adolescence and attain the mature adulthood of galactic civilization. Carl Sagan has even mused that the failure of civilizations to attain this mature biotechnological adulthood may be partially responsible for the initial lack of success of our fledgling search for extraterrestrial intelligence. Perhaps they all destroyed themselves during their technological adolescence.

Such realizations are inevitably seditious, as are our dreams for human envoys in space, the sons and daughters and cousins who will be the first extraterrestrial beings with whom we interact. These dreams lead us to the realization that the time has come to seek a newer world, to dare to start the world over. As the power of humanity is growing, so is the collective discord among peoples and states and within states among classes, cultures, and races. An alternative to these behavioral monuments to ethnocentric and egocentric aggrandizement must be considered. Suggestions should at least be forthcoming, whether or not they accurately reflect eventual solutions. Einstein said:

We are living in a period of such great external and internal insecurity, and with such lack of firm objectives, that the mere confession of our convictions may be significant, even if these convictions . . . cannot be proven through logical deduction.

Solutions will arise out of the realization that without justice there are social disease and social disintegration. This is the essential and, incredibly, largely unrecognized reason for law, social convention, political theory, philosophy, and even theology. It is also a central point of theoretical contention in competing theories of economics.

We should, therefore, finally recognize that the only natural purpose of an ideal community contract of government is to foster and promote justice. The natural duty of government is to protect the legal equality of persons, societies, and states.

Once again the view from space is instructive. From space Earth may still appear to be a house of many rooms, but they all are rooms under one recirculating roof, a roof under which the partitions cannot be discerned, a roof that can be burnt out by becoming the victim of the hypothetical nuclear flashpoint. Thus, what was once considered merely a utopian dream is rapidly becoming an urgent necessity. The only alternative to prolonged conflict and ultimate destruction of the human experiment is a new and revolutionary concept of law, one that transcends national boundaries and planetary surfaces. It must embrace the three great tenets of metalaw: Guaranteed individual sovereignty (do unto others as *they* would have you do); noninterference in the natural evolution and adaptation of other societies (do unto others as *they* would have you do); and renunciation of the use of force ("in spatial relationships of any kind, no force of any kind may be used").

These are the inescapable requirements for sapient existence, symbiosis, and survival. Assuming the survival of our species, these requirements are destined to alter radically the way we see ourselves. By identifying the right to govern as rising from the people as a whole—the fourth political dimension—we might begin to see ourselves, singly and collectively, as both the center of a multidimensional universe and as only one intelligent entity within a cosmic community of intelligent entities. We can begin to regard ourselves as sovereign citizens of the universe, all made of a simple, energetic fabric.

We are living examples of gravity and mass interacting with subatomic nature in a way that produces endless manifestations, including galaxies, planets, and people. We are one ethereal interface between space, time, and matter, bearing true witness to the fact that there is a matrix of consciousness within the cosmos, capable of comprehending the diverse unity of symbiosis and complexification—the true *e pluribus unum* of the cosmos.

As Arthur Clarke noted in *2010;* "Now the long wait was ending. On yet another world, intelligence had been born and was escaping from its planetary cradle. An ancient experiment was about to reach its climax."

As humanity moves to populate the stars, it is our generation that must constitute the jurisprudential context that will shape and define that climax here on planet Earth. How will we rate as founding fathers and mothers?

Epilogue: A Convention for Spacekind

Treaty Governing Social Order of
Long-Duration or Permanent Inhabitants
of Near and Deep Space

States parties to this treaty, encouraged by the increasing international commitment of valuable resources to the advancement of human occupation of space, and inspired by expanding long-duration human habitation of near-earth orbit facilities, and

Recognizing the empirical distinctions between value-forming processes of humans functioning in an Earth-indigenous environment and those occurring in a biotechnically integrated, alien, and synthetic life-support system of an off-Earth habitat; and

Believing that exploration, exploitation, and occupation of near and deep space by humankind should be conducted with a recognition and understanding of the breadth of biological variations upon which humankind's cultures are premised; and

Desiring to contribute to the unfolding knowledge of human values and behavior patterns reflected in the broad spectrum of personal and social relationships encountered while occupying near and deep space; and

Believing that such recognition and understanding of the distinguishing biological underpinnings of human activities in space will contribute to, and help strengthen, compatible relations among people and civilizations on Earth; and

Recalling the Treaty on Principles Governing the Activities of States in the Exploration and Use of Outer Space, Including the Moon and Other Celestial Bodies, signed at Washington, London, and Moscow on 27 January 1967 and entered into force 10 October 1967; and

Taking into particular account the United Nations Agreement on the Rescue of Astronauts, the Return of Astronauts, and the Return of Objects Launched into Outer Space; and

Being convinced that a Treaty Governing Social Order of Long-Duration or Permanent Inhabitants of Near and Deep Space will further the purposes

266

and principles essential to the transition of an earthbound culture to a bioculture reflecting the uniqueness of outerspace existence, have agreed to the following:

ARTICLE 1

The exploration and use of near and deep space, including all celestial bodies accessible by humankind, shall be carried out for the benefit and in the interest not only of the inhabitants of Earth, who shall be called earthkind, but of inhabitants of near and deep space as well, who shall be called spacekind. Such areas of habitation shall be considered the province of spacekind in the first instance, and of earthkind in the second. There shall be free access by both earthkind and spacekind to all areas of space and celestial bodies, consistent with the best interests of the mental and physical welfare of spacekind and its existing habitats, regardless of their political or Earth-sovereign origins.

ARTICLE 2

Space habitats, including orbiting platforms and those existing on or beneath the surface of celestial bodies, shall not be subject to claims of national sovereignty or citizenship deriving from or exercised by nation-states or regional jurisdictions located or originating on Earth. Spacekind occupying such habitats shall exercise independent cultural and political sovereignty and in no matter shall space habitat sovereignty or inhabitant citizenship be related to any territory or geographical boundaries on Earth. Subject to certain provisions set forth below relating to jurisdictional transitions between space habitats and Earth, the conduct and activities of earth–space travel shall be subject to the Outer Space Treaty of 1967, the Agreement on the Rescue of Astronauts, the Return of Astronauts, and the Return of Objects Launched into Outer Space, the Convention on Registration of Objects Launched into Outer Space and all other applicable international and space law.

ARTICLE 3

States parties to this Treaty shall conduct their relations among each other and severally and collectively with spacekind in a manner consistent with international law, the Charter of the United Nations or any successor organization, and consistent with developing law among spacekind, in the interest

of maintaining peace and security, and promoting cooperation and understanding not only among earth cultures but also between earth cultures and
cultures unique to space.

ARTICLE 4

The use of military personnel for scientific research for any other nonhostile
and peaceful purposes requiring interaction with space habitats, communities and inhabitants shall not be prohibited: *Provided,* however, that there
shall be no bilateral or regional military relationships or alliances whatsoever
established between any one or more states parties to this treaty and any
space habitat and its inhabitants. A military alliance may be established
between space habitat communities and the United Nations or its successor
organization only for the protection of Earth or space habitats and their
inhabitants against threats or hostile action originating from cultures, civilizations or political entities not deriving ultimately from earthkind or Earth-
indigenous public or private organizations or consortia.

ARTICLE 5

States parties to this treaty shall regard spacekind as envoys of a culture or
civilization different from those of earthkind. In the event of accident, distress, emergency landing on the territory of any state party hereto, or on the
High Seas of Earth, or in the event of any unforeseen or fortuitous situations
experienced by representatives of spacekind on earth or in space, all reasonable steps shall be undertaken by parties to this treaty to assist such representatives and return them to appropriate authorities and jurisdictions on
Earth or in space, as hereinafter described.

   States parties to this treaty shall inform immediately the other states
parties to this treaty of any phenomena they discover in near or deep space
or on the surface of Earth which could constitute a danger to the life or welfare of representatives of spacekind.

ARTICLE 6

Each state party to this treaty shall bear international and interspace responsibility for its own national activities in space that may adversely affect any
space habitat or its inhabitants. All commercial activities shall be conducted
in strict accord with the principles set forth herein. Regardless of whether
such activities are carried out by governmental agencies or nongovernmen-

tal entities, each party to this treaty shall assure severally that such national or regional activities in near and deep space in which it is involved are conducted in conformity with existing international and prevailing interspace law, including the provisions set forth herein. When activities which substantially affect the sociopolitical independence and general welfare of space habitat communities and spacekind are conducted in space by an Earth-indigenous international organization, responsibility for compliance with this treaty shall be borne both by such international organization and by the states parties to this treaty that are participating in such organization.

ARTICLE 7

In the conduct of all space-related activities directly involving space habitats and spacekind representatives, states parties to this treaty shall be guided by the principles of cooperation and mutual assistance, and shall temper their relationships with due regard for the cultural independence of spacekind.

States parties to this treaty shall pursue studies of near and deep space in such a manner as to avoid harmful interference and adverse changes in the ecosystems and cultural integrity of spacekind habitats which might be caused by the introduction of harmful alien material, or the imposition of insensitive and harmful alien cultural characteristics that are not consistent with individual freedom and the cultural independence of the habitat society. If a state party to this treaty has any reason to believe that an activity or experiment planned by it or its nationals in near or deep space might cause potentially harmful interference with space habitats or spacekind cultures, it *shall* undertake effective international consultations among other states parties hereto, as well as with the spacekind cultures which may be affected by such activity or experiment. Any state a party hereto may demand reasonable consultation with any other state party to this treaty and any spacekind community regarding an activity or experiment suspected of being potentially harmful to Earth, the space community or to earthkind or spacekind generally.

ARTICLE 8

In order to ensure the integrity of the peaceful purposes and intents embodied in this treaty, all states parties hereto that establish space habitats of a long-duration or permanent nature shall establish them in such a manner that they shall be open for cultural examinations and military investigation by representatives of other states parties to this treaty on the basis of reciprocity. Such examination and investigation shall not occur as a matter of right hereunder beyond the second generation of spacekind born to any subject space habitat community. States parties to this treaty shall give the subject space habitat community and its founding state party hereto reasonable advance notice of any examination or investigation, or attendant visit, to the space habitat community, in order that appropriate consultations may be held and that maximum precaution may be taken to assure safety and to avoid unnecessary interference with normal operations of the community or culture to be examined, investigated, or visited.

ARTICLE 9

States parties to this treaty agree that there shall be established an expert organization, under the aegis of the United Nations or its successor entity, to be called the International Organization for Sentient Space Activities (IOSSA). The principle purposes of this organization, to be established under separate charter, are threefold: (1) Provide an interdisciplinary, international academy to review constantly all aspects of interactive relationships between earthkind and spacekind that occur either in outer space or on the surface of Earth; (2) grant international agreements of recognition and capacity (IARCs) to those space communities that meet the requisites for home rule established in the charter of IOSSA; and (3) refer case situations to the International Court of Justice and any correspondent or successor court of transnational law wherein the propriety and predictable compatibility of such interactive relationships are at issue among expert representatives of states parties to this treaty as well as those representing outer space cultures and space community inhabitants. The academy shall serve as the sole expert advisory body to the court in such matters.

The international academy shall establish jurisdictional frameworks and legal regimes to encompass activities involving interactions among permanent or long-duration inhabitants of outer space and Earth indigenes, regardless of the physical location of the interactions.

Postscript: The Spacekind Declaration of Independence Completed

... We hold these truths to be self-evident, that earthkind and spacekind are created equal to their own respective environments, that once having been raised above their biological origins to a recognizable level of sentience and sapience they are endowed by their Creator with certain inalienable rights, and that among these rights are survival, freedom of thought and expression, and the evolution of individual and community knowledge. That to secure these rights, governments are instituted among sentient beings, deriving their reasonable and responsive powers from the consent of the governed and by protective inference from those life forms without the capacity to communicate interspecies. That whenever any form of government becomes destructive of these ends, it is the right of the governed to alter or abolish it, and to institute a new set of values and political framework, laying its foundation on such principles and organizing its duties and authority in such form as to them shall seem most likely to effect both their physical safety and sense of well-being through cultural evolution. Prudence, indeed, will dictate that political, economic, and ideological traditions long established should not be changed for light and transient causes; and accordingly all experience has shown that earthkind, and now spacekind, are more disposed to suffer, while evils are sufferable, than to right themselves by abolishing or radically restructuring the forms to which they are accustomed. But when there occurs a long train of abuses, usurpations, and insensitivity to the needs of future generations evolving in a unique life-support environment, pursuing invariably the policies of colonial dependency and biological parochialism, it is their right, their obligation, to destroy such usurpations, insensitivity, and unresponsive institutions, and to provide new value standards that will ensure their security from abuses by progenitor cultures and governments of earthkind. Such has been the sufferance of space community migrants who are now evolved to spacekind, and who now of necessity are constrained to alter the existing foundations of relationships among earthkind and spacekind. The history of governments and private enterprise in space development industries is a continuing history of injuries and usurpations, all having in direct object the maintenance of an absolute tyranny over space communities and spacekind. To prove this, a list of grievances is unnecessary. A candid world need only remind itself of the historical patterns of earthkind when nations have pursued economic, ideological, and religious expansion into the less technologically developed continents and societies of Earth. The plea of this declaration is to break the cyclic violence, warfare, and destruction of civilizations which follow with certainty from the establishment of colonies. We have petitioned for redress in the most humble terms: Our repeated petitions have been answered only by repeated neglect. We have warned the governments and appropriate controlling interests of earthkind from time to time of their determined insistence to extend their total jurisdiction over space communities and spacekind functioning in an Earth-alien environment. We have reminded them of the circumstances of our emigration and settlement in space, and those of our predecessors. These warnings and reminders, too, have met with the deafness of prevailing justice and a failure to recognize the responsibilities of consanguinity in succeeding generations of earthkind. We must, therefore, denounce the causes and acquiesce in the necessity of our separation, and hold them, as we hold the rest of galactic intelligence, enemies in war; in peace, friends.

We, therefore, the representatives of space migrants, space communities, and spacekind descendants of earthkind, appealing to the Creator for the rectitude of our intentions, do, in the name and by the authority of spacekind settled and living in space communities, solemnly publish and declare that these communities and their inhabitants are free and independent; that they are absolved from all allegiance to the governments and organizations of earth; and that all political and ideological subservience of spacekind to earthkind is and ought to be totally dissolved; and that as free and independent communities of spacekind they have full power to protect themselves, establish peaceful relations, contract commercial and defensive alliances, and to do all other acts and things which independent communities in space, as well as on Earth, may do. And for the support of this declaration, with a firm reliance on the protection offered through the creative intent, we mutually pledge to each other our lives, our fortunes, and our sacred honor.

Bibliography

Adams, Robert McC. "The Natural History of Urbanism." *Smithsonian Annual 2: The Fitness of Man's Environment,* 39–59, Washington, D.C.: Smithsonian Institution Press, 1967.

Akins, Faren, Mary Connors, and Albert Harrison. *Living Aloft: Human Requirements for Extended Spaceflight.* Washington, D.C.: U.S. Government Printing Office, 1985.

Altered States of Awareness: Readings from Scientific American. Introduction by T. J. Teyler. San Francisco: W. H. Freeman and Company, 1972

Annes, Colleen, and David Jones. "The Evolution and Present Status of Mental Health Standards for Selection of USAF Candidates for Space Missions." *Aviation, Space and Environmental Medicine.* August 1983, 730–733

Asimov, Isaac. Introduction to *Living in Outer Space,* by George S. Robinson. Washington, D.C.: Public Affairs Press, 1975.

Beck, Benjamin B. *Animal Tool Behavior: The Use and Manufacture of Tools by Animals.* New York: Garland Publications, 1980.

Berger, Peter. *The Social Construction of Reality.* New York: Doubleday Publishers, 1966.

Bisplinghoff, Raymond. "Twenty-Five Years of NASA." Paper delivered at the 21st Goddard Memorial Symposium, 24–25 March 1983. In *Space Applications at the Crossroads: Proceedings of the American Astronautical Society,* edited by J. H. McElroy and E. L. Heacock, 29–40. San Diego, Calif.: Published for the American Astronautical Society by Univelt, 1983.

Bluth, B. J. "Human Systems Interfaces for Space Stations." Paper delivered at the American Institute of Aeronautics and Astronautics Space Systems Conference, 12–14 June 1984.

———. "Consciousness Alteration in Space." In *Space Manufacturing 3: Proceedings of the Fourth Princeton/AIAA Conference on Space Manufacturing Facilities,* 14–17 May 1979, 1430–1437, edited by Jerry Grey and Christine Krop. New York: American Institute of Aeronautics and Astronautics, 1979.

Brady, J. V. *Human Behavior in Space Environments.* Baltimore: Johns Hopkins University Press, 1980.

Brady, J. V., and H. H. Emerson. "Behavior Analysis of Motivational and Emotional Interactions in a Programmed Environment." In *Nebraska Symposium on Motivation,* edited by Daniel J. Bernstein. Lincoln: University of Nebraska Press, 1981.

Brierly, J. L. *The Law of Nations: An Introduction to the International Law of Peace.* Oxford: Clarendon Press, 1981.

Bronowski, Jacob. *The Ascent of Man.* Boston: Little, Brown and Company, 1974.

Brown, Lester R. *Building a Sustainable Society.* New York: W. W. Norton & Company, 1981.

Bucke, Richard Maurice. *Cosmic Consciousness: A Study in the Evolution of the Human Mind.* 4th ed. New York: E. P. Dutton & Company, 1923.

Burke, James. *Connections.* Boston: Little, Brown and Company, 1978.

Calvin, Melvin, and Oleg G. Gazenko, eds. *Foundations of Space Biology and Medicine.* 3 vols. in 4. NASA SP 374. Washington, D.C.: U. S. Government Printing Office, 1975.

Capra, Fritzof. *The Tao of Physics.* 2d ed. Berkely: Shambala Publications, 1975.

Cardozo, Benjamin N. *The Nature of the Judicial Process.* New Haven: Yale University Press, 1921.

Cavalli-Sforza, L. L., and M. W. Feldman. *Cultural Transmission and Evolution: A Quantitative Approach.* Princeton: University Press, 1981.

Cheston, Stephen T., and David L. Winter, eds. *Human Factors of Outer Space Production.* American Association for the Advancement of Sciences Selected Symposium No. 50. Boulder, Colo.: Westview Press, 1980. A quotation from D. A. D'Atri on the psychological responses to crowding was taken from this valuable overview of the psychosocial aspects of biojuridics in space.

Cicero, Marcus Tullius. *De re publica,* bound with *De legibus.* Translated by Clinton Walker Keyes. Loeb Classical Library No. 213, Cambridge: Harvard University Press, 1959.

Clarke, Arthur C. *2001: A Space Odyssey.* New York: New American Library, 1968.

———. *Man and Space.* New York: Time-Life Books, 1974.

———. *2010: Odyssey Two.* New York: Ballantine Books, 1982.

Cocca, Aldo Armando. "The Advances in International Law through the Law of Outer Space." *Journal of Space Law* 9 (1981): 13–20.

Cohen, Morris L. *Legal Research in a Nutshell.* St. Paul: West Publishing Company, 1981.

Collins, Michael. *Carrying the Fire.* New York: Farrar, Straus & Giroux, 1974.

Coon, Carleton S. *The Story of Man.* 3d ed. New York: Alfred A. Knopf, 1969.

Cooper, Henry S. F. *A House in Space.* New York: Holt, Rinehart and Winston, 1976.

Crane, Robert. "Soviet Attitude Toward International Space Law." *American Journal of International Law* 56 (1962): 685–723.

Cunningham, Walter. *The All-American Boys.* New York: Macmillan, 1977. This book is perhaps the most comprehensive and revealing in print on the real behind-the-scenes nature of the early space program and astronaut corps.

Dahlberg, Frances, ed. *Woman the Gatherer.* New Haven: Yale University Press, 1983.

Davies, Paul. *The Runaway Universe.* New York: Harper & Row, 1978.

————. *God and the New Physics.* New York: Simon and Schuster, 1984. Several quotations from physicists such as Niels Bohr, J. A. Wheeler, and Eugene Wigner are taken from this highly readable book, a thoughtful, authoritative treatment of the philosophical and theological significance of science and cosmology.

DeSaussure, Hamilton, and Peter Haanapel. "Determination of Applicable Law to Living and Working in Space." In *Proceedings of the Twenty-Fifth Colloquium on the Law of Outer Space,* 223–228. New York: American Institute of Aeronautics and Astronautics, 1983.

Dionisopoulos, P. Allan, and Craig R. Ducat. *The Right to Privacy.* St. Paul: West Publishing Company, 1976.

Douglas, William O. *Towards a Global Federalism.* New York: New York University Press, 1968.

Dubos, René. Prologue to *How Humans Adapt: A Biocultural Odyssey,* edited by Donald J. Ortner. Washington, D.C.: Smithsonian Institution Press, 1983.

Dyson, Freeman. *Disturbing the Universe.* New York: Harper & Row, 1979.

Eisenberg, John F., and Wilton S. Dillon, eds. *Man and Beast: Comparative Social Behavior.* Washington, D.C.: Smithsonian Institution Press, 1971.

Emerson, Thomas I., David Haber, and Norman Dorsen. *Political and Civil Rights in the United States.* 2 vols. Boston: Little, Brown and Company, 1967.

Emme, Eugene M. *Aeronautics and Astronautics: An American Chronology of Science and Technology in the Exploration of Space 1915–1960.* Washington, D.C.: NASA, U.S. Government Printing Office, 1961.

Eterovich, Francis H. *Approaches to Natural Law: From Plato to Kant.* New York: Explosive Press, 1972.

Fasan, Ernst. *Relations with Alien Intelligences.* Berlin: Verlag Arno Spitz, 1970.

Fechner, Gustave. *Elements of Psychophysics.* New York: Holt, Rinehart and Winston, 1966.

Ferguson, Marilyn. *The Aquarian Conspiracy: Personal and Social Transformations in the 1980s.* Los Angeles: Jeremy P. Tarcher, 1981. This book proved a treasure trove of research clues and interdisciplinary melding. Several quotations have been taken from it, including those of Brian Josephson, Jack Sarfatti, Stephen J. Gould, Niles Eldrige, Thomas Berry, and Ilya Prigogine.

Forte, David F. "On Teaching Natural Law." *Journal of Legal Education* 29 (1978): 413–437.

Freeman, Marsha. "The NASA Story." *Fusion*, September 1980, 25–33.

Freitas, Robert A., Jr. "The Legal Rights of Extraterrestrials." *Analog,* April 1977, 54–67.

"From Aviatrix to Astronautrix." *Time,* 29 August 1960, 41.

Fuller, Lon. *The Morality of Law.* New Haven: Yale University Press, 1964.

Future Directions for Life Sciences in NASA. Washington, D.C.: U.S. Government Printing Office, 1978.

Gabrynowicz, Joanne Irene. "The Human Side of the Law." Unpublished manuscript, 1986. An interesting synthesis, worthy of publication. A quotation from Buckminster Fuller concerning the integrity of triangles was taken from this manuscript.

Gazenko, Oleg G. *Summaries of Reports of the Sixth All-Soviet Union Conference on Space Biology and Medicine.* 2 vols. Kaluga, USSR, 1979.

Gazenko, Oleg G., A. M. Genin, and A. D. Yegorov. *Major Medical Results of the Salyut-6/Soyuz 185-Day Space Flight.* NASA NDB 2747. Washington, D.C., 1981.

Gerbner, George, and Marsha Siefert. *World Communications.* New York: Longman, 1984.

Gingerich, Owen, ed. *The Nature of Scientific Discovery: A Symposium Commemorating the 500th Anniversary of the Birth of Nicolaus Copernicus.* Washington, D.C.: Smithsonian Institution Press, 1975.

Glazer, J. Henry. "Domicile and Industry in Outer Space." *Columbia Journal of Transnational Law* 17 (1978): 67–117.

———. "Astrolaw Jurisprudence in Space as a Place: Right Reason for the Right Stuff." *Brooklyn Law Journal* 11 (1985): 1–20.

Glenn, Jerome C., and George S. Robinson. *Space Trek: The Endless Migration.* Harrisburg, Pa.: Stackpole Books, 1978.

Green, Philip. *The Pursuit of Inequality.* New York: Pantheon Books, 1981.

Grey, Jerry. *Enterprise.* New York: William Morrow & Company, 1979.

———, ed. *Space Manufacturing Facilities 2.* New York: American Institute of Aeronautics and Astronautics, 1977.

Grey, J. A., and V. D. Nebylitsyn. *Biological Bases of Individual Behavior.* New York: American Institute of Aeronautics and Astronautics, 1972.

Gribbon, John. "Earth's Lucky Break." *Science Digest,* May 1983, 36–42.

Gurovskiy, N. N. *Outlines of the Psychophysiology of the Work of Cosmonauts.* Moscow: Meditsina Press, 1976.

Gurovskiy, N. N., F. P. Kosmolinskiy, and L. N. Mel'nikov. "Designing the Living and Working Conditions of Cosmonauts." From an unpublished NASA translation of *Proyektirovaniye Usloviy Zhizni I Roboty Kosmonavtov,* NASA TM-76497. Moscow: Mashinstroyeniye, 1980.

Haley, Andrew G. *Space Law and Government.* New York: Appleton-Century-Crofts, 1963. This book was one of the first two to discuss the subject of space law. Our debt to Haley in fashioning our own synthesis and elaborating its foundations is inestimable. For many years Haley was the lone pioneer of the new study of metalaw; as the book indicates, his 1956 article "Basic Concepts of Space law" in the old *Jet Propulsion* Journal was the first of its kind. Haley's archives are stored at the National Air and Space Museum of the Smithsonian Institution. Quotations taken from his book include those of former Chief Justice Earl Warren and Francisco de Vitoria.

Halle, Louis. "Our Imminent Colonization of Space." *Harvard Magazine,* March 1979, 43–46.

Hardin, Garrett. *Nature and Man's Fate.* New York: Holt, Rinehart and Winston, 1959.

Helmreich, Robert L. "Psychological Considerations in Human Space Missions." In *Human Factors of Outer Space Production,* edited by Stephen T. Cheston and David L. Winter. Boulder, Colo.: Westview Press, 1980.

Heppenheimer, T. A. *Colonies in Space.* Harrisburg, Pa.: Stackpole Books, 1977.

Hirsch, Richard, and Joseph John Trento. *The National Aeronautics and Space Administration.* New York: Praeger Publishers, 1973. An excellent study of the origins and intended organization of the United States space program.

Ivanov, Ye. A., Ye. V. Khrunov, L. S. Khachatur'yants, and V. A. Popov. *The Human Operator in Space Flight.* Moscow: Mashinostroyeniye, 1974.

Iyer, Raghavan. *Parapolitics: Toward the City of Man.* New York: Oxford University Press, 1979.

Jaynes, Julian. *The Origin of Consciousness in the Breakdown of the Bicameral Mind.* Boston: Houghon Mifflin Company, 1977.

Johnson, Richard D., and Charles Holbrow. *Space Settlements: A Design Study.* NASA SP 413. Washington, D.C.: U.S. Government Printing Office, 1977.

Johnston, Richard S., and Lawrence F. Dietlein, eds. *Biomedical Results from Skylab.* NASA SP 377. Washington, D.C.: U.S. Government Printing Office, 1977.

Knight, Alice Valle. *The Meaning of Teilhard de Chardin: A Primer.* Old Greenwich, Conn. Devin-Adair Company, 1974.

Kuhn, Thomas S. *The Structure of Scientific Revolutions.* 2d ed., enl. Chicago: University of Chicago Press, 1970.

Lem, Stanislaw. *Memoirs of a Space Traveler: Further Reminiscences of Ijon Tichy.* Translated by Joel Stern and Maria Swiecicka-Ziemianek. New York: Harcourt Brace Jovanovich, 1983.

Leonard, George B. *The Transformation: A Guide to Inevitable Changes in Humankind.* Los Angeles: J. P. Tarcher, 1972.

Lerner, Max. Foreword to *The Aquarian Conspiracy: Personal and Social Transformations in the 1980s,* by Marilyn Ferguson. Los Angeles: J. P. Tarcher, 1981.

Levine, Arthur L. *The Future of the U.S. Space Program.* New York: Praeger Publishers, 1975.

Ligneul, Andre. *Teilhard and Personalism.* Translated by Paul Joseph Oligny and Michael D. Meilach. New York: Paulist Press, Deus Books, 1968.

Lumsden, C. J., and E. O. Wilson. *Genes, Mind and Culture: The Coevolutionary Process.* Cambridge: Harvard University Press, 1981.

MacDonald, Margaret. "Natural Rights." In *Human Rights,* edited by A. I. Melden. Belmont, Calif.: Wadsworth Publishing Company, 1970.

McDougal, Myres S., Harold D. Lasswell, and Ivan A. Vlasic. *Law and Public Order in Space.* New Haven: Yale University Press, 1963. This book and Haley's *Space Law and Government* are the two pioneering works in space law. The unique contribution of McDougal, Lasswell, and Vlasic is their phenomenological approach to jurisprudence and to what Haley called metalaw. This phenomenology was based on the categories of communications theorist Harold Lasswell. Our own phenomenology, though simplified, updated, and with more of a slant toward natural law, was based in large measure on this work.

McLuhan, Marshall. *Understanding Media: The Extensions of Man.* New York: McGraw-Hill, 1964.

Maslow, Abraham H. *Toward a Psychology of Being.* New York: Van Nostrand Reinhold Company, 1968.

Melnikov, L. N. "Works of the Eleventh Reading of K. E. Tsiolkavsky." In *Problems of Space Biology and Medicine,* edited by Melvin Calvin and Oleg Gazenko. 3 vols. in 4, NASA SP 374. Washington, D.C.: U.S. Government Printing Office, 1975.

Midgley, Mary. *Beast and Man: The Roots of Human Nature.* Ithaca, New York: Cornell University Press, 1978.

Naisbitt, John. *Megatrends: Ten New Directions Transforming Our Lives.* New York: Warner Books, 1984.

Nathan, Otto, and Heinz Norden, eds. *Einstein on Peace.* New York: Avenel Books, 1981.

Nicogossian, A. E., and J. F. Parker. *Space Physiology and Medicine.* Washington, D.C.: U.S. Government Printing Office, 1982.

Nordenstreng, Kaarle, and Lauri Hannikainen. *The Mass Media Declaration of UNESCO.* Norwood, N.J.: Ablex Publishing Company, 1984.

Oberg, James E. *Red Star in Orbit.* New York: Random House, 1981.

Obregon, Mauricio. *Argonauts to Astronauts: An Unconventional History of Discovery.* New York: Harper & Row, 1980.

O'Neill, Gerard K. *The High Frontier: Human Colonies in Space.* New York: William Morrow & Company, 1977.

Ortner, Donald J., ed. *How Humans Adapt: A Biocultural Odyssey.* Washington, D.C.: Smithsonian Institution Press, 1983.

Pember, D. R. *Mass Media Law.* 3d ed. Dubuque, Iowa: William C. Brown Publishers, 1984.

Peter, Laurence J. *Ideas for Our Time.* New York: William Morrow & Company, 1977. This is a book of quotations from which several epigrams and some other textual references came. Quotations from this source were chosen primarily as anecdotes to illustrate explanations or lines of reasoning that we are forwarding.

Pfeiffer, John E. *The Emergence of Man.* New York: Harper & Row, 1969.

———. *The Emergence of Society: A Prehistory of the Establishment.* New York: McGraw-Hill, 1977.

Pound, Roscoe. *Social Control through Law.* New Haven: Yale University Press, 1942.

Prigogine, Ilya, and Isabelle Stengers. *Order Out of Chaos: Man's New Dialogue with Nature. New York: Bantam Books, 1984.*

Pucetti, Roland. *Persons: A Study of Possible Moral Agents in the Universe.* London: Macmillan & Company, 1968.

Radcliffe, Cyril John. *The Law and Its Compass.* Evanston, Ill.: Northwestern University Press, 1960.

"Report of the Special Subcommittee of the Selection of Astronauts." *Qualifications for Astronauts.* Washington, D.C.: U.S. Government Printing Office, 1962.

Rifkin, Jeremy. *Entropy: A New World View.* New York: Viking Press, 1980.

Robinson, George S. *Living in Outer Space.* Washington, D.C.: Public Affairs Press, 1975.

Rosen, Stanley G. "Mind in Space." *USAF Medical Service Digest* 27 (1976): 4–17.

Rosenfeld, Stanley B. "Some Conflicts in the Law Relating to Working in Space." In *Proceedings of the Twenty-Fifth Colloquium on the Law of Outer Space,* 273–278. New York: American Institute of Aeronautics and Astronautics, 1983.

Ross, Herbert H. *Biological Systematics.* Reading, Mass.: Addison-Wesley, 1974.

Rossiter, Clinton, ed. *The Federalist Papers.* New York: New American Library, 1961.

Sagan, Carl. *The Cosmic Connection: An Extraterrestrial Perspective.* New York: Doubleday & Company, 1973.

———. *The Dragons of Eden: Speculations on the Evolution of Human Intelligence.* New York: Random House, 1977.

———. *Cosmos.* New York: Random House, 1980.

Schell, Jonathan. *The Fate of the Earth.* New York: Alfred A. Knopf, 1982.

Schultz, Duane. *Theories of Personality.* Belmont, Calif.: Wadsworth Publishing Company, 1976.

Scott, James B. *The Spanish Origins of International Law.* Oxford: The Clarendon Press, 1934.

Singer, Philip, and Carl R. Vann. "Extraterrestrial Communities: Cultural, Legal, Political, and Ethical Considerations." In *Cultures beyond the Earth,* edited by Magoroh Maruyama and Arthur Harkins. New York: Random House, 1975.

Skinner, B. F. *Beyond Freedom and Dignity.* New York: Alfred A. Knopf, 1971.

Sloup, George P. "Factors Leading to the Development of the Jurisprudence of Astrolaw." In *Proceedings of the Twenty-Seventh Colloquium on the Law of Outer Space*. New York: American Institute of Aeronautics and Astronautics, 1985.

―――. "Determination of Applicable Law to Living and Working in Outer Space: The Municipal Law Connection and the NASA/Hastings Research Project." *Lincoln Law Review*. 14 (1983): 43–52.

Sommer, Robert. *Personal Space: The Behavorial Basis of Design*. Englewood Cliffs, N.J.: Prentice-Hall, 1969.

Spangler, David. *Emergence: The Rebirth of the Sacred*. New York: Dell Publishing Company, 1984.

Spencer, Janet T., and Robert L. Helmreich. *Masculinity and Femininity: Their Psychological Dimensions, Correlates, and Antecedents*. Austin: University of Texas Press, 1978.

Starr, S. Frederick. "Technology and Freedom in the Soviet Union." In *High Technology and Human Freedom,* edited by Lewis H. Lapham. Washington, D.C.: Smithsonian Institution Press, 1985.

Sterns, P. M., and L. I. Tennen. "International Recognition of the Art of Living in Space: The Emergence of Settlement Competence." In *Proceedings of the Twenty-Second Colloquium on the Law of Outer Space,* 221–223. New York: American Institute of Aeronautics and Astronautics, 1980.

Stine, G. Harry. *The Third Industrial Revolution*. New York: G. P. Putnam's Sons, 1975.

Stone, Christopher. *Should Trees Have Standing? Toward Legal Rights for Natural Objects*. Los Altos, Calif.: William Kaufmann, 1974.

Tanner, Nancy M. *On Becoming Human*. New York: Cambridge University Press, 1981.

Tax, Sol. *Horizons of Anthropology*. Chicago: Aldine Publishing Company, 1964.

Teilhard de Chardin, Pierre. *The Phenomenon of Man*. Translated by Bernard Wall. New York: Harper & Row, 1959.

―――. *The Future of Man*. Translated by Norman Denny. New York: Harper & Row, 1964.

―――. *Building the Earth*. Translated by Noel Lindsay. Wilkes-Barre, Pa.: Dimension Books, 1965.

―――. *Human Energy*. Translated by J. M. Cohen. New York: Harcourt Brace Jovanovich, 1969.

Thompson, William Irwin. *At the Edge of History: Speculations on the Transformation of Culture*. New York: Irvington, 1971.

Toffler, Alvin. *Future Shock. New York: Bantam Books, 1971.*

―――. *The Third Wave*. New York: Bantam Books, 1981.

Tucker, Robert B. "Interview with Ilya Prigogine." *OMNI,* May 1983, 84–94.

Tunkin, G. I. *Law and Force in the International System*. Moscow: Mezhdunarodnye otnoshniia, 1983.

Vereshchetin, V. S. "Legal Status of International Space Crews." In *Proceedings of the Twenty-First Colloquium on the Law of Outer Space,* 164–171. New York: American Institute of Aeronautics and Astronautics, 1979.

Wagar, Warren. *The City of Man.* Baltimore: Penguin Books, 1963. This book is a comprehensive history of cosmopolitan thought, which was a valuable resource guide and source of quotations on global community.

Way, H. Frank, Jr. *Liberty in the Balance.* 5th rev. ed. New York: McGraw-Hill, 1981.

Why Man Explores. Washington, D.C.: NASA, U.S. Government Printing Office, 1977. This little book was transcribed from a NASA symposium that took place 2 July 1976 in conjunction with the landing of the Viking spacecrafts on Mars. Quoted from it are Philip Morrison and Jacques Cousteau.

Wilson, E. O. *Sociobiology: The New Synthesis.* Cambridge: Harvard University Press, 1975.

———. *On Human Nature.* Cambridge: Harvard University Press, 1978.

Wolfe, Tom. *The Right Stuff.* New York: Farrar, Straus & Giroux, 1979.

Index

Humankind, 70, 72, 244
Human productivity in space, 75,
   76, 111, 200
Hunting, 10–11
Huntoon, Carolyn L., 62
Huxley, Aldous, 139
Huxley, Julian, 7

IAF. *See* International Astronautical
   Federation
IARC. *See* International Agreement
   for Recognition and Capacity
ICAO. *See* International Civil Avia-
   tion Organization
ICSU. *See* International Council of
   Scientific Unions
IGY. *See* International Geophysical
   Year
Industrial revolutions, 36–37, 39,
   69
Information revolution, 38–39, 133
Institute of International Law, 29
Intelligence: for assembling of
   energy, 24; earth-alien extrater-
   restrial, 72; human conscious-
   ness and, 32, 74; and Space
   Age exploration, 33–34, 35,
   38; and space migration,
   65–66
INTELSAT. *See* International Tele-
   communications Satellite Orga-
   nization
International Agreement for Recog-
   nition and Capacity (IARC), pro-
   posed, 204, 205, 224
International Astronautical Federation (IAF), 38, 41, 167, 224–
   25, 226
International Bill of Human Rights,
   156, 242
International Civil Aviation Organization (ICAO), 222
International Colloquia on Law of
   Outer Space, 224–25, 226
International Council of Scientific
   Unions (ICSU), 38, 40

International Court of Justice, 205,
   221, 223
International Covenants of Civil and
   Political, and Cultural, Social,
   and Economic Rights of the
   International Bill of Rights, 156,
   242
International Geophysical Year
   (IGY), 39, 40–41, 42
International Institute of Space Law,
   41, 167
International law, 148, 167; as
   metalaw, 220; and peaceful
   coexistence, 171; public and
   private, 155–56; as rule of
   force, 179, 220; Soviet view
   of, 178; third world and, 175;
   U.S. commitment to, 176
International Organization for Senti-
   ent Space Activities (IOSSA),
   204, 224
International Polar Years, 36, 38
International system: organizational
   and legal activities, 218–19;
   and transition to space habita-
   tion, 226; UN as subsystem of,
   221. *See also* United Nations
International Telecommunications
   Satellite Organization
   (INTELSAT), 225
International Telecommunications
   Union (ITU), 38, 155, 225
IOSSA. *See* International Organiza-
   tion for Sentient Space Activi-
   ties
Irwin, James, 121, 138
Isolation tests, 53–54, 142
ITU. *See* International Telecommuni-
   cations Union
Iyer, Raghavan, 245

Jaspers, Karl, 252
Jefferson, Thomas, 26, 34, 84, 95,
   184, 213–14, 216, 243
Jessup, Philip C., 156
Jesus Christ, 141, 234

John Paul II, Pope, 172
Johnson, Roy, 47
Josephson, Brian, 108
Jurimetrics, 34, 93
Jurisdictional astroregulations, 152–53
Jurisprudence: astrolaw, 235; ecological, 131, 134, 228; functions, 83; interplanetary, 14, 133; natural laws and, 18; neurological, 132–33; new studies in, 34; origins, 8; and space station society, 83–84
Jus, defined, 231
Jus humanitatis, 244–45

Kekkonen, Urho Kalera, 188, 189
Kennan, George F., 178
Kennedy, John F., 19, 34, 54, 55, 148, 172, 191
Knowledge, xiii–xiv, 11–12
Korovin, Vladimir, 172
Kuhn, Thomas, 150, 229

Lasswell, Harold, 26, 131
Law: anthropocentrism in, 234, 247; broad categories of, 154–56; defined, 117, 148; new research in, 34–35; reactionary nature of, 181; scientific definition of, 258
Law of the sea, 169, 170, 186, 187, 191
Legal positivism, 210, 211
Lem, Stanislaw, 94
Lenin, Vladimir Ilyich, 250–51, 252
Lerner, Max, 107
Liability Convention (1971), 181, 182–83
Liberty, 31, 95; constitutional ideals of, 210; legal definition of, as a social-transitional concept, 26–27
Lindbergh, Charles, 144
Locke, John, 189, 191, 192, 213, 252

Low, George M., 54
Ludwig, Arnold M., 139–40

McCall, Robert, xv
MacDonald, Margaret, 253
McDougal, Myres, 26, 27, 28, 131
McLuhan, Marshall, 39, 69, 71, 82, 114, 219
Madison, James, 149, 150, 216
Marx, Karl, 27
Maslow, Abraham, 121, 127, 138, 139, 140, 141, 143
Mayflower Compact, 198
Melnikov, L. N., 128
Mercury project, 35, 48–49, 50–51, 52, 77
Meta, 227, 228, 229, 262
Metalaw, xviii, 167, 220, 228, 249, 256, 260; as basis for constitutions, 213; defined, 211, 247; fundamental components of, 257; major tenets of, 264; in space, 221, 233
Metaphysical-transcendental level, of social ecology, 26, 28
Metaphysics, 211, 228
Mill, John Stuart, 188, 214, 220
Mitchell, Edgar D., 138, 139
Mohammed, 141, 234, 237–38
Mohler, Stan, 135
Molodtsov, S. V., 185, 188, 189
Montesquieu, Charles-Louis, Baronde, 213
Moon Treaty, proposed: and future space communities, 200–201; problems with, 186–87; provisions of, 186, 193, 194; Soviet Union and, 190; U.S. and, 192, 203
Moore, Charles, 252
Morowitz, Harold, 15–16
Morrison, Philip, 4
Moscow Space Policy Symposium, 166
Moses, 141, 234, 238

Naisbitt, John, 38, 110
NASA. *See* National Aeronautics and Space Administration
National Academy of Sciences, 55, 56, 57, 77
National Aeronautics and Space Act (1958), 46, 47, 48, 167, 168
National Aeronautics and Space Administration (NASA), 45; and commercialization of space, 193; dual military-civilian program of, 46–47, 58, 63; functions of, 46; Human Productivity Program, 76, 200; jurisdictional astroregulations, 152–53; nutritional program, 90; office of international relations, 225; planned space station, 198; and selection of astronauts, 48, 52–54. *See also* Space Shuttle Astronaut Program
National Aeronautics and Space Council, 46, 47
National Science Foundation, Polar Research Board, 197
National sovereignty, 167, 170; human rights versus, 243; third world concerns over, 176–77; threat to survival from global form of, 177
Natural law, 18; bases of, 178; basic rights of, xix; classical conception of, 211–12; defined, 151; Enlightenment School of, 212–13; Federalists and, 149–50; and human welfare, 244; and natural rights, 254; origin, 232; positive law and, 229; rule of reason and, 230; substantive, 178; U.S. Constitution and, 214–16. *See also* Natural rights
Natural rights: compromising of, 252; constitutional guarantee of, 232; international guarantees of, 241–42; for social

group, 234, 247; of spacekind, 241, 243; survival of, 253–54
Neanderthal man, 9
Neurological anatomies, 136–37
New World, English settlements in, 197–98
NGOs. *See* Nongovernmental organizations
Niebuhr, Reinhold, 261, 262
Nonequilibrium, 108–9
Nongovernmental organizations (NGOs), 224
Nordenstreng, Kaarle, 171, 172, 179
Novas, 3
Novus ordo, 219
Nutrition, for space habitation, 89–91

Obregon, Mauricio, 45
Occupational Safety and Health Act, application to space, 162
Office of Technology Assessment, 112
O'Neill, Gerard, 63, 162
Organization of American States, 155
Ortner, Donald J., 95
Orwell, George, xiii, 148
Outer Space Treaty of 1967, 46, 191; and international space law, 167; interpretation of, 170; on jurisdiction over space travelers, 151–52, 153, 155; and *jus humanitatis,* 244–45; principles, 168–69, 183; quasi-constitutional function, 181; self-government intent of, 202–3

Paradigm shifts, 71, 121, 139, 140, 142
Paris Conventions, 29
Parochialism, social, 25, 26; ecumenism versus, 27, 38; global, 40; and territorial sovereignty, 28–29

Peaceful coexistence, 166–67, 171–72
Peak experience, 121, 138; characteristics of, 140; potential effects of, 141; screening for susceptibility to, 142; value of, 143
Perpetual motion, 5
Personhood, 254
Pfeiffer, John, 9, 11, 13
Physics, 15–16, 231
Plato, 211, 229
Polymerization, 5, 8, 74
Positive law, 229
Positivism, 229, 231, 244
Pound, Roscoe, 229
Prigogine, Ilya, 5, 6, 16, 71, 140–41, 255, 258, 263
Private domestic law, 155
Private international law, 155–56
Psychological considerations, for space habitation, 118–22
Psychophysical, defined, 132–33
Psychotherapy, for Soviet space inhabitants, 125
Public domestic law, 154–55
Public international law, 155
Pucetti, Roland, 255
Pursuit of happiness, 26, 95
Punctuated equilibrium, 114

Quantum theory, 16, 107–8
Quasi contract, 230
Quasi law, international treaties as, 180–81

Radcliffe, Cyril John, 230
Radiation exposure, 84
Raleigh, Sir Walter, 197–98
Rambault, Paul C., 88
Reagan, Ronald, 42, 59, 186
Registration Convention, 181–82, 183
Relativity, 19, 230, 242
Religion: freedom of, for space, 108; privacy in, 237–38

Res communis: defined, 185; and law of the sea, 186, 187; Soviet-U.S. differences on, 190, 191, 192; third world and, 188, 190
Res communis humanitatis, 204
Rescue and Return Treaty (1968), 181, 182
Resonance: absence of, 111; efforts to produce, 28, 33; and survival, 112–13
"Right stuff," 32–33, 52
Ripley, S. Dillon, 75
Roddenberry, Gene, 9
Rogers, Carl, 139
Roosevelt, Franklin D., Four Freedoms, 176, 240, 242
Rosen, Stanley G., 121, 137
Rossiter, Clinton, 149
Rostow, Walter, 251
Rousseau, Jean Jacques, 188, 213
Rule of force, 178, 179, 220
Rule of law, 178, 179, 180, 220, 249
Rule of reason, 230
Ryumin, Valery, 87, 116

Sadat, Anwar, 238
Sagan, Carl, 8, 264
Salyut 6 mission, 80
Sarfatti, Jack, 108
Satellite communications, 167
Satellite killers, 170
Satyagraha, 238, 251
Schell, Jonathan, 172, 177
Schmitt, Harrison, 62, 65
Schweickart, Russell L., 55, 56, 100, 121, 138
Scott, David, 121
Scott, James B., 232
Self-actualization, 127, 137, 139, 143
Self-government, space communities, 198; city-state jurisdiction for, 199–200, 202; municipal law for, 199; realms of, 204–5

basic, 26, 28; interdisciplinary nature of, 243; survival versus cooperative, 30–31, 33
Van Allen belt, 84
Vann, Carl R., 94, 96–97, 98
Vlasic, Ivan, 26, 131
Voas, Robert, 50
Vereshchetin, Vladlin S., 201–2, 203
Von Braun, Wernher, 42, 88
Von Pirquet, Clemens, 92

Wagar, Warren, 251, 252, 261–62
WARC. *See* World Administrative Radio Conference
Warren, Earl, 249
Waterman, Alan, 40
Way, H. Frank, Jr., 210, 214, 243
Weightlessness, 81–82, 91
Wells, H. G., 97, 258–59
Western Union Telstar, 168
Wheeler, J. A., 108
White, Edward, 138
Whitman, Walt, 239
WHO. *See* World Health Organization

Wigner, Eugene, 108
Wilson, Edward O., 74
Wilson, James, 216
Wilson, Woodrow, Fourteen Points of, 176
WMO. *See* World Meteorological Organization
Wolfe, Tom, 24, 32–33
Women astronauts, 53–54, 63
World Administrative Radio Conference (WARC), 167
World Data Centers, 40
World Health Organization (WHO), 222
World International Space Agency, proposed, 226
World Meteorological Organization (WMO), 38, 225
Writing, invention of, 11–12, 17

Young, John, 55, 99

Zhukov, G. P., 166